W9-CWQ-187

Microsoft® Works for Windows™

Microsoft® Works for Windows™

JoAnne Woodcock

PUBLISHED BY
Microsoft Press
A Division of Microsoft Corporation
One Microsoft Way
Redmond, Washington 98052-6399

Library of Congress Cataloging-in-Publication Data
Woodcock, JoAnne.
    Microsoft works for windows / JoAnne Woodcock.
        p.   cm.
    Includes index.
    ISBN 1-55615-397-X
    1. Microsoft Works (Computer program) 2. Microsoft Works for
Windows.   I. Title.
QA76.76.I57W66   1992
005.369--dc20   91-37626
                                                             CIP

Printed and bound in the United States of America.

1 2 3 4 5 6 7 8 9   MLML   6 5 4 3 2 1

Distributed to the book trade in Canada by Macmillan of Canada, a division of
Canada Publishing Corporation.

Distributed to the book trade outside the United States and Canada by Penguin
Books Ltd.

Penguin Books Ltd., Harmondsworth, Middlesex, England
Penguin Books Australia Ltd., Ringwood, Victoria, Australia
Penguin Books N.Z. Ltd., 182–190 Wairau Road, Auckland 10, New Zealand

British Cataloging-in-Publication Data available.

Hayes® is a registered trademark of Hayes Microcomputer Products, Inc. IBM® is a
registered trademark of International Business Machines Corporation. Microsoft®
and MS-DOS® are registered trademarks and Toolbar™ and Windows™ are trademarks of Microsoft Corporation. ZIP Code® is a registered trademark of the United
States Postal Service. Paintbrush™ is a trademark of ZSoft Corporation.

Acquisitions Editor: Marjorie Schlaikjer
Project Editor: Peggy McCauley
Manuscript and Technical Editor: Editorial Services of New England

For Kate and Mark

Contents

Acknowledgments

Effusive acknowledgments can sound insincere, so this page will dispense with uncomfortable flattery and simply acknowledge the large debt owed to two teams of skilled professionals. They helped turn these pages from a manuscript into a book.

On the West Coast, at Microsoft Press, thanks go to Marjorie Schlaikjer, acquisitions editor; Peggy McCauley, project editor; and Sally Brunsman, managing editor. Far to the east, associated with Editorial Services of New England, are: Michelle Neil, project manager; JT Aldridge, technical reviewer; Kathy Wiesner, copy editor; and Justin Cuyler, who kept track of all the graphics. If you find this book useful, both teams deserve much of the credit.

Thanks are also in order for another group, the people without whom there would be no book: the real WorksWizards, the developers who created Works for Windows.

JoAnne Woodcock
September 1991

Introduction

Microsoft Works for Windows puts a new face on a venerable product that has been available for years in a number of different forms — as Works for the Apple II, Works for the Macintosh, and Works for IBM and compatible computers. What makes Works for Windows (from here on, Works for short) so special? It's lively, it's graphical, and it's easier to use than ever before. It also "talks" to Windows and other Windows programs — with no attention from you whatsoever — giving you the benefits of consistency, predictability, and — again — ease of use.

Works, as you no doubt know, is a type of program called integrated software. Integration refers to the fact that it gives you, in one package, the benefits of three applications: a word processor, a spreadsheet, and a database. These three applications are carefully designed to work with one another — they are integrated — so that you don't have to worry about where your data is stored, what form it's stored in, or how you can blend two different types of data in one document. Works can do it. As integrated software, Works also features a single set of basic commands and a single approach to using your computer, yet it enables you to create documents as varied as a financial statement, a parts inventory, and the thesis for your college degree.

WHO THIS BOOK IS FOR

Works is for people who care more about using a computer than understanding its insides, and this book is for people who want to know how to use Works. The idea is not to make you a computer expert, but to give you the information you need to feel comfortable using Works. (Eventually, you might feel comfortable enough to push its capabilities to the limit to make your own work easier and faster.) For the majority of computer-based tasks, Works gives you everything you need to get the job done. To use Works, all you need is a basic understanding of what it can do, how you use it, and when to apply a particular feature to the task at hand. That, in a nutshell, is the goal of this book.

WHAT YOU'LL FIND IN THIS BOOK

People differ, sometimes considerably, in the way they learn a new skill. Some like to dive in and strike out for parts unknown; others prefer to know where they're going and what's involved in getting there. To accommodate both approaches, Part I gives you an overview of both Windows and Works so you can see what they are and, roughly, how they work together.

In Part II, you begin a more extensive tour of each Works application. Because computers, like cars, are "hands-on" machines, you'll learn the basics by jumping directly into the applications and creating sample documents. As you work through the book, you'll use these sample documents for practice as you learn to control each application and adapt it to fit your needs. As you work, the chapters will describe what to do, why, and under what circumstances. Practice sessions alone, however, cannot teach you every feature of Works or its three applications, so once you know your way around, you can refer to the end of Chapters 5 through 10, where you'll find a guide to each application's menus and commands. These guides will serve as a reference section. They describe the application's features so that you'll know which commands to use when you're on your own and ready to try something new. When you finish Part II, you should be able to create, modify, print, and save documents with ease in each of the Works applications.

Part III, the last few chapters of the book, takes you from using Works as a collection of separate applications to using Works as a means of passing data back and forth — from one document to another and from one Works application to another. Along the way, you'll also learn about transferring data via the phone system, with the aid of a modem and the Windows communications program, Terminal. By the time you finish with Part III, you should be able to take control of your data by moving it wherever you want, whenever you want.

All this capability is yours thanks to a really special program called Microsoft Works for Windows. Enjoy the experience.

Part I

Getting Started

Part I introduces you to Windows, Works, and a special set of tools called the WorksWizards, which can help you create an address book, mailing labels, or a form letter. The three chapters in Part I are designed to help you become comfortable with both Works and the Windows environment in which it runs.

1

From Windows to Works

You're probably eager to get started with Works for Windows, but first you should learn a bit about Microsoft Windows. Why? Because Works and Windows are like a duck and water: They go together naturally. Even the official name emphasizes this relationship; it is Works *for* Windows.

This does not mean, however, that you *must* learn Windows to use Works. Nor does it mean that using Works effectively means mastering two programs rather than one. If you want, you can use Windows merely as a springboard to Works. If computers or Windows are relatively new to you, take the brief tour that begins in the next section. The time taken will be time well spent.

NOTE: *This book assumes that both Windows and Works are already installed on your system. If they are not, turn to Appendix A for guidance on installing both programs.*

WINDOWS

Windows is a working environment that surrounds MS-DOS, the operating system that controls basic functions within your computer. (Hereafter, we'll refer to MS-DOS simply as DOS.) Why do you want or need Windows? There are many reasons, most of them having to do with how efficiently your computer and programs run. In your daily work, however, you'll find that the most compelling reason by far for using Windows is this:

```
C:\>_
```

This is the famous (or infamous) DOS prompt from which you give your computer commands, such as:

```
C:\>xcopy \examples\*.* a: /d:11-30-91 /s /e /v
```

Granted, this command was deliberately chosen to look complex. But it is a real DOS command, one that copies files. Some people enjoy such commands and affectionately refer to working at the DOS prompt as efficient. Others, less charitable, deem the same process user-hostile. This is where Windows comes in.

If you're at your computer, start it if you haven't already. If Windows doesn't appear, type the following at the DOS prompt.

```
C:\>win
```

Within a few seconds, you see a display like this:

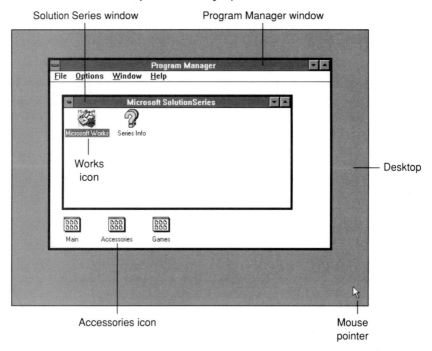

You've just entered the world of *graphical user interfaces*, where a mouse becomes your friend and the DOS prompt gives way to pictures. Working with your computer has now evolved from typing cumbersome strings of characters to using a far more visual point-and-click approach. You are presented with available options and Windows waits patiently until you make a choice.

Four characteristic features of Windows are labeled for you in this illustration: the *mouse pointer*, an open area called the *desktop*, one or more open *windows*, and several graphics called *icons*.

NOTE: *If your display does not exactly match the one in the illustration, don't be concerned. Windows is very flexible and might look slightly different on your system.*

What Is a Window?

What, exactly, is a window, aside from being a feature from which Windows takes its name? Visually, a window is a rectangular portion of the screen framed in a double-lined border. Functionally, a window is a part of the screen that Windows reserves for displaying a particular program or, within a program, a particular document, such as a letter.

One of the great strengths of Windows is its ability to keep track of two, three, or more programs at the same time. To avoid chaos, Windows runs each program you start in its own *application window*. Likewise, if you want to work with one program but several documents, Windows (and Windows programs) displays each in its own *document window*.

The Desktop

Surrounding the onscreen window is an empty area called the *desktop*. Windows uses a desktop as a metaphor to help you visualize your screen as the electronic equivalent of the desk on which you work. You can arrange several types of "objects" on the desktop — a clock, a calculator, a letter, a budget, and so on — although, unlike on a real desktop, each of these objects appears in a separate window. You can, however, move these items around to suit your preferences, exactly as you can on a real desktop.

The Mouse and How to Use It

> **NOTE:** *This book assumes that you have a mouse and gives keyboard equivalents only where using the keyboard is faster or more efficient than using the mouse. If you don't have a mouse, refer to your documentation or use the Windows Help facility (as described later) to become familiar with keyboard equivalents. (See "Help, a Special Menu," later in this chapter.)*

When you use a mouse, a small pointer on your screen moves as you move the mouse on your desktop. When you move the mouse, the pointer moves the same relative distance, and in the same direction, on the screen.

Once you've positioned the pointer, you use the left mouse button to carry out one of three basic mouse actions:

- Click — quickly press and release the left mouse button once.

- Double-click — quickly press and release the left mouse button twice in succession.

- Drag — place the mouse pointer on the object, and then press and hold the left mouse button while moving the mouse on your desk.

The Program Manager

The Program Manager is the core program of Windows. From it, you can start the applications that help your computer become a productive part of your life. Because the Program Manager is so useful, its window is the one you normally see whenever you start Windows.

Here's a closer look at a typical Program Manager window:

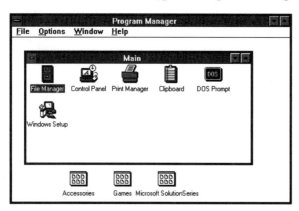

Within the Program Manager window in the illustration (and, probably, on your own screen), you see a second, smaller window. This second window represents a *program group* that contains a set of related programs. Windows organizes programs into groups to keep order and enable you to find your programs quickly. Within the program group window, you see several icons — small graphic images that Windows uses to represent programs and, in other situations, items such as disk drives and files.

When Windows is installed, it creates three program groups:

- Main, which gives you access to a set of Windows utility programs, including one called File Manager that offers an alternative way of starting Windows programs

- Accessories, which includes a set of useful programs such as Write (a word processor), Paintbrush (a drawing program), and Terminal (a computer communications program)

- Games, which offers potentially addictive amusement in the form of Solitaire (a card game) and Reversi (a form of Go)

You might also see groups named Windows Applications and Non-Windows Applications. For Works and two related programs named Microsoft Money (a checkbook manager) and Microsoft Publisher (a desktop publishing program), Windows creates a special group named Microsoft Solution Series.

Program groups can be displayed as open windows or as small icons, like this:

Games

Opening a Program Group

In the form shown above, a program group's window is said to be *minimized*. The program group is available, and you can open its window whenever you want, but because the program group is not currently active, Windows has tucked it away at the bottom of the Program Manager window.

You should have one or more minimized group windows on your screen. Open them all:

    ☐ Point to a group icon and double-click the left mouse button. Repeat for each program group.

Moving Among Group Windows

The group windows you've opened should be overlaid like shingles on a roof. Notice that only the window on top has any color to its border. This color (dark on a non-color screen) indicates the current, or active, window — the one that will be affected by any commands you issue.

You can change to a different group window in any of three ways. Try one or all of them to see which best suits your style of working:

■ Place the mouse pointer anywhere in a window that is not active. Click.

■ Hold down Ctrl and press Tab repeatedly to cycle from group to group.

■ Open the Window menu by clicking on it or by pressing Alt and the underlined letter, W, in the menu name. The menu shows you a numbered list of open windows, like this:

Choose the window you want by clicking on its name or by pressing the underlined number to its left.

Whichever method you choose, notice that the new window comes to the top of the "stack."

NOTE: *Windows often responds to key combinations, rather than individual keys. In this book, such combinations are hyphenated (for example, Ctrl-Tab, for the key combination mentioned above). When you see these combinations, remember to press both keys at the same time.*

Starting a Program

You've got plenty of group windows open, but the real reason for using the Program Manager is to start programs. To see how it's done, start the Windows accessory called Clock. It's interesting to look at and easy to manipulate. First, find Accessories and make it the active window. Now

☐ Double-click on Clock.

The clock appears on your rather crowded desktop. Just for fun, change the Clock's face from analog to a more computer-appropriate digital display:

☐ Open the Clock's Settings menu by clicking on it or by pressing Alt-S.

☐ Choose Digital by clicking on it or by pressing D.

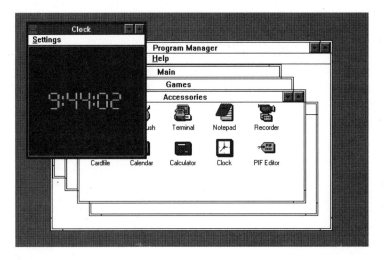

Managing Windows

When you have more than one window open, you want to be able to use them efficiently: close them, change their sizes, rearrange them, and move them out of the way by turning them into icons at the bottom of the screen. Windows lets you do all this with the help of a mouse and several different window elements.

The following illustration labels the window elements that most concern you:

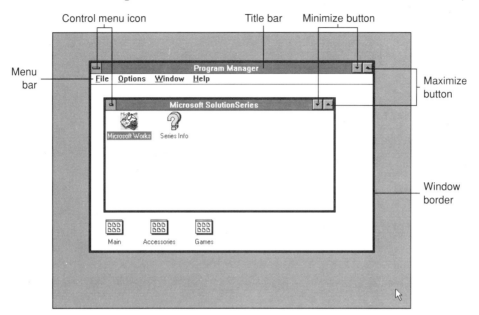

Now, let's take a quick — hopefully memorable — tour of Windows' high points. Grab your mouse and let's go.

Sizing a Window with Borders

A double-lined border frames every window on your screen. You can move either a side or a corner to change the size of a window. When you're sizing a window, the mouse pointer appears as a double-headed arrow on the side or corner you are pulling or pushing into position. The mouse pointer looks like this:

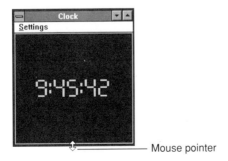

— Mouse pointer

To change the height or width of a window, you move one of the side borders. To change both dimensions of a window — for example, to make it shorter and narrower at the same time — you move a corner.

Verify that the Clock is still the active window. Move a corner to make the Clock smaller:

☐ Place the mouse pointer on the bottom right corner.

☐ Press and hold the left mouse button and push the corner up and to the left until the outline of the Clock is about the size of a business card.

☐ Release the mouse button.

Your Clock should look something like this:

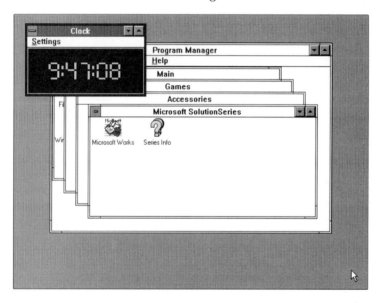

Moving a Window with the Title Bar

The *title bar* appears at the top of every window. As its name indicates, the title bar identifies the program or document in the window. The title bar is also the key to moving a window around on the desktop.

The Clock is now a handy size for displaying the time in some out-of-the-way corner, so move it away from the center of the screen:

☐ Place the mouse pointer on the title bar of the window (on the word *Clock* is a useful place).

□ Press and hold the left mouse button, and drag the grayish outline to the bottom right corner of the desktop.

□ Release the mouse button, and the Clock jumps to its new location.

With the Clock out of the way, you can tinker with the Program Manager's display for awhile:

□ Click in the Program Manager window.

Giving Commands with the Menu Bar

A menu bar appears just below the title bar in any application window (a window in which a program is running). Each program has its own menus, as you can see by comparing the menu bars of the Program Manager window and the Clock window. Menus always contain lists of commands to choose from. In many respects, they are equivalent to typing commands at the DOS prompt.

Earlier you learned how to use the Window menu to change to a different group window. The same procedure applies to choosing any menu or command in either Windows or Works: Either click on the menu name, or press Alt and the underlined letter in the menu name.

Use the Window menu once again, this time to rearrange the group windows in the Program Manager:

□ Point to the Window menu and click.

Notice that the first two items on the Window menu are Cascade and Tile. When windows overlap, as they do now in the Program Manager, they are cascaded like shingles on a roof. You can see only the icons in the window on top. If you tile the open windows (which you'll do next), Windows arranges them side by side so that the contents of each are visible.

Before you begin tiling the windows, notice the key combinations Shift-F5 (shown as Shift+F5 on the screen) and Shift-F4 to the right of Cascade and Tile. Notations like these on a menu indicate shortcuts you can use directly from the keyboard. Tile the open windows on your screen:

□ Place the mouse pointer on Tile and click, or press Shift-F4.

Almost immediately, the screen changes to look like this:

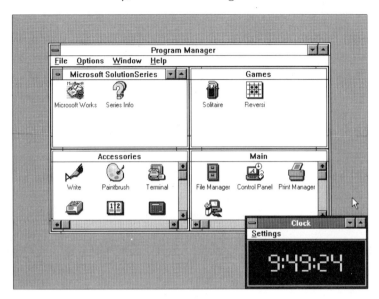

Return to cascaded windows by using the keyboard shortcut:

☐ Press Shift-F5.

Controlling a Window with the Control Menu

A Control menu icon appears in the upper left corner of every application and document window:

If you use a mouse, the Control menu icon is a quick way to close a window. You don't need so many open windows in the Program Manager, so close a few:

☐ Point to the Control menu icon in the active group window (not Program Manager). Double-click.

Close one or two other group windows, including Accessories if you want; the Clock won't stop running. When you're through,

☐ Return to the Clock window by clicking on it or by pressing Alt-Esc.

Growing and Shrinking Windows

Like magic cookies in Wonderland, Windows' Maximize and Minimize buttons have a profound effect on size. Looking like side-by-side Scrabble tiles in the top right corner of the Clock window title bar, the Minimize button is identified by a downward-pointing triangle, the Maximize button with an upward-pointing triangle. You can use these buttons only if you have a mouse. With the keyboard, you must use the Control menu.

To practice, first make the Clock window smaller by minimizing it:

□ Point to the Minimize button and click.

The Clock becomes an icon in the lower left corner of the desktop.

When the Clock, or any other application, is minimized, it is out of the way, yet it remains active and continues to keep time. You don't have to stop, start, and stop an application each time you want to switch from it to another application and back again.

After you've minimized an application, you'll probably want to restore it to its former size at some point:

□ Point to the minimized Clock and double-click.

Maximizing a Window: And now maximize the Clock window:

□ Point to the Maximize button and click.

The Clock immediately grows to fill almost the entire screen:

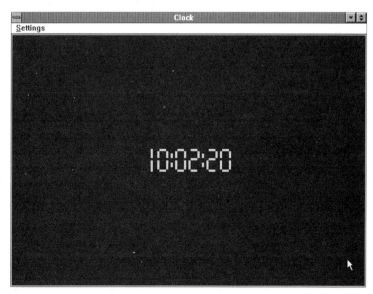

Although the display is way too big for a simple clock, do remember how to maximize a window. You'll find that this type of full-screen display is very useful when you're working with even a moderately long document in an application window.

 It's possible to "bury" an open application window underneath others when resizing windows. The window remains open, even though it is not visible on the desktop. To get to it, you can restore the maximized window and then choose the window you want, press Alt-Esc to cycle through all open application windows, or choose Switch To from the maximized window's Control menu and choose from the list of open tasks it displays.

Restoring a Maximized Window: When a window is maximized, as the Clock is now, notice that the Maximize button changes to display two arrows, one pointing up and the other down:

You have no need for a Maximize button now, so Windows has changed it to a Restore button. You can use this button to return the Clock to its former size:

□ Point to the Restore button and click.

To stop the Clock (or any other program completely), you *close* it:

□ Double-click on the Control menu icon.

This is a quick way to choose the Close command from the Control menu. Use it whenever you finish with a program. If you've left some unsaved changes in an open document, the program will ask what you want to do with them before it shuts down.

That nearly concludes your whirlwind tour of Windows. Now for another jaunt, this time to look at a feature that can help you out in a jam.

Help, a Special Menu

Windows is easy to use and it also offers a great deal of power and flexibility, but you don't have to repeatedly turn to the documentation, try to figure out what to do on your own, or memorize every possible Windows feature. You can ask for help whenever you want.

Windows, like Works and many other Windows applications, offers *on-line Help* that you can refer to not only when you need information about a specific feature, but also when you want to explore the program on your own, at your own convenience.

To see what Help looks like:

☐ Make Program Manager the active window if necessary.

☐ Open the Help menu.

You'll see this menu:

The types of help you can request include an index of Help topics, help on using the keyboard, a review of Windows procedures ... even help on using Help.

NOTE: *The only choice on the Help menu that is not directly related to Help is called About Program Manager. Choose this item to see copyright information or, more importantly, to find out how Windows is running on your computer (the* mode *it is in), how much available memory you have, and what percentage of your system's resources are available.*

Because Help is so useful, both Windows and Works let you request help without opening the Help menu. Simply press the F1 key, and the Help window will appear.

Using Help

To dig a little deeper into Help, choose Basic Skills from the Help menu:

☐ Click Basic Skills, or press B.

Within a few seconds, this window appears:

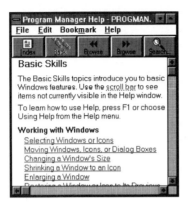

Notice the buttons and menu names in the Help window. Help is an application in its own right, rather than a simple text-display module, so it offers you an assortment of buttons and menus that let you control the window and use Help selectively.

Scroll Bars

Along the bottom and right sides of the Help window, you should see two *scroll bars:*

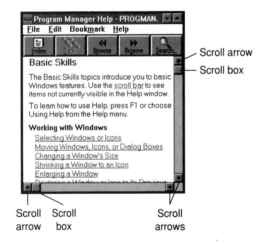

Scroll arrow
Scroll box

Scroll   Scroll   Scroll
arrow   box   arrows

Scroll bars appear both in Windows and Windows applications whenever the onscreen window is too small to display its entire contents. The horizontal scroll bar moves (scrolls) the view from side to side, and the vertical scroll bar moves the view up and down. Each scroll bar contains the same elements, and you use them in the same ways.

Clicking a scroll arrow in the vertical scroll bar moves you up or down one line at a time. Clicking a scroll arrow in the horizontal scroll bar moves you left or right one character at a time. Pointing to a scroll arrow and holding down the mouse button scrolls the screen continuously in the direction you indicate. Try using a vertical scroll bar:

☐ Click the down scroll arrow a few times.

☐ Click the up scroll arrow to return to the "top" of the window.

NOTE: *The horizontal scroll bar in Windows Help is displayed but is not functional because you don't need it. Windows Help is designed to display all text within the window. In other programs, including Works, however, you'll find this scroll bar very useful.*

The *scroll box* in each scroll bar serves a double purpose. First, its position in the bar shows your relative position in a document. Second, the scroll boxes help you move rapidly through a document:

☐ Drag the scroll box to various points on the scroll bar to see different parts of the Help window.

☐ Click above the scroll box to scroll up one screenful.

☐ Click below the scroll box to scroll down one screenful.

When you finish experimenting, return to the beginning of the Help topic.

Navigating in Help

Notice that Help is displayed in three ways: in normal, underlined, and dotted underlined text. (The underlined and dotted underlined words are also probably in a different color if you have a color monitor.) The normal text describes Help and gives you instructions. You read it as you would read the paper, a book, or a letter.

The underlined text is special. To borrow a word from science-fiction tales, underlined text "warps" you to a new Help topic. In the Basic Skills window, for example, you see a number of underlined categories, including *Selecting Windows or Icons* and *Moving Windows, Icons, or Dialog Boxes.* Choose one of these to get to that Help topic:

☐ Place the mouse pointer on *Selecting Windows or Icons.* (Notice that the mouse pointer turns into a hand with a pointing finger.) Click to see the topic.

Very quickly, the display changes:

Take some time now to scroll through the Help on selecting windows and icons. As you go, notice that certain words, such as *select* and *window,* are displayed with a dotted underline. These are glossary items that Help can define for you:

☐ Place the mouse pointer on a glossary term. (Again you see a hand with a pointing finger.) Press and hold the left mouse button.

A small box containing a definition appears on your screen:

When you're finished, release the mouse button, and the definition will disappear. To leave Help:

☐ Double-click on the Control menu icon in the top left corner of the Help window.

NOTE: *If you don't have a mouse, choose Keyboard from the Help menu and spend some time leafing through the keyboard Help topics. To keep a list of keystrokes for later reference, print the list you want by choosing Print Topic from the Help window's File menu.*

This concludes your look at Windows. From here on, you'll be working with Works. Because you are now familiar with the Windows environment, you should find Works as comfortable as old sneakers . . . right from the start.

WORKS

In the remainder of this chapter, you'll start Works, take a look around, and learn how to set up Works so that your screen resembles those illustrated in later chapters. Along the way, you'll see how the Windows look extends to applications designed to work with it, and you will come to view Windows and Works not as computer programs to be memorized and mastered, but as tools that help you define a productive way of working. That's what computers are all about anyway: providing the tools that let you concentrate on what you want to do, rather than on how you're supposed to do it.

Starting Works

As already mentioned, when you install Works, Windows creates a program group named Microsoft Solution Series. Check your desktop for the Microsoft Solution Series group and make it the active window:

When you install Works, the Setup program creates two icons, one for Works itself and another — a question mark — named Series Info. If you double-click on the Series Info icon, a Help window opens and displays information about Works and its relatives in the Series. Right now, however, start Works:

☐ Double-click on the Works icon.

Your disk drive hums into action, and the Program Manager is quickly replaced by a licensing message, followed by this opening screen:

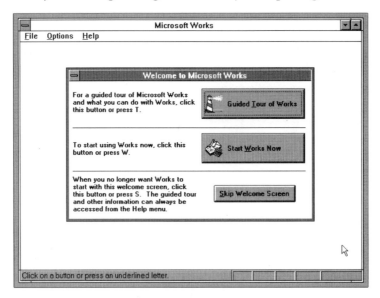

To make you feel comfortable from the start, the Works opening display lets you choose to tour Works to see what it's like or start Works and get right down to business. You'll soon find this display unnecessary — and even a little bothersome — so the third button lets you choose to skip this opening screen altogether. Leave it for now.

The Works guided tour is a self-contained and self-explanatory look at major attractions, so it's a good idea to try it out at some point. If you're following this introduction to Works on your computer, however, skip the tour for now, and choose the second button on the Works opening screen:

□   Click the Start Works Now button.

This is what you see:

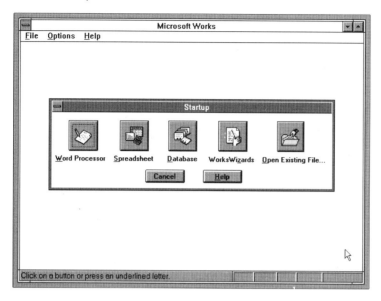

This is the Works application window, the place in which you'll start up the word processor, spreadsheet, database and WorksWizards. At the bottom of the window, you see a one-line *status bar*. As you work with Works, the text at the left side of the status bar will change to display short, informative messages. Here, for example, it tells you to *Click on a button or press an underlined letter*. For a quick reminder, the status bar can be very useful.

In the center of the window, Works normally displays a box, called a *dialog box*, titled Startup. A dialog box is the Works (and Windows) method of showing you options, displaying messages, or requesting information. This dialog box lets you choose the type of work you want to do:

- Word Processor, Spreadsheet, and Database open the respective modules and display a document window in which you can create a new document.

- WorksWizards takes you to a special — and colorful — set of tools that help you create mailing labels, an address book, or a form letter. You'll use a WorksWizard in Chapter 3.

- Open Existing File lets you choose a previously stored file and, at the same time, start the module with which the file was created. For example, if you choose a spreadsheet file, the spreadsheet module will start so you can work on the file.

NOTE: *If you don't see the Startup dialog box or the status bar, don't be concerned. You'll soon find out how to make both appear.*

The remainder of this chapter looks at the Works menus. To open these menus, you have to close the Startup dialog box, so:

☐ Click the Cancel button.

The Works window now covers almost all of the screen, but you can see part of the desktop around the edges. If you want, you can return to the Program Manager or another program by clicking in a visible part of its window or by pressing Alt-Esc. Usually, however, you'll want to make the most of your screen, so expand Works to fill the screen by clicking its Maximize button.

Your onscreen window should look familiar. Like Windows, the Works application window contains a title bar identifying the program, a menu bar, an icon for the Control menu, and two sizing buttons (currently, Minimize and Restore).

The Works Menus

In addition to the Control menu, the Works application window offers three menus in the menu bar: File, Options, and Help. The Control menu, like its relatives in Windows, helps you manage the application window and switch to other active programs. The File and Options menus contain commands you see within the Works modules as well, so a quick survey will be enough for now. As you'll see, the Help menu is similar to Windows Help.

The File Menu

Although you'll normally use the Startup dialog box, the File menu offers another means of starting a Works application. You can also specify whether you want to work on a new file or one you've already created. Open the File menu:

☐ Click on File.

You see this menu:

The first two choices on the File menu let you choose to create a new file (document) or open one that already exists. These commands are the equivalents of choosing the Word Processor, Spreadsheet, Database, and Open Existing File buttons on the Startup dialog.

The Close, Save, and Save As commands respectively let you close an open file, save a file under an existing name, and save a file under a new name, in a different directory, or on a different disk. These three commands are currently dimmed (grayed out) to indicate that you cannot use them now — because you can't close or save a file when you haven't yet opened one.

The Save Workspace command lets you tell Works to remember which documents you have open and how you've arranged them in the application window. This feature lets you preserve a given situation so that you can return to it at another time and pick up where you left off.

The final command on the File menu, Exit Works, is the command you use to quit Works and return to Windows. If you want, you can double-click on the Control menu icon to do the same thing. Close the File menu for now:

◻ Click anywhere in the Works window, press Esc twice, or press Alt once.

The Options Menu

When you haven't yet started a Works application, the Options menu includes only one command, Works Settings. You use this command to set up Works the way you want. To see the options:

◻ Choose the Works Settings command.

A dialog box like this appears:

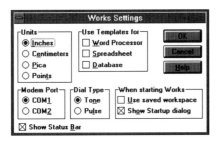

Dialog boxes in both Works and Windows vary according to their purpose. Some, such as the Startup and Works Settings dialog boxes, present sets of options. Others, as you'll see when you begin working with Works, offer lists of choices or ask you to type information, such as the name of a file.

Every dialog box contains at least one button, usually labeled OK, that you can click to signal "I'm done." Most contain more than one. This dialog box, for example, has three of these buttons: OK, Cancel, and Help. Cancel, as you've seen, cancels a dialog box and, hence, the command or option presented. The Help button takes you directly to help on using the dialog box, which can be very useful when you need more information.

Notice that some options in the dialog box are preceded by circles, others by squares. The circles are *option buttons* you can click to choose a particular item. The squares are *checkboxes* you can click to turn an item on or off. Although they seem to serve the same purpose, option buttons and checkboxes differ:

■ A dark circle appears in the option button of a chosen item. When option buttons appear next to sets of related items, you can choose only one. You cannot, for instance, choose both inches and centimeters as units of measurement.

■ An X appears in a checkbox to show that an option is turned on. When checkboxes appear next to sets of related items, you can turn on more than one. You can, for example, check both Use saved workspace and Show Startup dialog in the box entitled *When starting Works.*

At the bottom of the dialog box is the item Show Status Bar. When the status bar is turned off, you lengthen the usable space on your screen by one line.

To ensure that your screen matches the illustrations shown in this book, check the Show Startup dialog and Show Status Bar settings. If you don't see an X in the box,

□ Turn the option on by clicking in its checkbox.

To carry out the command, whether or not you changed settings:

□ Click OK.

The Help Menu

You've seen Windows Help, so there's not much left for you to learn about Works Help except what it has to offer. Now is as good a time as any, so open the Help menu. The following list drops down from the menu bar:

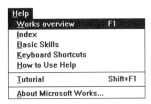

The first Help topic is a Works overview. To the right of the topic name you see *F1*, the keyboard shortcut that takes you to the overview without opening the menu. Notice that the status bar now reads *Displays this Help topic.*

Works Help resembles Windows Help, so once you're familiar with one, you're familiar with the other. As you use the Works word processor, spreadsheet, and database, you'll notice that the Help menu changes slightly to provide assistance specifically for each of these areas. (The Help menu is not included in WorksWizards because the wizards guide you step by step and are easy to use.)

From the Help menu, you can also request the Works Tutorial, a self-teaching aid that walks you through Works and its three applications. The tutorial shows you what Works can do and lets you try your hand at using the program. Although the tutorial is somewhat constrained in the sense that it follows one clearly defined path through Works and it does not allow you to do much experimenting along the way, its descriptions are clear, the graphics are pleasant, and the lessons are well-presented. If you've never used an on-line tutorial, and especially if you tend to dislike "programmed learning," you should try the Works tutorial. You can stop whenever you like, work at your own pace, and skip lessons that don't interest you.

If you're going directly to Chapter 2, close the Help menu and leave the screen as it is. If you want to quit Works for a while, double-click on the Control menu icon.

2
Using Works

You probably purchased Works because it's an integrated software program — a single program you can use to print, sort, organize, and calculate your data in most of the ways that matter to you.

Works offers the services of a word processor, a spreadsheet, and a database — three programs that you would otherwise have to purchase separately. Because they are combined in a single package, the Works applications offer a big advantage over stand-alone programs: consistency. You learn one basic set of commands and one basic way of interacting with the program, and then you apply what you know to any of the three applications.

This chapter will give you a look at all three Works applications so you can become acquainted with Works as a whole before you get down to the business of digging into each of the applications in Part II.

A PLACE TO START

Most people are familiar with word processing, so the word processor is a good application to explore first. To keep the screen simple, start the word processor by telling Works you want to open a new file:

- □ Start Works if necessary.

- □ Choose Word Processor from the Startup dialog. If you're continuing from Chapter 1, choose Create New File from the File menu, and then click the Word Processor button in the dialog box that appears.

Works displays the following:

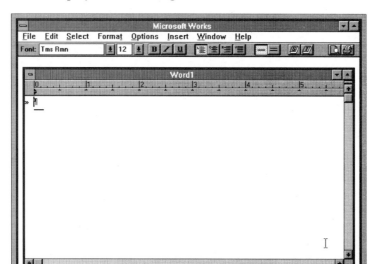

Now you are in the word processor, and the screen quickly becomes much more detailed than it was before. Notice that you have two windows open, the application window and a smaller document window within it. Each window has its own border, title bar, and control buttons.

In the document window, Works displays *Word1* in the title bar. Word1 is the default name for your first new word processing document — letter, memo, report, and so on — in a Works session. Until you name and save a new file, Works always gives it a generic name and number like this. When you do save a file, Works assigns the extension WPS to a word processing document. In the spreadsheet, Works uses the extension WKS; in the database, it uses WDB.

A fair amount of unused space surrounds these windows, so maximize them both to take advantage of your entire screen. (Maximize the application window first.) The screen should look like the one at the top of the following page.

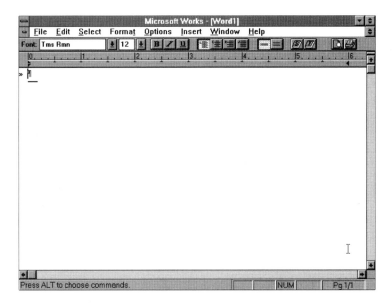

Notice that the two windows become much less distinct when they are maximized. Even though you still have two separate windows, they seem to have blended seamlessly into one. Because the document window no longer has a title bar of its own, the document name, Word1, is displayed in square brackets in the title bar of the application window.

The Application Window

Across the top of the application window is a more extensive set of menu names than the three you see when starting Works. At the left edge of the menu bar is a second Control menu icon. Because your document window is maximized and has no title bar of its own, you use this icon for managing the document window. The Control menu icon above it is, as usual, for managing the Works application window. To the right of the menu bar is a Restore button. Again, this controls the document window. The Restore button above it controls the Works window.

Just below the menu bar is one of Works most useful onscreen features, the *Toolbar:*

With the Toolbar you can quickly and easily carry out common actions with the mouse. Instead of choosing commands from a menu, you simply click on a button on the Toolbar to achieve the same result. Once you become accustomed to its speed and responsiveness, the Toolbar quickly becomes indispensable.

Document Windows

Your document window, which was displayed within its own border before the windows were maximized, now begins at the top of the onscreen ruler (just below the Toolbar).

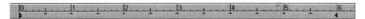

Like the Toolbar, the ruler is responsive to the mouse and lets you quickly carry out commands you would otherwise choose from menus. The ruler appears only in the word processor. It allows you to set tab stops and indent paragraphs. You'll see more of the ruler in Chapter 4.

At the top left corner of the document window's workspace is a blinking vertical line called the *insertion point.* This line marks the place where text will appear when you begin typing. Try typing some text. If you make a mistake, backspace to the error and retype.

☐ Type the words

```
This is the first document I've created with the Works word processor.
```

As you type, the insertion point moves to the right, staying one space ahead of each new character.

The Changeable Pointer

Somewhere else in the document window you should also see the mouse pointer. (If you don't see it, move the mouse around a little bit.) The mouse pointer changes shape in different parts of the screen. In the word processor, it takes three important shapes:

■ A vertical line with short crossbars at the top and bottom. This is called an I-beam cursor.

■ The arrow, which you have already seen.

■ A "cross" of sorts, with parallel lines as the horizontal bar and a double-headed arrow as the vertical bar. This is called a split cursor.

NOTE: *If you see dots between words or small arrows on the screen as you work through this chapter, don't worry. These are spacing characters. Chapter 4 tells you how to turn them off and on.*

Each of these shapes performs a different task. Within the document workspace, the mouse pointer is an I-beam cursor. You can use it to move the insertion point and to select text for editing:

- ☐ Place the pointer just in front of the *d* in *document*. Click the left mouse button and the insertion point jumps to that position.

- ☐ With the pointer on the word *document*, double-click. A dark highlight covers the entire word, indicating that it is selected.

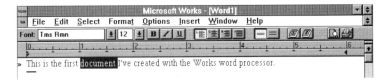

In the scroll bars, the menu bar, and the ruler, the mouse pointer takes on its usual form (the arrow):

- ☐ Move the pointer to the menu bar. Notice that the pointer changes to an arrow. Point to a menu and click to open it.

- ☐ Move the pointer into the document workspace. Click to close the menu.

Here, you've used the mouse pointer for its usual point-and-click function. Because a menu was open, and Works expected you to choose a command, the mouse pointer remained an arrow even though you moved it back into the document workspace. When you closed the menu, indicating you were finished with it, the mouse pointer returned to its I-beam shape.

Finally,

- ☐ Move the mouse pointer to the small rectangle (the split box) just above the up scroll arrow in the vertical scroll bar.

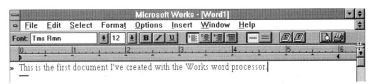

□ When you see the split cursor, drag it down toward the middle of the screen. Release the mouse button.

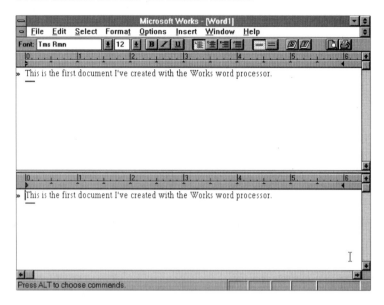

Here, the mouse pointer split a window into two. When you split a window, you can scroll each window independently to view different parts of a long document.

□ To remove the split and return to a single window, place the mouse pointer on the horizontal *split bar* separating the two windows. Double-click or drag the split bar off the screen.

As you'll see, the mouse pointer assumes other shapes in the spreadsheet and database. When you explore the applications in detail, you'll see how the shape of the mouse pointer gives you visual clues to what it can do.

Managing Document Windows

Every time you open a document, whether it's a new or existing file, Works opens a new document window. As in Windows, you can choose to cascade document windows, overlapping them on the screen, or you can choose to tile them, placing them side by side in the available space. You can maximize a document window to fill the application workspace, or you can minimize it and reduce it to an out-of-the-way icon.

To see how easily you can work with multiple documents, open a second window:

□ Choose Create New File from the File menu and click the Word Processor button to create another word processing document.

□ When the second window opens, distinguish it from the first by typing

`This is my second document.`

Right now, the windows overlap, so you can't see the text in the first document you created. To see them both:

□ Choose Tile from the Window menu.

Immediately, the screen changes to look like this:

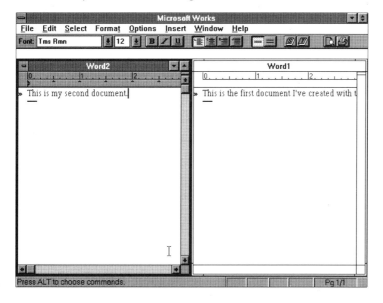

Tiling windows makes it easier to work with two or more documents. The highlighted menu bar tells you that Word2 is the active document window. Each window is equipped with its own title bar, scroll bars, and control buttons, so you can manipulate each in any way you choose. To switch from one document to another, click in the window you want.

Notice, however, that the text in your first document is no longer completely visible. The window is too small to display the entire line. You could use the scroll bars to view the rest of the text, but that would become tedious if you were working with a multiline document, so Works provides an easier way:

☐ Click in the Word1 window to make it active.

☐ Choose Wrap for Window from the Options menu.

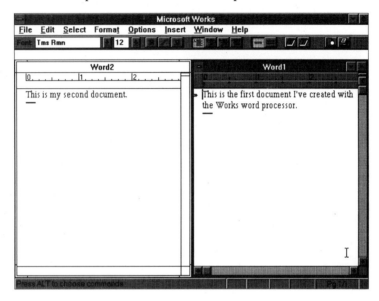

Now you've instructed Works to "wrap" the text of your document, fitting it into the window area so that all words are visible. See what happens when you change the window's size:

☐ Move the right window border so that the window is about 2 inches wide.

Works rebreaks the lines to display all of your text. Such a narrow window is usually impractical, though, so:

☐ Drag the border back to return the window to its former size.

PRACTICING WITH THE APPLICATIONS

Part II gives you an in-depth look at each of the Works applications and what you can do with them. Before you dive in, though, you'll find it helpful to see how they resemble one another and how they differ. That's what you'll do in the remainder of this chapter. Don't worry about memorizing details for now. They'll come soon enough.

In the Word Processor

Oddly enough, even though computers originated as mathematical machines, they are most commonly used these days for processing words, not numbers. Of all applications, the word processor is used more often than any other.

The Works word processor is remarkably adaptable in many ways, particularly in its ability to insert drawings, spreadsheet charts, and database records into a document. You can even create *links* to charts and other items so that changes in them are automatically reflected in the word-processed document to which they are linked.

You're working with the word processor now, so let's take it on an extended test run. To clear the screen a bit, close the second document window without saving your sample text:

◻ Make the Word2 window active.

◻ Double-click on its Control menu icon or choose Close from the File menu.

◻ When Works displays a dialog box asking if you want to save the changes to Word2, click No.

This is the way to "toss out" an unnamed document you don't want any longer. Tile the remaining document window.

Shaping and Viewing Text

Now try out the Toolbar:

◻ Select the word *first* by placing the mouse pointer on it and double-click. The highlight expands to cover the entire word.

☐ Make the word boldface, so it appears in dark type. Point to the button labeled B (for Bold) and click.

☐ Place the mouse pointer in a blank part of the window and click to move the highlight away from the word *first.*

Now see what your document would look like if you printed it:

☐ Point to the Preview button on the Toolbar (the second-to-last button, showing a diagram of a page and a magnifying glass) and then click.

The screen changes to show you a page with your small bit of text on it:

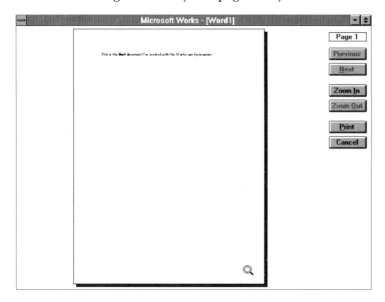

The words are indecipherable, but you can change that:

☐ Click the button labeled Zoom In or move the mouse pointer over the page and click.

☐ To make the words even larger, click the Zoom In button again or click on the page again.

Each time you zoom in on the page, Works magnifies the words for you. The first time, it zooms in halfway; the second time, it zooms in all the way. To reverse course and see the entire page again:

- ☐ Either click the button labeled Zoom Out or click on the preview page itself twice in succession.

- ☐ To leave the Preview feature, click the Cancel button.

That's enough of the word processor for now. If you don't want to leave the Wrap for Window option turned on, open the Options menu and click on the item again.

In the Spreadsheet

The Works spreadsheet lets you work with numeric data — finances, budget projections, salary information, and the like. Because much of the work you do with numbers involves calculations, the spreadsheet enables you to build formulas to add, subtract, multiply, work out percentages, and so on. For certain calculations, such as averages, loan payments, and return on investments, the spreadsheet also includes standard formulas called *functions* that you can use by simply plugging your own numbers into the formulas and letting Works take care of the rest.

You can experiment with different possibilities (the so-called "what if" scenarios) to see which of several alternatives works best for you. For example, you can calculate the difference in payments on a loan extending 5, 10, and 15 years. How do those payments fit into your current operating budget? Which payment comes closest to your projected future income? For that matter, what is your projected future income? The spreadsheet can't decide any of these things for you, but it can help you see the figures more clearly, especially if you use it to transform those numbers into a graph or chart that shows pictorially what you think you see numerically.

You can start the spreadsheet while the word processor is running:

- ☐ Choose Create New File from the File menu.

- ☐ Click Spreadsheet when Works asks what type of file to create.

A new document window appears, this one containing a blank document named Sheet1 and a rectangular grid of small boxes called *cells*:

Each of the cells on your screen can contain a numeric value, an item of text, or a formula that performs a calculation. Notice the letters across the top of the window. Each letter refers to one vertical *column* of cells on the spreadsheet. Similarly, you can see numbers running down the left-hand side of the window. Each of these numbers refers to one horizontal *row* of cells. Because each cell occupies a unique position in the spreadsheet, each has its own "address" that describes the column and row in which the cell appears. For example, the cell in the top left-hand corner of the spreadsheet (currently outlined by a double-lined box) is cell A1 because it is in column A, row 1. You and Works use these cell addresses whenever you want to refer to a specific cell or group of cells.

Recall that the mouse pointer looks like a slender I in a word processor document. In the spreadsheet, it looks like a chubby cross. Once again, however, the mouse pointer shows its changeability. Move it around on the screen and you'll notice it changing shape, depending on the screen region it touches.

Entering and Calculating Numbers

You've probably noticed that the Toolbar in the spreadsheet looks a little different from the Toolbar in the word processor. Specifically, several buttons toward the right side of the Toolbar have changed. As a reminder, this is what the Toolbar looks like in the word processor:

This is what the Toolbar looks like in the spreadsheet:

In the word processor, two buttons control the spacing of lines in a paragraph, one button starts a spell-checking program, and another calls up a thesaurus that lets you find synonyms for words. These buttons aren't needed in the spreadsheet, so they're replaced by buttons that let you display numbers as dollar amounts, as percentages, or with commas as separators. The button with the Greek sigma (Σ) lets you total a group of numbers with pushbutton ease, and the button labeled with a small bar chart lets you turn a group of numbers into one of several types of charts.

You can try out some of these buttons now. First, verify that the highlight is in the top left-hand corner of the grid (cell A1). Now enter some numbers on the spreadsheet:

☐ Type *123* in cell A1. Press the Down arrow key to enter the number, and at the same time, move the highlight down one cell.

☐ Type *456* in cell A2. Press the Down arrow key again.

☐ Type *789* in cell A3 and press Enter.

This is what the cells should look like:

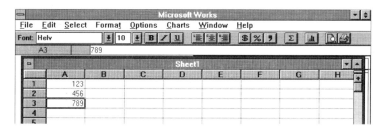

The numbers are rather plain at the moment. Try telling Works to display dollar values instead:

☐ Place the mouse pointer on cell A1. Press the left mouse button and drag the mouse pointer down until the highlight covers cells A1 through A3.

☐ Click the Currency button (labeled with a $) on the Toolbar.

Next tell Works to chart the numbers:

☐ If necessary, drag the highlight to cover cells A1 through A3. Click the Chart button (third from the right) on the Toolbar.

A new document window opens, displaying a chart like this:

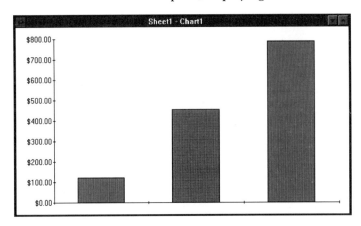

You've now turned the numbers into a graphic display. Return to the spreadsheet layout:

☐ Open the Window menu and choose Sheet1.

You've seen enough of the spreadsheet for now, so close it and get rid of your experiments:

☐ Choose Close from the File menu.

☐ Choose No when a dialog box appears and asks if you want to save the changes to Sheet1.

Now on to the database.

In the Database

With the word processor you can write anything from a letter of complaint to a bid proposal. With the spreadsheet you can track numbers ranging from pennies to your Fortune 500 stocks. What's left? A place to keep lists. You can keep lists of any kind, for any purpose — groceries if you want — but you will most likely keep lists of entries you want to sort in some way, from names and addresses to warehouse inventories, catalog items, or a lifetime list of bird species spotted in your back yard. All of these lists can be turned over to the Works database, a far more organized and efficient listmaker than most humans.

A database of any sort is a set of *records* related to a particular topic. Each record forms a unit of information made up of one to several *fields*, each containing one piece of data about the record. For this chapter, you'll create a short sample database with three fields — Last, First, and Dept — which form records for several people employed by Company X:

Last	First	Dept
Dillion	Marianne	Accounting
Tanaka	George	Accounting
Mayer	Oscar	Sales
Donatello	Raphael	Graphic Arts
Smith	Georgia	Sales

The spreadsheet helps you by calculating formulas and creating charts. Similarly, the Works database does more than list items. It can sort them for you, find specific entries, and even examine records to find those that match qualifications you specify. If you want, the database can calculate averages, find the highest and lowest values in a given field, and generate a report for you.

To start the database:

□ Choose Create New File from the File menu.

□ Click Database when Works asks what type of file to create.

Once again the screen changes, as does the document name (Data1) and the Toolbar. Here, as in the word processor, you see an insertion point. Works presents you with a blank slate, but unlike the word processor, the database opens on a blank *form*. This is where you create the fields that will hold the data for each of the records in your database. You can arrange the fields in any way, much as you would when creating a paper-based form for employee information, test scores, insurance coverage, or any other set of records.

Unlike the other Works applications, the database works in four *views*. Here, you see its *form view*. In form view you can create a form and enter information one record at a time. Several buttons in the Toolbar let you quickly change views: *list view* displays groups of records in a spreadsheet-like format; *query view* lets you search for and display specific records; and *report view* generates a printable report listing the records and calculations you choose to include. The following figure shows the buttons in the Toolbar:

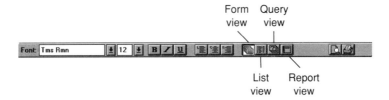

Entering Records and Viewing a Database

Try creating a form for the fields in the sample database shown earlier. The insertion point should be in the top left-hand corner of the form view window. Don't worry about arranging the fields artistically at this point; simply start typing:

☐ Type *Last:* (don't forget the colon; it tells Works to create a field) and press Enter. Works displays a dialog box like this, asking how large you want the field to be:

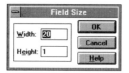

☐ Press Enter to accept the suggested size. A dotted line appears after the field name, and the insertion point drops to the next line.

☐ Type *First:* and press Enter twice to create the field and accept the suggested size.

☐ Create a third field, *Dept:*, as you did the other two.

Now you're ready to enter some data:

☐ Click on the field named Last: (or press the Up arrow key and Right arrow key). A large highlight appears on the dotted line after *Last:*. Type *Dillion* and press the Tab key.

☐ When the highlight moves to the next field, *First:*, type *Marianne*. Press Tab and type *Accounting* in the *Dept:* field.

☐ Press Tab to start a new record. Create records for the following entries. Press Enter when you complete the last record.

```
Tanaka        George        Accounting

Mayer         Oscar         Sales

Donatello     Raphael       Graphic Arts

Smith         Georgia       Sales
```

Now, to see what your database looks like:

☐ Click on the List view button in the Toolbar.

The screen changes to a list of records:

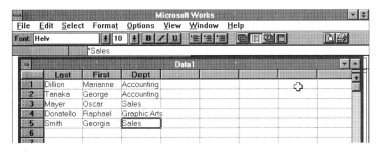

Suppose you want to see the records for only those employees who work in Accounting:

☐ Click the Query view button in the Toolbar.

☐ When the screen changes to show a blank version of your form, click or press Tab (if necessary) to move the highlight to *Dept:*. Type *Accounting*. Press Enter.

☐ Switch back to List view by clicking the List view button.

This time you see only selected records: those for Marianne Dillion and George Tanaka, the only employees in the database who work in Accounting.

Combining Data

As a final exercise, try moving a few records from your database into the word-processed "document" you created earlier. In the past, transferring data between documents created by different applications was one of the most difficult and frustrating activities in personal computing. With Works, it's a breeze, thanks to Windows and a very special Windows feature called the *Clipboard.*

The Clipboard

Chapter 1 explained that Windows and Works form a partnership to help you get things done. Although you can't see the Clipboard, it is an important part of Windows. Essentially, the Clipboard is a portion of your computer's memory that Windows sets aside specifically for holding data that you want to move from one document to another. After you place information on the Clipboard, whether it's text or a graphic, one paragraph or several pages, that information remains in memory and is available to programs that can accept it until you place new data on the Clipboard.

To move data from document to document, you use a process called *cut and paste.* Cut and paste is the electronic equivalent of scissors and tape. You've no doubt had the fun of snipping apart a letter, report, or proposal and reorganizing it or inserting parts of a different document by putting the pieces back together. You use cut and paste in Windows and Windows applications in much the same way, but without the mess. Windows, in fact, is better than real-life cut and paste, because it lets you *copy* and paste as well.

You can rearrange or duplicate information across documents with only three basic commands: Cut, Copy, and Paste. All three appear on the Edit menu in Works and most other Windows applications. Cut, as its name implies, removes information and places it on the Clipboard. Copy duplicates information, placing a copy on the Clipboard but leaving the original where it belongs. Paste inserts the contents of the Clipboard into an open document.

Using the Clipboard

You've already built a small set of records in the Works database, and you've got an open "letter" in the word processor. Your screen should be showing the List view in the database, with two selected records on it: the names of the employees in the Accounting department of Company X. To insert those records into the open document in the word processor:

- □ Drag the mouse pointer to extend the highlight to cover the six cells containing the names and departments of the two employees.

- □ Choose Copy from the Edit menu.

- □ Return to the word processor by choosing Word1 from the Window menu.

□ Press Enter to move the insertion point to a new line.

□ Choose Paste from the Edit menu.

The two records appear in your word-processed document, neatly laid out on separate lines. That's all there is to it. To see what the document would look like in print, click on the Preview button in the Toolbar or choose Print Preview from the File menu. To take a closer look, use the Zoom In button to see the text:

Easy as pie.

Your real exploration of Works and its capabilities begins in the next chapter, so it's time to clean up the screen:

□ Click the Cancel button or press Esc to leave Print Preview.

□ Double-click the Works window's Control menu icon.

□ Choose No when Works asks if you want to save the changes to Word1 and Data1.

You're back to Windows and ready to move on.

3

Using WorksWizards

Chapters 1 and 2 introduced you to Windows and the Works environment. In this chapter, you'll see how to bootstrap yourself to instant productivity with the help of three mini-programs called the WorksWizards. Friendlier than the average puppy, the WorksWizards are prefabricated sets of instructions that walk you through the process of creating an address book, a form letter, and a set of mailing labels. The WorksWizards are so easy to understand that they need little in the way of explanation or introduction, other than to say that they take most of the work and nearly all of the guesswork out of creating some common document types.

The best way to get acquainted with the WorksWizards is by jumping in and using one, so start Works if it isn't already running. If the welcome screen appears, click the Start Works Now button.

CALLING A WORKSWIZARD

You can call for your wizards at any time with the click of a button. After starting a Works session, choose WorksWizards from the Startup dialog box:

If you decide you need a WorksWizard later in a session, choose it from the dialog box that appears when you choose Create New File from the File menu in any Works application:

In this chapter you'll use a WorksWizard named Address Books that helps you create a form you can use to enter and update a list of names and addresses. To start the example,

◻ Click the WorksWizards button in the Startup dialog box, or choose Create New File from the File menu and click the Works-Wizards button in the dialog box that appears.

Works then displays another dialog box, asking which type of WorksWizard you want to use:

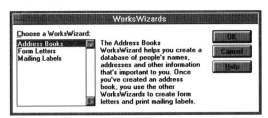

The Address Books WorksWizard is highlighted in the Choose a Works-Wizard box. The text in the middle of the dialog box describes the WorksWizard. Before making your selection, see what the other WorksWizards do:

◻ Point to Form Letters and click once with the mouse or use the Down arrow key to move the highlight. The text in the dialog box changes to describe this WorksWizard.

◻ When you finish reading about form letters, use the mouse or the Down arrow key again to highlight Mailing Labels.

To use either the Form Letters or Mailing Labels WorksWizard, you must already have created an address book of names and addresses. Unless you've already created such a list with the Works database, Address Books is your starting point in using the WorksWizards, so

☐ Double-click on Address Books to start the WorksWizard.

Within a few seconds, Works builds a more interesting graphical display than it normally presents:

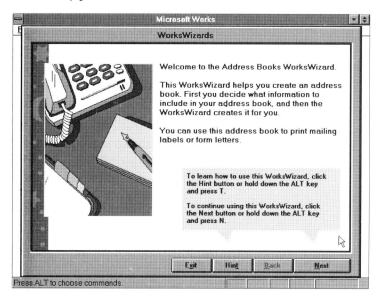

USING A WORKSWIZARD

The TV-like screen, titled WorksWizards, that you see within the Works window is an *instruction box*. For each major step in using a WorksWizard, Works displays a different instruction box containing explanatory text and asking you to make choices. The buttons at the bottom of the screen are your controls. They can be used as follows:

- To quit at any point, click the Exit button.

- To ask for more information, click the Hint button.

- To return to the previous instruction box, click the Back button (currently dimmed because there is no previous box to return to).

- To go on to the next instruction box, click the Next button.

On every part of the screen, especially in the bordered box at the bottom, you can see how much help a WorksWizard gives you as you use it. Because the WorksWizards offer so much information, this chapter won't waste your time with details that would only repeat what you see.

To see what the Address Books WorksWizard has to say about itself,

□ Click the Hint button.

Works displays a screenful of information about the control buttons. When you've read enough,

□ Click the Close Hints button. (The More button becomes active if a WorksWizard offers more than one screenful of hints.)

CREATING AN ADDRESS BOOK

When you use the Address Books WorksWizard, the WorksWizard asks your preferences before it designs that form into which you can later type names and addresses. For this example, create a personal address book to hold the names and addresses of your friends and relatives:

□ Click the Next button to move on to the second instruction box.

□ Click the button next to Personal.

Works now displays a box telling you what types of information you can include:

> Choose this option to keep track of addresses, phone numbers, birthdates, and information such as who you've sent thank you notes to.

Even though they are "programmed" instructions, WorksWizards don't lock you into choices as soon as you make them. Here, for example, you can click on the other buttons to see how the entries in a personal address book would differ from those in a business or organization address book:

□ Click on the button next to Business to see what types of information you can include.

▢ Click on the button next to Organization/Club for a description of that option.

▢ When you're finished reading the explanation, click on the button next to Personal again, and then click the Next button to move on to the next instruction box.

In the top half of the new instruction box the WorksWizard tells you which items it will include in your address book. If you don't want to include any of these fields, you can click in its checkbox to eliminate it. The fields are standard, though, so for this example keep them all.

In the lower half of the instruction box the WorksWizard offers you four additional options. Of these, two are particularly useful,

▢ Click in the Address2 checkbox to guarantee a place for apartment numbers, P.O. boxes, and the like.

▢ Click in the checkbox for Phone to include phone numbers as well as addresses.

▢ Click the Next button to move on.

You've included the basics for an address book, so the next instruction box simply asks if you want any other options. If you answer No, the WorksWizard will move on to the next step, creating a form for your data. Answer Yes, instead, to see what else you can add:

▢ Click Yes.

Now you find that you can add birthdates, work information, and other useful facts. If you want, go ahead and personalize your address book:

▢ Click the Next button. The WorksWizard displays a list of eight employment-related options.

▢ Click in the checkbox next to any items you want to add.

▢ Click the Next button. Now you see a list of family-related items. Again, click in the checkbox next to any you want.

☐ Click the Next button again. The WorksWizard tells you you've reached the last option, and it's ready to create your address book:

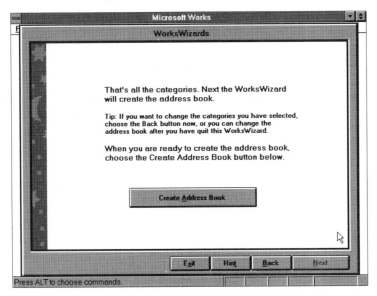

The screen says that you can make changes to the address book after you leave the WorksWizard. Making changes now is easier, however, so if you want or need to make a change, or if you simply want to review your choices, click the Back button as many times as necessary to return to the instruction box where you want to make a change. When you're satisfied with all your choices,

☐ Click the Next button (if necessary) to return to the screen in the preceding illustration.

☐ Click the Create Address Book button in the middle of the screen.

For the next minute or so you'll probably feel as if you're watching the computer equivalent of pressing the fast forward button on your VCR. The WorksWizard displays an hourglass and a message asking you for patience, and the screen explodes into action as the WorksWizard steps through a rapid, if somewhat dizzying, display of all the menu commands it needs to use to create the form you specified. At the end of it all, you see a screen like this:

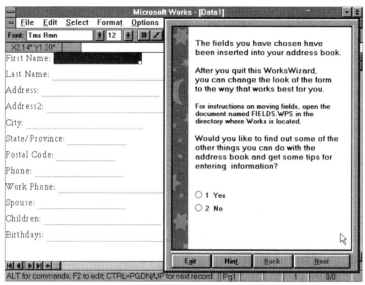

Look at the title bar, and you'll notice something familiar, the filename Data1. If you were too busy watching the screen change to think about what the WorksWizard was doing, you can tell now that it was working in the database. Essentially what you did by unleashing the WorksWizard was speed up and simplify the process of creating a form for a database of names and addresses. The WorksWizard started with a basic set of instructions, asked and remembered your preferences, and built the form you wanted. All that's left for you to do is enter the data.

The WorksWizard's job is about done. If you want more information about completing your address book, the WorksWizard offers some tips on using it. Until you're comfortable enough with any procedure to walk through it almost without thinking, advice can be handy, so,

    □ Click Yes and then click the Next button to see what the Works-
       Wizard has to say.

The WorksWizard displays two screenfuls of information telling how to use your completed address book as the basis for creating form letters and mailing labels with its companion wizards, and a third screenful that points you to information on printing and sorting the names and addresses you enter. Don't worry about memorizing or copying down the information. You'll find out all you need to know later in this book, and in the meantime, you have the manual that came with Works, and when you leave WorksWizards, on-line Help is only a mouse click away. To finish up,

□ Click the Next button to see the WorksWizard's next message:

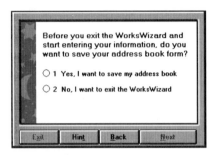

The WorksWizard has created a form for you, but it hasn't saved the form on disk. You can choose to save the form now, with the help of the WorksWizard, or save it later, on your own. Saving is simple either way, but from within the WorksWizard, you can save the form only in the MSWORKS directory, which the WorksWizard chooses for you. If you save after you exit the WorksWizard, you can use the Save As command from the File menu to save your form on any disk or in any directory you choose. For this example, use the WorksWizard to save the form:

□ Click on the button next to Yes, I want to save my address book, and then click the Next button. The message changes to one telling you that the WorksWizard is ready to save your form:

☐ Click the Save button, and you see this screen:

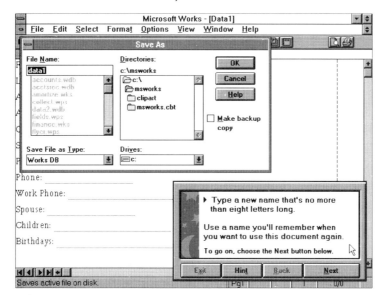

The Save As dialog box you see at the top of the screen is provided by Works. The WorksWizard has invited Works to join the party, and Works has responded with a dialog box asking, "OK, what do you want to name the form?" This is the same dialog box you see when you choose Save As from the file menu in the other Works modules.

By examining the Save As dialog box, you can see that Works displays the default name DATA1, and it proposes to save your form along with a group of sample files (ACCOUNTS.WDB, ACCTSREC.WDB, AMORTIZE.WKS, and so on) in one of its own directories. When you're working with Works outside of a Works-Wizard, you can jump from disk to disk, and directory to directory, to save files wherever you want. Here, however, Works and the WorksWizard only allow you to type a name for the file. If you want, you can later use Windows or DOS to copy or move the file to another disk or directory. For now, however,

☐ Type a descriptive name, such as *personal*, that's no more than eight characters long.

□ Click the Next button, and the WorksWizard will display this message:

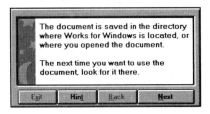

The document is saved in the directory where Works for Windows is located, or where you opened the document.

The next time you want to use the document, look for it there.

| Exit | Hint | Back | Next |

□ Click the Next button, and it's hurrah and goodbye. You've finished, so click the Exit button to send the WorksWizard home.

When the screen clears, Works displays your new address book form, ready and waiting for you to enter your data.

A QUICK LOOK AT YOUR FORM

The form that Works displays on your screen shows a separate line for each option you chose while using the WorksWizard. You can also see that the WorksWizard made some decisions as to the length of each line (that is, the size, or width, of each *field*). In Chapter 2, you used the default field size of 20 characters. Here, you have smaller sizes for fields such as First Name, State/Province, and Postal Code. Fields like these normally don't require a full 20 characters, so the WorksWizard pared them down for you.

If you don't like the field sizes, you can change them at any time by typing a new width in the dialog box displayed by the Field Size command on the Format menu. Until you begin working with the database application on your own, however, you might prefer to leave the fields as they are. Even if Works can't display an entire entry, it will remember and use the entry correctly. Chapter 9 tells you more about modifying the layout, font, and field sizes of a database form.

ENTERING DATA IN FORM VIEW

You're all set to create a personal database. The example in Chapter 2 showed you how to enter database records in form view, so if you want to start putting Works to work, maximize the application window and enter some records of your own:

□ If you must move the highlight to the first field, do so by pressing the Up arrow key or by clicking on the dotted line next to the field name.

□ To enter data, press the Tab key to move from field to field, or to move from the last field in one record to the first field in a new record.

□ To delete a field entry, highlight it and choose the Clear Field Entry command from the Edit menu. Until you're more familiar with databases, avoid any commands that cut, insert, or delete either fields or records.

To scroll through your records in form view, use the following buttons on the horizontal scroll bar:

If you click the button that takes you to the last record in a database, Works always displays a blank form. Click the button for the previous record to see the last actual entry in the database. When you're finished scrolling, choose the Save command from the File menu to tuck your database safely away on disk.

TIP Works is very sensitive to mouse actions when you're working with a database form. As a result, you can inadvertently move a field by clicking on it. You won't hurt anything other than the appearance of your form, but to avoid the possibility, use an arrow key instead.

ENTERING DATA IN LIST VIEW

If you prefer, you can also enter records in list view, which presents your database in a spreadsheet-like grid of rows and columns. List view has the advantage of displaying multiple records at the same time. Because you can see more than one record, you can easily click in different fields to correct typing errors or change information. To try entering data in list view,

□ Click the List View button in the Toolbar. It's to the immediate right of the Form View button that is currently "pressed down" on your screen.

- ☐ If necessary, drag the scroll box in the horizontal scroll bar all the way to the left, and click in row 1 under First Name to position the highlight.

- ☐ Type the first name of the first person you want to include in your database.

- ☐ Press the Tab key to move to the Last Name field, and type the person's last name. Continue in the same way, pressing Tab whenever you want to move to a new field. Skip over unnecessary fields by pressing the Tab key more than once. When you reach the end of one row, a quick way to move to the beginning of the next is to press Home (to return to the first field in the current row), and then press the Down arrow key (to move down to a new row).

The following illustration shows parts of two sample records in list view:

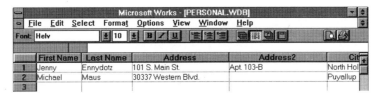

Use the horizontal scroll bar to view parts of a record that are not currently displayed. To clear a field, highlight it and choose the Clear Field Entry command from the Edit menu. As mentioned earlier, avoid any commands that cut, insert, or delete either fields or records until you're more familiar with the database. Choose the Save command from the File menu to save your work on disk for another day and time.

THE OTHER WORKSWIZARDS

The two other WorksWizards, Mailing Labels and Form Letters, can work their magic only if you've already completed and saved an address book database. The address book doesn't have to be one you've created with the Address Books WorksWizard; you can use the Mailing Labels and Form Letters WorksWizards with lists of clients, business contacts, and other groups you've created directly from the database application. Because the WorksWizards are designed to work together, however, relying on them for these three tasks can minimize the snags and minor inconsistencies that could otherwise make creating form letters and mailing labels time-consuming and tedious.

Form Letters

A form letter is a "boilerplate" document that you personalize with different names and addresses before you send it out. The process of individualizing such letters is often called *merge printing*, and a program that can handle the job for you is said to include a *print merge* feature. In Works, you can create such documents on your own in the word processor or with the help of the Form Letters WorksWizard.

Whether you use the word processor or the Form Letters WorksWizard, you must start with two existing documents: a database of names and addresses like the one you just created and a letter you want to personalize. To create a form letter, you first insert *placeholders* that tell Works where to insert names, addresses, and other variable information. Then you select (if necessary) the individuals or companies that are to receive the letter.

The WorksWizard can help you by inserting placeholders for the return address and salutation and by helping you pick out selected recipients for the letter. It does not, however, help you create the letter itself, nor does it print the finished letters. For printing, you rely on the Print command on the File menu in the word processor. See "Previewing and Printing" in Chapter 13 for detailed printing instructions.

Mailing Labels

Envelopes can sometimes be a nuisance to print, especially if you have to feed them into the printer individually. The Mailing Labels WorksWizard helps you turn a database of names and addresses into neatly printed sheets of mailing labels that you can simply peel off and stick onto your envelopes. For mass mailings, you might well prefer this approach for convenience and to save time.

The Mailing Labels WorksWizard creates a special "labels" document for you in the word processor. In this document, the WorksWizard sets up the format and content for each label (first name, last name, and so on) according to your specifications. The WorksWizard then goes on to apply the print settings — page length and width, label spacing, and number of labels per row — that will enable Works to align and print the labels correctly. You print labels, as you print form letters, after you leave the WorksWizard. For more information on printing mailing labels, see "Mailing Labels and Envelopes" in Chapter 13.

The WorksWizards are not difficult to use, so if you want to experiment with them, go ahead. The experience you've already gained with the Address Books WorksWizard should help you feel right at home with the Form Letters Works-Wizard and the Mailing Labels WorksWizard.

Part II

The Works Modules

Part II gives you in-depth looks at the three Works modules: the word processor, spreadsheet, and database. In these chapters, you'll learn the ins and outs of using each application. In the process, you'll see ways to apply Works to a variety of tasks from writing a letter to keeping financial records to maintaining an inventory.

4
The Word Processor

One of the pleasures of using a word processor is the ability it gives you to concentrate on what you want to say, without giving a thought to how those words appear on your screen. Close your eyes if you want and start typing. Works will faithfully remember every key you press, without ever breaking into your thoughts by stopping at the end of a line or blindly running your words onto the platen when you reach the end of a page.

From beginning to end, word processing breaks down into four main categories: writing, revising, formatting, and printing. This chapter is organized in the same four categories. The writing you must do yourself: A word processor can't help you think, nor can it make the words flow when the creative pipeline is clogged, but a good one can automate the mechanical tasks required to produce and reproduce your prose.

WYSIWYG

You're seeing correctly. WYSIWYG (pronounced "wizzywig") stands for What You See Is What You Get. It also describes the Works word processor. Unlike some non-Windows programs, Works shows onscreen basically what your document will look like when printed — what you see is what you get.

While WYSIWYG might not seem like such a big deal right now, you'll find that, in addition to making your screen a friendlier place to work, it also helps you to envision what your documents will look like when you print them. Thanks to WYSIWYG, you can see what a heading in large, bold, underlined capitals will look like. You can also see what will happen if you combine different styles of type. Although Works can't help your sense of style and proportion, its WYSIWYG capability will, at the least, help you see what you're doing and avoid wasting paper on unsuccessful printouts.

GETTING STARTED

In this chapter and throughout the remaining chapters in this book, you'll see examples to try on your own computer. Occasionally, you'll be told to save a sample document. To keep your hard disk tidy, take the time now to create a directory — a file drawer, if you will — for these examples. Later on, you'll be able to delete the examples easily without worrying about deleting valuable files or leaving the odd stray example lying around on the disk:

☐ If Windows is running, choose DOS Prompt from the Main program group. (If you're already at the DOS prompt, skip this step.)

☐ When the DOS prompt appears, type the following command. Be sure to include the backslash.

```
C:\>md \wksbook
```

☐ Press Enter to complete the command. If you started from Windows, type *exit* to return. If you started from DOS, start Windows.

Now start Works. Start the word processor with a blank workspace.

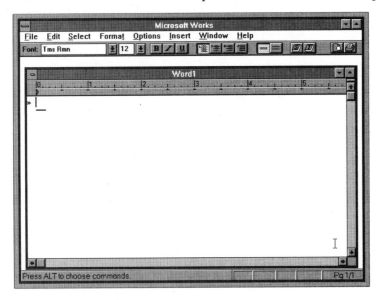

Maximize both the application and document windows to give yourself plenty of room.

STOPPING AND STARTING

There's a good chance that you will not always have the time to complete each chapter or example in a single session, so here's what to do to save any incomplete examples and return to the same place later on:

❑ Choose Works Settings from the Options menu. When you see the following dialog box verify that the Use saved workspace setting is checked.

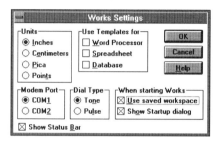

❑ If the setting is not checked, click on it, and then click on OK to close the dialog box and save the settings.

❑ When you want to quit, choose Save Workspace from the File menu.

❑ To quit Works, double-click the Control menu icon in the top left corner of the Works window.

❑ If you have any unsaved work, Works will display a dialog box asking if you want to save your changes. If you do, choose Yes.

The next time you start Works, it will restore your screen, example and all, exactly as you left it.

NOTE: *Use this same procedure with your own work whenever you must interrupt what you're doing but want to return to the same place when you next start working with Works.*

WRITING

In Chapter 3, you saw that a WorksWizard can help you create certain documents quickly and without bother. The Wizards aren't for all occasions, though. Most of the time, you'll create and lay out documents for which no Wizard is available, so it's time to get down to business with the word processor.

Type the following paragraphs. Press Enter only where you see [Enter] in the text. Don't worry about your lines running off the screen as you type and don't be appalled by the look of your document. You'll learn how to improve its appearance later. (Type the dash after *history* as two hyphens.)

```
To all our friends:[Enter]

You're invited to help us celebrate our 10th anniversary as a business here in
beautiful, rainy, western Washington.[Enter]

We're having the biggest, best blowout sale of our history—a real sales
extravaganza. Stock up on all your raingear needs: umbrellas, slickers,
ponchos, waterproof boots, hats, and more. At prices you won't believe. Fifty
percent off regular prices, fifty percent more off the last marked sticker
price on all sale items. Come see us now and save![Enter]

It's summer now, but remember: Fall is right around the corner.[Enter]
```

Your screen should look something like this:

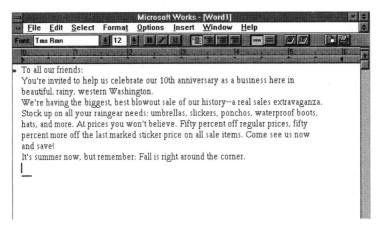

NOTE: *If you see characters that look different, or if your onscreen lines break in different places, don't think you've done something wrong. Works tailors itself to the capabilities of your computer and printer. The examples in this book show Works running on a computer connected to a Hewlett-Packard LaserJet printer equipped with the Tms Rmn and Helv typefaces (which determine the look of the characters onscreen). If you have a different printer, your lines may not wrap at the same places. As you work through the examples, remember that they are merely examples. Use them as guides, but feel free to experiment with settings or choices that produce comparable or better results on your equipment. After all, your goal is to see what Works can do for you.*

Wordwrap

As you typed, Works moved the insertion point to a new line whenever your words neared the right edge of the screen. This "intelligence" on the part of Works is typical of word processors and is known as *wordwrap*. One of the first differences you notice between using a typewriter and using a word processor, wordwrap eliminates the need to press the carriage return to keep lines from extending into the margin.

Special Characters

You now have several paragraphs on the screen, but they're not easy to tell apart. Works is using its default format for paragraphs: single-spaced, with no extra spacing above or below, and with no indent for the first line. Even if you opt for a format like this, however, there's an easy way to tell exactly where your paragraphs begin and end:

☐ Choose Show All Characters from the Options menu.

Now your display looks like this:

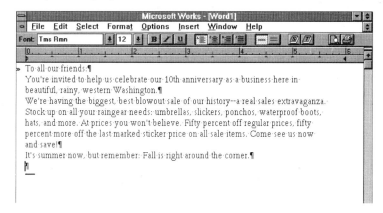

The small dot between words is the Works onscreen symbol for a blank space — the character you type whenever you press the Spacebar. At the end of each paragraph, you see a paragraph mark (¶) on the screen. A paragraph mark appears each place you pressed the Enter key while typing.

Works doesn't print these characters (or other special characters you'll encounter later), but it's often useful to display them while you're writing so that you can see exactly what you're doing. After you're comfortable with the word processor, you might want to turn off the display (by choosing Show All Characters again) to unclutter the screen.

Paragraphs

Paragraphs are the building blocks of any word-processed document. You're probably accustomed to thinking of a paragraph in the traditional sense: a unified block of text that presents a single idea or part of a topic. As a computer user, however, you have to extend this definition. Think of a paragraph as being any amount of text you want to present in a particular way — with special indents, for example, or extra spacing above and below — on a page.

As you typed, Works used the same single-spaced format for each paragraph. Whenever you press Enter, Works "clones" a new paragraph, giving it the same spacing and indentation as the previous paragraph. If you had started out with a double-spaced paragraph, Works would have double-spaced them all.

REVISING

It takes work to turn a first draft into a final draft. Most writing, in fact, boils down to the tedium of revising, rewriting, inserting, and deleting. Works can't help here, any more than it can help with the original draft, but it can make the revision process easier and cleaner than it is with a pen, pencil, or typewriter.

Moving Around and Selecting Text

Often, as you revise a document, you'll want to move the insertion point, select text, or do both. To move the insertion point with a mouse, all you do is point to the new location and click.

You'll probably want to use the keyboard for these tasks too, especially if you're really comfortable with a keyboard and decide to fix a typographical error or change a sentence or paragraph as you're writing. The following table shows some quick ways to move around in a document with the keyboard:

To Move	Press
Left or right one character	Left arrow key or Right arrow key
Up or down one line	Up arrow key or Down arrow key
Left or right one word	Ctrl plus Left arrow key or Right arrow key (Ctrl-Left or Ctrl-Right)
Up or down one paragraph	Ctrl plus Up arrow key or Down arrow key (Ctrl-Up or Ctrl-Down)
Beginning of line	Home
End of line	End
Start of document	Ctrl-Home
End of document	Ctrl-End

For many revisions, you'll both move the insertion point and select text. The following table shows you how to use the mouse and the keyboard to select varying amounts of text:

To Select	Mouse	Keyboard
One character	Drag insertion point over character	Hold down Shift; press Left or Right arrow key
One word	Double-click on word	Move insertion point to word; press F8 twice
One sentence	Drag insertion point over sentence	Move insertion point to sentence; press F8 three times
One paragraph	Move insertion point to left margin; when it becomes an arrow, double-click	Move insertion point to paragraph; press F8 four times
One line	Move insertion point to left margin; when it becomes an arrow, click once	Move insertion point to start of line; press Shift-Down arrow
Whole document	Hold down Ctrl and click in the left margin	Press F8 five times or press Ctrl-Home to move insertion point to start of document and then press Shift-Ctrl-End

To "deselect" text you highlighted with the mouse, click elsewhere in the document or press an arrow key. To deselect text you highlighted with the keyboard, press Esc and an arrow key.

Before you go on, practice moving the insertion point and selecting various amounts of text in the same document. When selecting text becomes almost instinctive, you'll really begin to feel at home with the word processor.

Adjusting Paragraphs

After you've typed a document, you're not stuck with the paragraphs you created. You can break one paragraph into two, combine two into one, and add new paragraphs wherever you want. Try this with your sample document:

☐ Place the insertion point before the word *umbrellas*.

☐ Press Enter to create a new paragraph.

□ Do the same with *slickers, ponchos, waterproof boots,* and *hats,* and in front of the words *At prices.* Don't worry about trailing punctuation in your list. You'll take care of it later.

Your first two paragraphs are pretty short now, so combine them:

□ Place the insertion point before the paragraph mark after the period at the end of the first sentence.

□ Press Delete and the Spacebar.

That's better. Your document should now look like this:

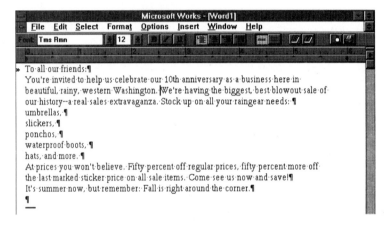

Adding Text

Adding new text is the easiest type of revision you can make with Works. Suppose, for example, you want to add a new sentence to your practice document:

□ Use the mouse or keyboard to place the insertion point at the beginning of the sentence *Come see us now and save!*

□ Type *Sizes for children and adults.* Press the Spacebar to add an extra space after the new sentence.

When you insert new characters, Works normally moves the existing text to the right to make room for the new text, so adding text to a document is simple.

Replacing Existing Text

For some revisions, you'll want to replace, rather than add, text. You can do this in two ways. Open the Options menu. Near the bottom, you'll see the Typing Replaces Selection option and the Overtype option. Each of these two options toggle between two methods of replacing existing text.

Typing Replaces Selection

The Typing Replaces Selection option deletes selected text as soon as you begin typing new text to replace it. Works adjusts the spacing to fit, so it doesn't matter whether the deleted text is longer or shorter than the new text. For example:

☐ Click Typing Replaces Selection from the Options menu if you don't see a checkmark next to this item.

☐ Select the words *regular prices, fifty percent more off the last marked sticker price on all sale items.*

☐ Replace this wordy mess by typing *everything in the store.*

The old text disappears, to be replaced by the new text. Now your document looks like this:

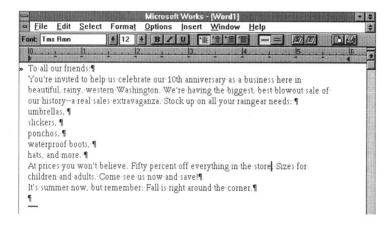

Overtype

In contrast, the Overtype option replaces existing characters with new ones as you type. To try it:

☐ Click Typing Replaces Selection on the Options menu to turn replacement off.

☐ Move the insertion point to the space before *won't* in *prices you won't believe.*

☐ Turn on Overtype either by pressing the Insert key or by choosing Overtype from the Options menu. Notice that the letters OVR appear in the status bar to show that overtype is turned on.

☐ Type *ca* in place of *wo.*

The word *won't* turns into the word *can't* with a few keystrokes.

When you turn on the Overtype option, you must remember this: Length matters. Works deletes one character of existing text for each new character you type. Suppose, for example, you wanted to change the sentence *The canary ate the cat.* Turning on Overtype and replacing *canary* with *parrot* would produce *The parrot ate the cat.* But replacing *parrot* with *duck* would produce *The duckot ate the cat.* When you toggle Works to Overtype, remember that you've done so. If you're a touch typist accustomed to working from drafts on paper, it can be extremely frustrating to glance at the screen and find you've overtyped an entire sentence or paragraph when you meant to insert text.

To avoid possible confusion in later examples:

- Turn off Overtype by clicking on the Options menu or by pressing Insert again.

Deleting Text

Professional writers have professional editors who find and delete unnecessary words, sentences, and even whole sections of an article or book. If you're working with Works on your own, you'll probably have to be your own editor — a thankless task when you've struggled with a document. Often, however, careful editing pays off in clearer, more understandable text.

For example, your practice document doesn't really need the words *a real sales extravaganza,* so delete them:

- Select the text, including the hyphens at the beginning.

- Press Delete.

Using Undo

Although deleting your golden prose seems final, it doesn't have to be. You can "undelete" text if you change your mind, as long as you haven't made any other changes to your document in the meantime. Suppose you decide you liked the upbeat sound of *a real sales extravaganza:*

- Restore the text by choosing Undo from the Edit menu or, for a quicker method, press Alt-Backspace.

The words return to the sample document, exactly where they were before you deleted them.

As you'll see in other examples, the Undo command reverses more than deletions. Essentially, Undo reverses the effect of any editing operation that alters the appearance or content of a document. Use Undo when your fingers outpace your thoughts and you find you've made a change you didn't mean to make. Remember, though, that you can't undo selectively. You can reverse only your last change.

Before you go on:

- □ Delete the punctuation at the ends of the lines reading *umbrellas, slickers, ponchos, waterproof boots,* and *hats, and more.*

Moving Text

Chapter 3 introduced you to the Clipboard and to the concept of cut and paste. In the next exercise, you'll use cut and paste to reorganize a document. You'll remove text as you did when you deleted, but this time you'll cut it from the document so you can paste it in somewhere else.

Before you start, open the Edit menu. Note that Paste is displayed in dimmed letters. Dimmed commands, you may recall, are those you can't use in the current situation. Here, Paste is dimmed because you haven't cut or copied any text yet. The Clipboard is empty, so Works has nothing to paste into your document. You'll change that now:

- □ Select the sentence *Come see us now and save!* (Include the space before the sentence in your selection.)

- □ Choose Cut from the Edit menu or, as a shortcut, press Ctrl-X.

The text disappears as it did when you deleted earlier. This time, however, the cut text is on the Windows Clipboard. From the Clipboard you can paste text back into any area of a document:

- □ Move the insertion point to the end of the document, after *Fall is right around the corner.*

- □ Choose Paste from the Edit menu or press Ctrl-V.

Now the end of your document looks like this:

> At·prices·you·can't·believe.··Fifty·percent·off·everything·in·the·store.··Sizes·for·children·and·adults.¶
> It's·summer·now,··but·remember:··Fall·is·right·around·the·corner.│Come·see·us·now·and·save!¶

Cut and paste is that simple. Bear in mind, however, that the Clipboard holds only one item at a time. Thus, if you cut one block of text and then go on to cut (or copy) another, the second block of text replaces the first on the Clipboard. The first block of text is gone, and you cannot retrieve it.

 If you want to check the contents of Clipboard, minimize Works and open Clipboard from the Main group in the Program Manager. A small window will appear, displaying the current contents of the Clipboard. To return to Works, close the Clipboard window by double-clicking its Control menu icon, and then maximize the Works icon displayed at the bottom of your screen.

Copying Text

You move information onto the Clipboard in one of two ways: by cutting it with the Cut command on the Edit menu or by copying it with the Copy command on the same menu. When you cut information, you remove it from the document; when you copy, you duplicate that information. In other respects, Cut and Copy are the same.

Suppose you have some ideas about revising the first paragraph of your document, but you'd like to keep the original to compare the two. You can copy the paragraph to the Clipboard, paste it back into the document, and make revisions to one while leaving the other intact:

☐ Select the paragraph beginning with *You're invited.*

☐ Choose Copy from the Edit menu, or use the keyboard shortcut, Ctrl-C.

☐ Place the insertion point in front of *umbrellas* and choose Paste from the Edit menu (or use the keyboard shortcut, Ctrl-V).

The paragraph you copied is pasted into the document below the original. If you find it difficult to distinguish one paragraph from the other:

☐ Press Enter to add a blank paragraph.

☐ Place the insertion point in front of *umbrellas* and press Enter again.

Now your copied paragraph is visually set off from the rest of the document:

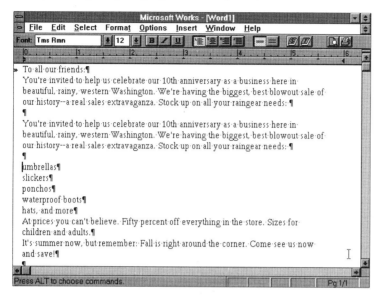

Practice making revisions to this duplicate paragraph before moving on to the next topic. Try inserting, deleting, cutting, and pasting. Here's a sample paragraph to try your skills on. (Notice that one cut and paste takes a sentence from somewhere else in the document.)

> This year marks our 10th anniversary as a business here in beautiful, rainy, western Washington. You're invited to help us celebrate! We're having the biggest, best sale of our history--a real extravaganza. Come see us now and save! Stock up on all your raingear needs: ¶

Delete the edited paragraph and the extra paragraph marks when you're done. You'll try some other examples shortly, so save your sample document for now:

☐ Choose Save As from the File menu. Verify that the highlight is in the File Name box and type *raingear*.

☐ Under Directories, you probably see c:\msworks. You want to save the example in WKSBOOK, so double-click on the folder for drive C (c:\). The directories on drive C will appear.

☐ Scroll down if necessary until you see *wksbook*. Double-click to make it the current directory (the one in which Works will save your file). Click OK.

Works saves your file and tells you so by changing the filename in the document window's title bar from Word1 to RAINGEAR.WPS.

FORMATTING

The format of a document is the design you use to make it attractive and readable, to emphasize important points, and to ensure that your reader interprets your meaning correctly. Good formatting can mean the difference between a document that is read and one that is tossed aside.

The Toolbar

The Toolbar is your shortcut to the most common commands in the word processor. You'll use the Toolbar a great deal for formatting, revising, and printing documents with Works, so now's a good time to become familiar with the various boxes and buttons on the Toolbar.

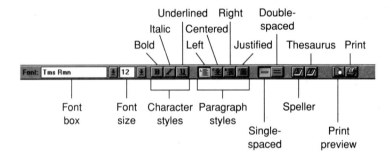

The following sections describe the Toolbar and the menu commands they represent.

You'll probably want to take the Toolbar for a test run, so:

☐ To make a clean workspace for yourself, open a new word processor document with the Create New File command on the File menu.

Fonts and Font Sizes

At the left end of the Toolbar are two boxes for fonts and font sizes. Fonts are different designs of type. Each font has a name such as Courier, Helv, Script, or Tms Rmn, and each creates characters with a particular look and style.

76

The Font box on the Toolbar displays the name of the font you're currently using. Try out your own fonts:

☐ Click the button to the right of the Font box to see a list of available fonts.

☐ Click on a font name other than the one that is highlighted.

☐ Type its name and press Enter.

☐ Do the same for the rest of the fonts.

Here's a sample of what you might see:

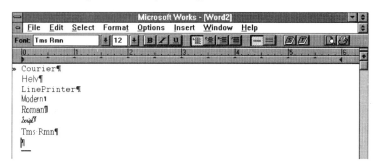

NOTE: *The font styles and number of fonts available depend on your printer and its capabilities, so don't be concerned if your list doesn't match the one in this book.*

Font Sizes

Font sizes, measured in units called points, determine the size your printed characters will be. There are approximately 72 points to an inch. Standard documents are printed in either 10-point or 12-point type, the latter being larger and easier to read.

The Font Size box to the right of the Font box displays the current font size. Try changing font sizes:

☐ Select one of the font names you typed.

□ Click the button to the right of the Font Size box to see what other sizes are available.

□ Click the size you want.

The result will be something like this. (Notice the change in Script.)

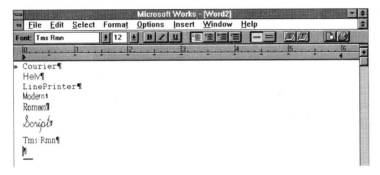

Character Styles

The main part of the Toolbar is devoted to five sets of buttons grouped by function. The first three buttons, labeled B, I, and U, assign special looks to selected characters. Try them out:

□ Select one of the font names you typed. Click the B button. Move the highlight to another line, and you can see clearly that the font name is now **bold**.

□ Select another font name and try the I button for *italic*.

□ Select yet another font name and try the U button for underlined.

The Font & Style Command

Fonts, font sizes, and character styles are also accessible through the Font & Style command on the Format menu. Choose the Font & Style command. You will see a dialog box like the one at the top of the following page.

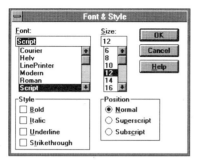

Notice that the dialog box presents the items available on the Toolbar and some additional formats, such as strikethrough and superscripting, that you use less frequently. As already mentioned, the Toolbar is a fast way to carry out some commands; it is not the only way.

Paragraph Styles

The four buttons labeled with lines of "text" and the letters *L, C, R,* and *J* affect the way selected paragraphs are aligned on the page. *L* produces left-aligned paragraphs, like the examples in this book. To see what the others look like:

□ Click Cancel to close the Font & Style dialog box.

□ Move the insertion point to the end of your document and press Enter to create a new paragraph. If necessary, choose your normal display font (such as Tms Rmn).

The C button centers paragraphs between the left and right margins of the page:

□ Click the C button and type the following:

```
Going Out of Business Sale![Enter]

Everything must go![Enter]

Ridiculous prices you won't believe![Enter]
```

The result is

Going·Out·of·Business·Sale!¶
Everything·must·go!¶
Ridiculous·prices·you·won't·believe!¶
¶

R, the opposite of *L,* produces right-aligned paragraphs — paragraphs in which the left edges are ragged but the right edges form a straight line down the page:

☐ Click the R button, press Enter to add some space, and type the following:

```
As a poet I'm a flop.[Enter]

Printing this just wastes the ink.[Enter]

But please, no laughs;[Enter]

You see, I think[Enter]

There's not much use for these paragraphs.[Enter]
```

The result is:

¶

As·a·poet·I'm·a·flop.¶

Printing·this·just·wastes·the·ink.¶

But·please,·no·laughs;¶

You·see,·I·think¶

There's·not·much·use·for·these·paragraphs.¶

Finally, *J* produces justified paragraphs — paragraphs in which both the left and right edges are even:

☐ Click the J button, press Enter, and type the following:

```
Justified paragraphs depend on the word processing program to decide where
and how to add extra spaces within the lines in order to align the edges
evenly. Sometimes, though, these extra spaces can make a document look,
well, "spaced out."[Enter]
```

¶

Justified· paragraphs· depend· on· the· word· processing· program· to· decide· where· and· how· to· add· extra· spaces· within· the· lines· in· order· to· align· the· edges· evenly.· Sometimes,· though,· these· extra· spaces· can· make· a· document· look,· well,· "spaced· out."¶

The next two buttons have parallel lines on them. They let you choose whether paragraphs are single-spaced or double-spaced:

☐ Place the insertion point in the last (justified) paragraph you typed. Click the button with the widely spaced lines to double-space the paragraph. Click the other spacing button to return to single-spaced lines.

The Indents & Spacing Command

You can also change the appearance of paragraphs with the Indents & Spacing command, which is found on the Format menu. Choose the command, and you see the following:

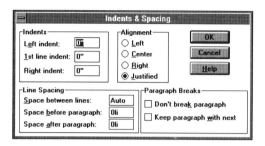

Like the Fonts & Style command, the Indents & Spacing command gives you access to more options than the Toolbar has room for. Here, for example, you can choose the Line Spacing box to triple-space your text and add extra space above or below your paragraphs. The other options are covered later in the chapter.

Special Tools

The buttons labeled S and T call up the Works spelling checker and thesaurus. The spelling checker can scan your document for typographical errors. You can also access these tools through the Check Spelling and Thesaurus commands on the Options menu.

The Thesaurus is particularly useful when you're stuck for a synonym. For example:

☐ Close the Indents & Spacing dialog box if necessary.

☐ Place the insertion point anywhere in the word *align*. Click the Thesaurus button and Works displays the following:

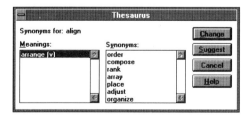

☐ Click the Cancel button to get rid of the display. You'll learn more about the Thesaurus in Chapter 6.

Printing

The final two buttons on the Toolbar let you view and print your document. The button with the magnifying glass puts you in the word processor's Print Preview mode, discussed in Chapter 2. The final button, the one with a printer on it, prints the document, as you would expect.

You can also preview documents and print them with the Print Preview and Print commands, which can be found on the File menu.

The Ruler

Just below the Toolbar, at the top of the document window, you can see an onscreen ruler:

Your ruler, like the one illustrated, probably shows measurements in inches. If you want, you can use the Works Settings command on the Options menu to change the measurement unit to centimeters, picas (sixths of an inch), or points.

Three black triangles on the ruler show where your lines of text will start and end, relative to the left and right edges of the page. Two small black triangles should appear directly under the 0 on the ruler to mark the left edge of your document. A second, larger triangle should appear under the 6-inch mark, showing that Works will make each line 6 inches long (standard on a page 8 ½ inches wide).

Like most features in both Works and Windows, the ruler is "live" — it responds to the mouse. Like the Toolbar, it gives you fast access to menu commands, in particular the Indents & Spacing and Tabs commands on the Format menu.

Formatting Your Sample Document

Now it's time to get back to your sample document:

☐ Close your experimental workspace by choosing Close from the File menu.

☐ Choose No when Works asks if you want to save your changes.

Your RAINGEAR.WPS document should reappear on the screen.

NOTE: *If your sample document does not reappear on the screen, choose* C:\WKSBOOK\RAINGEAR.WPS *from the list of previously opened files at the bottom of the File menu. Works always lists the last four files you used; choosing a filename from this list is an easy way to open an existing file. To open a file that isn't listed, use Open Existing File from the same menu.*

Now for some formatting. Start out by double-spacing the entire document:

☐ Select the entire document by holding down Ctrl and clicking in the left margin and then click the Double-Space button in the Toolbar.

NOTE: *If you want to double-space the document using the Indents & Spacing command, which is found on the Format menu, type 2 in the box for Space between lines, and click* OK.

Character Styles

Character styles, such as italics and boldface, can add visual interest to a document and can help the reader correctly interpret your document. For example, see how the sentence "So you did that" changes meaning when you italicize different words: So *you* did that, versus So you did *that*.

You can add character styles to a document with the Toolbar, with special keyboard shortcuts (described below), or with the Fonts & Style command on the Format menu.

Add some character styles to your sample document:

☐ Select *a real sales extravaganza* and italicize it with the I button on the Toolbar or by pressing Ctrl-I.

☐ Select *Fifty percent off everything in the store* and boldface it with the B button on the Toolbar or by pressing Ctrl-B.

☐ Select *everything* in the words you just boldfaced and underline it with the U button on the Toolbar or by pressing Ctrl-U.

Paragraph Styles

Unlike character styles, which affect characters, words, or sentences within a paragraph, paragraph styles affect the look of entire blocks of text. Works gives you many ways to change the appearance of a paragraph. You've already seen different types of alignment and spacing. Some of the other formats are discussed in the following sections.

First-Line Indents: A first-line indent is the amount — typically one-half inch — that the first line of a paragraph is indented, relative to the other lines. To indent the first line of one or more selected paragraphs, you can use either the ruler or the Indents & Spacing command on the Format menu.

With the ruler, you use the first-line indent marker (the top triangle at the left edge of the ruler).

First-line
indent —
marker

Try indenting the first line in the first paragraph of your sample document:

☐ Place the insertion point anywhere within the paragraph beginning *You're invited.*

☐ Drag the first-line indent marker to the right, letting go at the one-half-inch mark on the ruler. (Grabbing only the first-line indent marker might take some practice.)

Immediately, the paragraph changes:

NOTE: *If you want to use the Indents & Spacing command, type .5 after 1st line indent in the Indents box.*

Paragraph Indents: Left and right paragraph indents determine how far an entire paragraph is indented, relative to the margins of the page. When you use left and right indents, you are adding to the amount of white space at the edges of the page. Here, for example, is a quotation with both left and right indents that set it off from the surrounding text:

Impassioned voices sometimes stir the emotions of readers long after the speakers themselves have blended into history:

> Let me be a free man--free to travel, free to stop, free to work, free to trade where I choose, free to choose my own teachers, free to follow the religion of my fathers, free to think and talk and act for myself--and I will obey every law, or submit to the penalty.

These were the words of Chief Joseph of Washington state. Such quotations cut through the clamor of everyday life and speak directly to the hearts of people everywhere.

On the ruler, you drag the left and right indent markers.

Left indent   Right indent
marker   marker

You can also use the Indents & Spacing command on the Format menu.

NOTE: *To give paragraphs a left indent of one-half inch, select them and press Ctrl-N. To indent farther, in half-inch increments, press Ctrl-N as many times as necessary. To undo one or more indents, press Ctrl-G.*

Use left indents to set off the itemized list in your sample document:

☐ Select the paragraphs from *umbrellas* through *hats, and more.*

☐ Drag the left indent marker to the one-inch location on the ruler. (The first-line marker will tag along.) If you prefer, press Ctrl-N twice.

The paragraphs look like this:

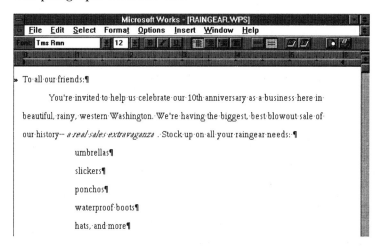

NOTE: *If you want to use the Indents & Spacing command, type* 1 *in the Left indent box.*

Tabs

Tabs are used to align items in columns, and they often make it easier to set up special alignments, such as bulleted lists:

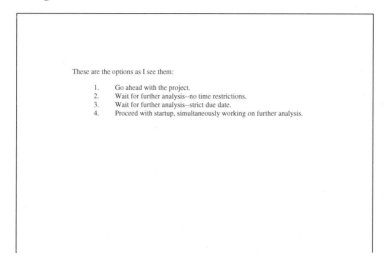

Works lets you set several types of tabs: left-aligned, right-aligned, centered, and aligned on a decimal point. This is what they look like:

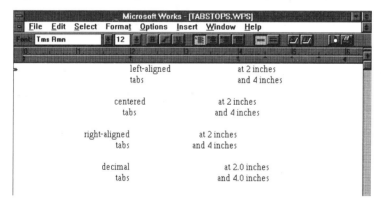

When you set tabs, you can also specify whether you want leader characters. These are characters that Works uses to fill in the space leading up to a tab stop — the type of characters you would use in a table of contents:

```
                         Progress Report:

              Graffitti Reduction Committee (GRC)


     Introduction........................................    3
     Overview............................................    5
     Action Items Scheduled this Quarter.................    9
     Goals Achieved......................................   22
     Budget..............................................   34
     Staff...............................................   36
     Action Items: Next Quarter..........................   39
```

If you don't set any tabs, Works sets them for you. The default tabs are left-aligned at half-inch intervals with no leader characters.

In the following examples, you'll use both the ruler and the Tabs command on the Format menu to set tabs in your sample document. First, turn the itemized list into a bulleted list:

□ If necessary, select the items from *umbrellas* through *hats, and more.*

□ Move the mouse pointer to the ruler, just below the 1.25-inch mark, and click.

Works inserts a left-aligned tab stop (the only kind you can set with the ruler) at that location.

□ Place the insertion point in front of *umbrellas*. Type a lowercase *O* and press Tab.

□ Do the same for the other items in the list.

For each tab you set, notice that Works displays the tab as a right-pointing arrow on the ruler; this is another of its special characters. Now your list looks like this:

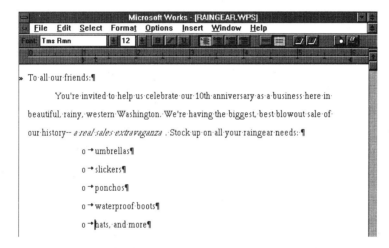

The items are much more noticeable now. If you want to see how your document looks so far, click the Print Preview button on the Toolbar or choose Print Preview from the File menu.

The bullets you just created work fine for single-line lists. For bulleted lists in which some or all entries are two or more lines long, combine a tab stop with indents to create the look you want. Drag the left indent marker to the location at which you want the text to begin, and then drag the first-line indent marker *to the left,* to where you want the bullet character to appear. Finally, set a tab stop at the same position as the paragraph indent. (For example, set the left indent to one-half inch, set the first-line indent to one-quarter inch, and set a tab stop at one-half inch.) For each entry in the list, type the bullet character, press tab to move the insertion point to the text position, and then type the text. The tab stop will control the beginning of the first line of text; the left indent will align all other lines beneath it.

NOTE: *If you want, you can also press Ctrl-H to have Works create this format for you. Works will assume you want to type the bullet at the left margin and align the text one-half inch to the right. To use this format, type the bullet character, press tab, and begin typing.*

You're almost finished. Add one more tab to your list, this time a right-aligned tab with periods as leader characters. You can't use the ruler for this, so:

- ☐ Select the list and choose Tabs from the Format menu.

- ☐ Type *5* in the position box. Choose Right in the Alignment box and 1 (the periods) in the Leader box. Click OK.

- ☐ Place the insertion point at the end of *umbrellas*. Press Tab and type *big and small*.

- ☐ Follow the same procedure for each item to make your list look like this:

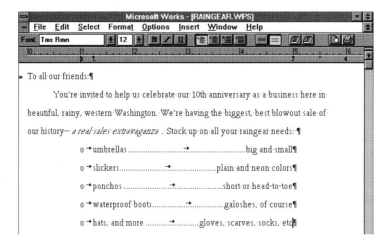

Finishing Touches

As a final exercise, add extra space above and below your bulleted list and surround the list with a border. By now, the steps shouldn't need much explanation:

- ☐ Select the first paragraph (*umbrellas*). Choose Indents & Spacing from the Format menu and type *2* for Space before paragraph in the Line Spacing box. Click OK.

- ☐ Select the last paragraph (*hats, and more*). Choose Indents & Spacing again, and type *2* for Space after paragraph in the Line Spacing box. Click OK.

□ Select the entire list. Choose Border from the Format menu. Choose Outline in the Border box and Normal for Line Style. Click OK.

The Border command, as you can see, adds a border around selected paragraphs. You can choose a normal border, as was done here, or one that is bold or consists of a double line. Borders, besides being fun to use, can add a little spice to your documents.

The right edge of your border looks a bit lopsided, so:

□ Select the entire list, if necessary, and move the right indent to the 5.1 mark (5.125 to be exact) on the ruler. A cosmetic touch, but useful.

Here's the result:

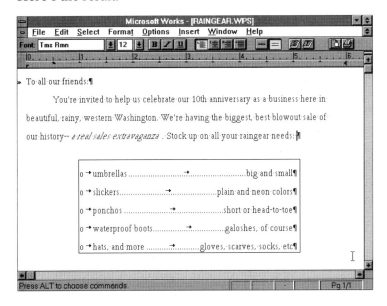

Save the document. This time, because you've already named the file, you can use Save instead of Save As on the File menu. Save As is for naming a file, renaming it, or saving it on a different disk or in a different directory. Save simply saves the file under its current name.

Use Print Preview to look at your document now. It might seem that it's taken quite a while to create this short flier, but you've covered a lot of word-processing ground at the same time. Your own documents will be much faster to produce.

5
Using Microsoft Draw

One of the most appealing features of the Works word processor is its ability to help you add emphasis and visual impact to your documents with drawings and graphics such as logos, maps, symbols, and even scenery. The key to spicing up the printed page in this way is the Works drawing program, Microsoft Draw.

If you're not artistically inclined, Draw offers a *clip art* library — a collection of ready-made illustrations, any of which you can display, select, and move into the document of your choice. If you're of a more creative bent, Draw offers a set of drawing tools — lines, arcs, squares, circles, and so on — that you can use as you would a group of drafting tools or templates. With Draw, you can create geometric forms with ease, design your own monograms and letterheads, and arrange text in circles, squares, and other patterns. In this chapter, you'll view some clip art and then use Draw to create a simple logo for the flier you worked on in Chapter 4.

IN PREPARATION

To begin, start Works if it is not already running. If the Welcome to Microsoft Works screen still appears at startup, turn it off by clicking the Skip Welcome Screen button at the bottom of the display.

Depending on how you've set up Works, you open RAINGEAR.WPS in one of two ways: with a saved workspace or without a saved workspace.

Starting with a Saved Workspace

If you followed the instructions at the beginning of Chapter 4, and you chose Save Workspace from the File menu before quitting, Works starts up by displaying the last document you worked on.

If the document that appears on your screen is not RAINGEAR.WPS, open the File menu. If RAINGEAR.WPS is on the list of previously opened files at the bottom of the menu, choose its name. If the filename does not appear on the list of previously opened files, use the Open Existing File command, as described in the next section.

Starting Without a Saved Workspace

If you did not save your workspace at startup, Works asks what you want to do by displaying its Startup dialog box:

To open RAINGEAR.WPS,

☐ Click Open Existing File.

Works displays a dialog box titled Open:

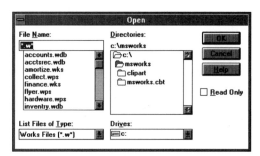

Notice that the highlight is in the box under File Name. The current directory is MSWORKS, but your file is in the WKSBOOK directory. The simplest way to open the file is to type both the directory name and the filename:

☐ Type \wksbook\raingear. (Don't forget the backslash at the beginning.)

☐ Click OK to open the file.

Sometimes you can't quite remember where you saved a file. To view files in a non-MSWORKS directory,

□ Double-click the root directory item (c:\) in the Directories box and choose from the new list of directories that Works displays.

To view files on a different drive,

□ Click the downward pointing arrow in the Drives box, and double-click the drive you want.

To view files with a particular extension,

□ Open the List Files of Type box, and click on the file type you want.

□ Choose the file you want when its name is displayed in the list under the File Name box.

After you've found and opened RAINGEAR.WPS, maximize the Works and document windows.

ACTIVATING DRAW

Draw is less visible than most programs: You can't start it directly from Windows or from Works. You can, however, call it while you're working with either a new or an existing word processing document like RAINGEAR.WPS.

When you insert a drawing into a document, Works inserts it at the current position of the insertion point. So before you jump into Draw, make room for your drawing-to-be:

□ Check that the insertion point is at the beginning of the docu-ment (in front of the first character of the first paragraph).

□ Press Enter to create a blank paragraph, and then move the insertion point up to the new paragraph.

To start Draw,

□ Choose Drawing from the Insert menu.

Your disk drive goes into action for a short while, and soon a new window appears:

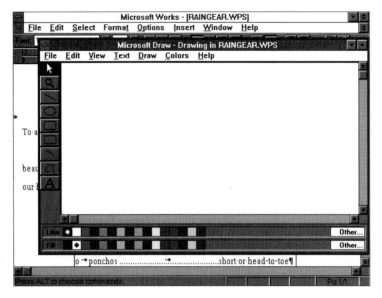

The blank workspace filling most of the window is your Draw canvas. Down the left side is a *toolbox* containing your drawing tools, and across the bottom is a *color palette* showing available colors for drawing lines and filling shapes. Less interesting, perhaps, but just as important, are the usual title bar and control buttons at the top of the screen, and the menu bar just below the title bar. Notice that the name of your word processing document appears in the title bar — Draw's way of telling you that any drawing you create will be inserted into RAINGEAR.WPS. Notice, too, that Draw includes a Help menu.

A Look at Some Clip Art

As already mentioned, Draw includes a library of predrawn graphics. This library contains about 50 different pictures, ranging from arrows of various shapes to more elaborate (and difficult to draw) pictures of buildings, cars, people . . . even a helicopter and a yacht. These pictures are stored in a directory named CLIPART within the main directory, MSWORKS, that the Works Setup program creates for you. To see some examples,

    □ Choose the Import Picture command from Draw's File menu.

The CLIPART directory should be listed in the Directories part of the dialog box that appears. To see the contents of this directory,

□ Double-click on *[clipart]*.

The Files portion of the dialog box now fills with a list of picture names, beginning with *2darrow1.wmf* (a two-dimensional set of curved arrows). To explore the clip art library,

□ Click below the scroll box in the vertical scroll bar to scroll the list one "boxful" at a time.

□ To see an interesting example of clip art, scroll to the end of the list and double-click on *yacht.wmf*.

The blank space in the Draw window quickly fills with a picture showing a luxurious yacht:

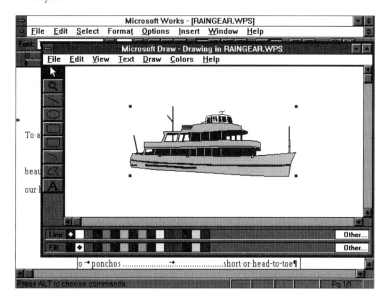

After you've displayed a picture from the clip art library, you can change its size, add other clip art to create a "scene," and (of course) move the results into a word-processed document. These procedures are described in the remainder of the chapter. Before you move on, you might want to see some other clip art:

□ Clear the screen by choosing Clear from the Edit menu.

□ Choose Import Picture again from the File menu, and double-click on the name of another picture.

As you'll soon see, you don't have to clear the screen each time you display a new picture, because Draw can overlay them, and you can easily move pictures to make room for others. For now, however, using the Clear command is an easy way to keep your screen uncluttered and clear the screen for the next examples. When you finish with the clip art,

◻ Clear the screen a final time to return to a blank display.

Draw Basics

Experimenting with Draw is fun. To create an image of your own with Draw, you must first know your tools, so start out by checking the contents of the Toolbox. The top two items, an arrow and a magnifying glass, are "management" tools. The arrow lets you select and manipulate shapes (called *objects* in Draw). The magnifying glass lets you zoom in and out to change the displayed size of an object. The rest of the tools create objects. These tools, starting from the top of the Toolbox, are named Line, Ellipse/Circle, Rounded Rectangle/Square, Rectangle/Square, Arc, Freeform, and Text.

Drawing an Object

To be sure Draw reacts as described here,

◻ Open the Draw menu and verify that a diamond shape appears next to both Framed and Filled on the menu.

Now use the Ellipse/Circle tool to see how Draw treats objects.

◻ Click on the Ellipse/Circle tool (fourth from the top) and move the pointer into the blank workspace.

Notice that the pointer becomes a set of cross hairs. As you create objects, you'll use the center of the cross hairs to mark your starting point. To draw an ellipse,

◻ Press the left mouse button and drag the mouse. Release the button when you've drawn an egg shape a few inches across.

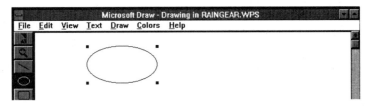

Changing an Object

When you released the mouse button in the previous example, four small black boxes appeared in a rectangle around your ellipse. These boxes are called *resize handles* and appear at the corners of an invisible box that Draw places around each object you create. You see the resize handles only when the object is selected, as your ellipse is now. You can drag one of the resize handles to change the size (or shape) of an object as follows:

- ☐ Select the Arrow, the object-manipulation tool, by clicking on the Arrow in the Toolbar or by clicking in any blank portion of the workspace.

- ☐ Selecting the Arrow "deselects" all objects, so place the pointer anywhere in the ellipse and click to select it again.

- ☐ Point to one of the handles and press the mouse button. Notice that the arrow pointer changes to an arrowhead. Drag the handle in any direction. As you drag the handle, an outline of the ellipse will follow the handle to show how its changing positions affect the shape of the object. When you've created an ellipse you like, release the mouse button.

Handling an Object

You've now seen why Draw refers to shapes as objects: When you manipulate a shape, Draw treats it as a unit, a whole item . . . an object. Consequently, you can place objects on top of each other, group them together, and manipulate them singly or together. To see how this works,

- ☐ Click on a rectangle tool.

- ☐ Place the cross hairs on your ellipse and draw a rectangle that extends beyond the border of the ellipse.

When you're finished, the rectangle lies on top of and partly covers the ellipse:

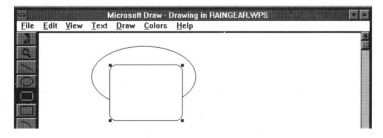

Now move the rectangle:

- ☐ Select the rectangle with the Arrow tool.

- ☐ Drag the dotted outline that appears completely off the ellipse.

When you release the mouse button, notice that Draw has completely separated the two shapes. Both the ellipse and the rectangle are whole and unchanged:

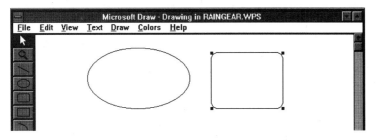

Selecting Multiple Objects

You can also treat separate objects as a group, either temporarily or permanently.

- ☐ Choose the Arrow tool if necessary.

- ☐ Place the pointer in a blank area of the workspace above and to the left of both the ellipse and the rectangle.

- ☐ Press the left mouse button and drag the mouse. As you drag the mouse, a dotted rectangle will form. This dotted outline is the *selection rectangle.* You use it to select a group of objects.

- ☐ Expand the selection to include both the ellipse and the rectangle you drew:

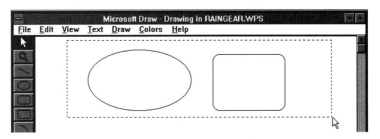

When you release the mouse button, resize handles appear around both objects to indicate that they are selected. They are still separate objects, but the selection rectangle tells Draw you want to work with both at the same time.

Managing Multiple Selections

Once you've selected a group of objects, you can move, color, copy, or delete them. Try moving and coloring the two objects:

- ☐ Place the pointer on either object.

☐ Press the left mouse button and drag slowly. As you drag the mouse, dotted outlines of the two objects follow the mouse pointer. When you release the mouse button, the ellipse and the rectangle move to new positions, maintaining their original relationship to one another.

☐ Point to the part of the color palette labeled Fill. The current fill color (probably white) is indicated by a diamond shape or check mark.

☐ Click on a different color.

 When you move selected objects, Draw will display a single dotted rectangle, instead of the outlines of both shapes, if you drag the selected objects too quickly. To see the outlines of individual shapes, move the objects slowly.

After you choose a color, a checkmark appears on the color in the palette, and Draw fills the shapes with the color you chose. To see how managing multiple objects differs from managing individual objects:

☐ Click in a blank area of the workspace to deselect the objects.

☐ Click on the rectangle to select it.

☐ Click on a different fill color in the palette.

This time only the rectangle changes color.

NOTE: *If you've been wondering about the difference between the Line and Fill palettes, select an object and then choose white for the fill and a bright color, such as red, for the line. Fill refers to the internal color of an object; line refers to the border.*

Grouping Objects

Now try grouping the ellipse and the rectangle:

☐ Select both objects as you did before with the selection rectangle. Notice the positions of the resize handles.

☐ Choose Group from the Draw menu or use the keyboard short-cut, Ctrl-G.

When you carry out the command, a single set of four resize handles appears around both objects. Draw is now prepared to treat the two objects as if they were one:

□ Point to one of the resize handles and drag it.

When you release the mouse button, Draw adjusts the sizes and shapes of both objects, once again maintaining their original relationship to one another.

In the next section you'll learn how to add some visual interest to a Works document by creating a logo for your RAINGEAR.WPS document. At the end of this chapter, you'll find a quick reference to Draw's menus and commands. To explore further, refer to the Help menu. You'll especially appreciate its How to section.

PUTTING DRAW TO WORK

Drawing programs are among the most enjoyable — and the most infuriating — programs to use. If you're a talented artist with a steady hand, you're sure to find more creative uses for Draw than you'll see in this practice session. Not everyone is a Michelangelo, however, so in the interests of sanity, we'll keep it simple.

Although your screen might be a mess at the moment, you don't have to quit Draw to start over:

□ If necessary, choose Select All from the Edit menu, or use the keyboard shortcut, Ctrl-A.

□ Press the Del key (the keyboard shortcut), or choose the Clear command from the Edit menu.

The flier you created in Chapter 4 is going to be sent out by a company named Bumbershoot Raingear. You'll create a logo that combines a simple graphic — part of an umbrella — and text spelling out the company name and address.

Start by maximizing the Draw window and verifying that the scroll boxes are at the top and left-hand edges of the scroll bars. Next,

□ Choose Show Guides from the Draw menu.

When the full window reappears, Draw displays two dotted guidelines in the center of the screen. These guides are comparable to the movable straight edges on drafting equipment. They indicate your position relative to the top left-hand corner of the drawing. Because the guides are movable, and because objects "snap to" them like filings to a magnet when you move the objects close enough, you can use the guides to position text and images with a high degree of precision. To use the guides,

□ Place the pointer on the vertical guide and press the left mouse button.

A decimal number appears above a right-pointing arrow to tell you how far the guide is from the left edge of the drawing area and in which direction Draw is measuring. The same type of information appears when you point to the horizontal guide and press the left mouse button.

To move a guide, point to it and drag it in the direction you want it to go. To start off, however, leave the guides where they are.

Creating a Drawing

This is the drawing and text you're going to create:

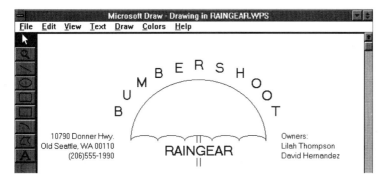

The drawing area available to you is much larger than the visible screen area, but to simplify matters and to ensure that your drawing will fit neatly into RAINGEAR.WPS, you'll create the drawing within a single window. At the same time, you'll make the objects large enough to be easily manipulated. This will result in a larger drawing than you really need, and in the future you will probably want to create drawings closer to the actual size you want. For this example, however, you'll find a larger drawing easier to work with.

The outline of an umbrella will be the centerpiece of your logo. Draw gives you two options for creating shapes: Framed (outlined) and Filled. You can combine these options to make three types of objects: framed, filled, and both framed and filled. These three types of objects look like this:

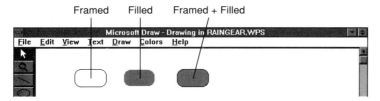

You'll use the Arc tool to make an outline with framed, but not filled, shapes:

▢ Open the Draw menu.

▢ If a diamond-shaped mark appears next to Filled, click on it to turn the option off. If a diamond-shaped mark does *not* appear next to Framed, click on it to turn it on.

Creating the Outline

If you've ever tried drawing the two halves of a valentine heart, a butterfly, or a pair of scissors, you know that it can be very difficult to make both halves identical. With Draw, the process is much easier because you can use the tools to create regular shapes. To use an even faster method, however, make half of the drawing, use Draw to copy the object, and then flip it to create a mirror image.

You'll need five curves across the bottom edge of the umbrella, so start with them. That way, you can later make the top curve of the umbrella fit exactly in one try:

▢ Choose the Arc tool.

▢ Place the center of the cross hairs about a quarter of an inch above the intersection of the two guides.

▢ Press the left mouse button and drag to create a small arc extending from the starting point to the horizontal guide.

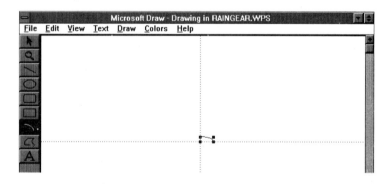

Now make Draw do most of the work:

▢ Verify that the arc is still selected.

▢ Copy the arc to the Clipboard with the Copy command on the Edit menu. (Use the keyboard shortcut Ctrl-C, if you prefer.)

□ Choose the Paste command (or press Ctrl-V) to paste the arc back into the window.

Flipping an Object

The arc doesn't do much for you as is. To continue creating the umbrella bottom,

□ Choose Rotate/Flip from the Draw menu.

A submenu opens offering four choices: Rotate Left, Rotate Right, Flip Horizontal, and Flip Vertical.

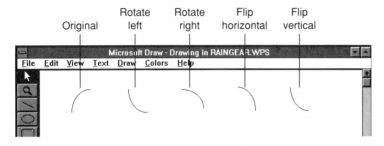

To make a side-to-side mirror image of the arc,

□ Choose Flip Horizontal.

□ Click in a blank area of the window, or choose the Arrow tool.

□ Select the new arc by placing the pointer on it, and drag the arc into position next to the original.

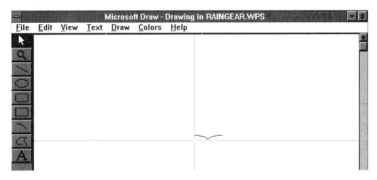

□ The original arc you copied is still on the Clipboard because you haven't replaced it yet, so paste another copy onto the screen.

□ Drag the new copy, without flipping it, and place it next to the first arc you pasted.

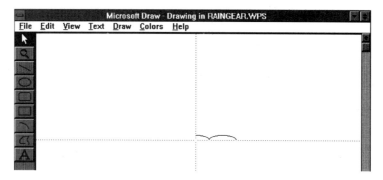

Now that you have a complete curve,

□ Use the Arrow tool to select both pasted halves.

□ Choose Group from the Draw menu to make the two halves a single object.

□ Choose Copy from the Edit menu to copy the curve to the Clipboard.

□ And, finally, paste the copy into the workspace, positioning it like this:

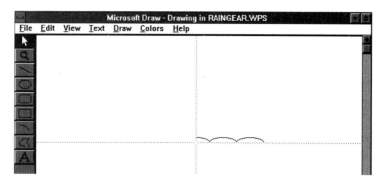

Positioning Objects

Now for the rest of the umbrella:

□ Choose the Arc tool again.

□ Position the cross hairs about an inch and a half from the top of the window and draw a new arc extending to the outside edge of the smaller curves you made.

□ Choose the Line tool.

□ Make part of the umbrella's handle by drawing a short vertical line slightly to the side of the umbrella's center. You might have trouble positioning the line accurately, if Draw is snapping the line to the guides and, possibly, to an invisible grid it maintains on the screen. To gain mobility, move the guides out of the way temporarily and turn off Snap to Grid on the Draw menu.

□ You need another vertical line about half an inch below the one you just drew. Draw another vertical line just beneath the first one.

□ Use the resize handles to push the top of the line down to create the gap you need.

That's half your umbrella. Now make the other half by flipping the image:

□ Select the entire umbrella.

□ You now want to work with all the pieces as a single object, so choose Group from the Draw menu.

□ Now copy the group to the Clipboard and then paste it back into the workspace.

□ Use Flip Horizontal from the Draw menu to flip the copy.

□ Drag the rest of your umbrella into position. Remember to grab one of the lines on your drawing to move the new group.

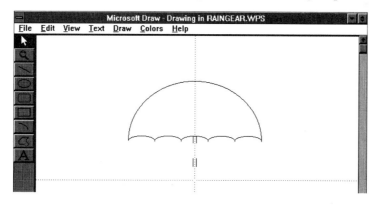

Adding Text

Now you'll use Draw to add the name and address of the company. For this exercise, you'll need the Text tool (the A icon in the Toolbox) and an appropriate font and font size. First,

☐ Open the Text menu and choose Font.

☐ If it's not already chosen, click on Helv. It's an attractive, no-frills font.

☐ Click on Size and choose 14.

Moving a Text Object

Now you'll add and arrange text in two different ways. First, the easy part — treating several characters as a single object:

☐ Choose the Text tool. Notice that the pointer is now an I-beam, as it is when you are working with the word processor. Move the I-beam to an area in the workspace with plenty of room. Click.

☐ Type *RAINGEAR* in all capitals.

☐ Select the text. Notice that Draw treats all the letters as a single object because you typed them all at the same time.

☐ Drag the text object into position, centering it under the umbrella.

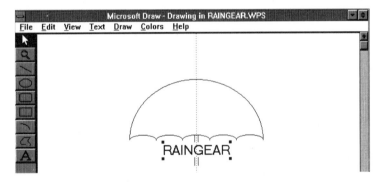

Characters as Objects

Now for the word *BUMBERSHOOT*. These letters are positioned in a curve over the top of the umbrella. You can't type in a curve, so you'll create each letter as a separate object and position them individually later:

☐ Select the Text tool.

☐ Position the pointer anywhere on the screen and type a capital *B*.

☐ Click in an open area of the workspace. Notice that resize handles appear around the *B*. Draw treats it as a single object.

☐ Use the same procedure to type the remaining letters in *BUMBERSHOOT,* making each letter a separate object. Because you'll be moving the letters soon, you can scatter them all over the screen.

Positioning Individual Characters

Moving the letters into position across the top of the umbrella is now simply a matter of dragging them individually into place. This is where patience and a steady hand come into play.

There are 11 letters, so you might want to start by placing the *R* at the top of the umbrella and arranging the remaining letters on each side. If you don't trust your ability to place each letter the same distance from the curve of the umbrella, create a second, slightly larger curve and position the letters on it. You can select the unneeded curve later and delete it with the Clear command on the Edit menu. Use the horizontal guide to check the alignment of letters in matching positions on each side of the curve. The finished logo looks like this:

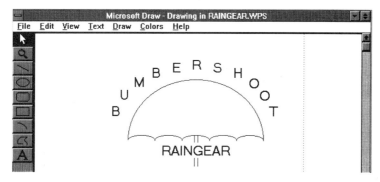

Finishing Up

Once you finish the logo, select it all and group the pieces to create a single object. This allows you to move, copy, or even delete it as a single item. If you want to work on some part of the logo later, you can choose the Ungroup command from the Draw menu and "deconstruct" the object into its separate parts.

Before you return to the word processor, there's one final touch to add: the address of the company and the names of the owners. You'll add this information in Draw rather than in the word processor because of the layout of your document.

When you insert the drawing into your document, Works will treat the entire drawing as part of a paragraph. You could use the word processor to add text beside the logo, but because of the way the word processor treats paragraphs and lines within paragraphs, you could not align the text evenly between the top and bottom of the drawing. While you're still working with Draw, however, the process is simple:

☐ Choose the Helv font and font size 10 from the Text menu.

☐ Choose the Text tool.

☐ Find a clear workspace and type each of the following lines as single objects:

```
10790 Donner Hwy.

Old Seattle, WA 00110

(206)555-1990

Owners:

Lilah Thompson

David Hernandez
```

☐ Using the guides, position the text objects on either side of the logo as shown.

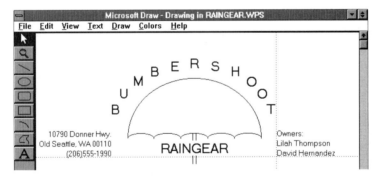

RETURNING TO THE WORD PROCESSOR

Now let's see what you've created. To return to the word processor and tell Draw to insert your artwork,

☐ Choose Exit and Return from the File menu.

Draw will display a dialog box asking if you want to update RAINGEAR.WPS. Update, in this instance, means to insert the drawing in RAINGEAR.WPS. This is what you want, so click Yes.

When your disk drive settles down, the drawing appears at the top of your flier. To see what your drawing looks like,

☐ Click the Print Preview button on the Toolbar.

When the preview page appears, don't be appalled if you see a text-and-graphic mess at the top of the page. Zoom in once or twice, and everything will become clear. When you're finished viewing the picture,

☐ Click Cancel to return to document view.

Notice that Works inserted your artwork at the current position of the insertion point in the word-processed document — the blank new paragraph you created before starting Draw. If the insertion point had been at a different position, Works would have placed the drawing there instead.

When creating your own artwork, remember to check the position of the insertion point before you start Draw. Although you can select a misplaced drawing, cut it to the Clipboard, and paste it in a new location, you can easily do without the extra steps — especially if your time is limited.

Scaling a Drawing

Remember that you deliberately made the logo larger than necessary. If you want, you can use the resize handles in Draw to shrink a picture before you import it into a document. If the picture contains text, however, as your logo does, resizing doesn't work. Draw shrinks shapes and other objects without a problem, but text retains its original size. There's another way to change the size of a drawing, though, that will work with your logo. You can tell Works to scale it down to a more respectable size. To scale a drawing,

☐ Select the drawing, if necessary, by clicking on it once.

☐ Choose the Picture command from the word processor's Format menu. Works displays a dialog box like this:

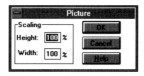

If you keep a drawing within the bounds of a single Draw screen, Works can usually import it into a document at or near its full size. Works scales down drawings larger than a single screen to fit within the margins of the page. In the

case of the Bumbershoot logo, Works did not need to scale down the drawing when importing it. On your own screen, you might see 97 or some other percentage, depending on the size of your own drawing and whether (or how much) Works reduced it to fit.

Scaled or not, once a drawing is in your document, you can decide on a specific size that suits your preferences. For this example, scale the drawing to 75 percent of the original:

□ Type 75 in both the Height and Width boxes of the Format Picture dialog box.

□ Click OK.

When Works redisplays the drawing, check the edges to be sure you haven't lost any of the drawing. If you specify a smaller size than Works can accommodate, it clips the drawing at the edges. This most often occurs with text. If this happens, scale the drawing up until all of it appears. Your finished drawing should look something like this:

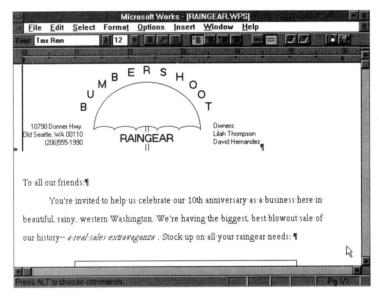

When you scale a drawing, you can specify different percentages to alter the ratio of height to width. If you do, however, be sure to preview the result before printing. Scaling unevenly can be desirable in some situations; in others, you might find squares printing out as rectangles or pies turning into eggs.

Positioning a Drawing

The position of your drawing is governed by the formatting of the paragraph mark at the bottom right corner. Currently, the paragraph is set for double spacing and left alignment because you created the new paragraph from an existing one with that formatting. You can change the drawing's alignment and add space below it with the ruler, the Toolbar, and the word processor's Format commands. As an experiment,

□ Drag the left indent marker to the 1-inch mark on the ruler.

Works immediately moves the drawing 1 inch in from the left margin. Now position the logo where you really want it:

□ Drag the left indent marker back to the 0 mark on the ruler.

□ Align the drawing with the right margin, rather than the left, by clicking the Right button on the Toolbar.

Next, make the drawing stand out by adding a little extra space below it:

□ Choose Indents & Spacing from the Format menu.

□ Type 2 in the Space after paragraph box. Click OK.

Notice that the highlight now extends two lines below the paragraph mark to show the space that you just added.

There's your logo: designed, imported, and neatly aligned in your word-processed document — an example of WYSIWYG in action. To print out the document,

□ Click the Print button on the Toolbar, or choose Print from the File menu. (If you're in Print Preview, click the Print button.)

Works displays this dialog box:

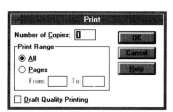

Specify the number of copies you want to print in the Number of Copies box. The Print Range, which doesn't apply here, lets you specify certain pages of a multiple-page document (for example, From page 5 To page 17). If you want to print out a fast, draft-quality copy, check the Draft Quality Printing box. A draft-quality printout leaves room for a drawing, but does not actually print the image. That's part of the reason a draft copy prints faster. You want to print a drawing right now so don't check the Draft Quality Printing box.

Correcting a Drawing

Sometimes, perhaps often, you won't be satisfied with a drawing when you print it. You can easily return to Draw and to the drawing you want to fix:

☐ Open the word-processed document containing the drawing.

☐ Double-click on the drawing.

That's it. When you double-click, Works starts Draw and displays the drawing you've indicated. You can move back and forth between Draw and Works whenever you want. To get back to the word processor, simply choose Exit and Return from Draw's File menu. To return to Draw, double-click on a drawing or choose Drawing from the word processor's Insert menu.

DRAW AND WINDOWS PAINTBRUSH

As you've seen, Draw is a program for creating images. What might not be obvious, however, is how Draw compares to a program like Windows Paintbrush, which also helps you express your creative urges. Yet this distinction is important, because knowing when to use Draw and when to use Paintbrush can help avoid hours of frustration.

When you want to create an image, decide first whether you want to create a *drawing* or a *painting*. On the surface, it would seem that drawing is something you do with a pen or pencil and painting is something you do with brushes. Remember, however, that Draw defines a drawing as a shape or collection of shapes. Paintbrush defines a painting as a collection of dots called a *bit map*. Draw specializes in shapes (or objects); Paintbrush specializes in bit maps.

To make the distinction in real-life terms, suppose you created two sets of squares — the first set by cutting them out of paper and the second set by carefully shaping several piles of sand. Each paper square is the equivalent of a Draw object. Each of the sand squares is a collection of "dots" resembling a Paintbrush image.

You can handle your paper squares much as you handle objects in Draw: You can grab one corner and move an entire square, and you can place one on top of another knowing each will remain whole and distinct. On the other hand, if you grab a corner of your sand square, only the corner will move — nothing more. If you place one sand square on top of another they will blend; their separateness will disappear.

This distinction would seem to favor Draw — and it does in many ways — but drawing programs and painting programs each have their own strengths. Drawing programs are appropriate when you want to manipulate images made of shapes in one way or another. Painting programs are best suited for freehand images — irregular shapes or images that you want to create, color, or alter a little bit (even a dot) at a time.

REFERENCE TO DRAW COMMANDS

The following table briefly itemizes Draw's menus and commands. Use this table when you are uncertain about what a command does or whether it will do the job you want. Because Help in both Works and Draw is so extensive, these lists can't duplicate the information you can find with a click of the mouse. Use them as reminders or as a general guide to Draw's capabilities.

The File Menu — for managing whole files

Update	Updates a drawing within a document without having to leave Draw. Update is something like a Save command for drawings.
Import Picture	Brings into Draw a clipart image or a picture you've created with another graphics program, such as Paintbrush.
Exit and Return	Takes you back to the word processor, at the same time letting you choose whether or not to update an inserted drawing.

The Edit Menu — for manipulating objects you've drawn

Undo	Cancels your last edit. Undo reverses only the last change Draw recognizes as a complete and single edit, so don't rely on it to undo two or more changes that, to your mind, are related.
Cut	Moves one or more selected objects to the Clipboard.
Copy	Copies selected objects to the Clipboard.
Paste	Pastes the contents of the Clipboard into a drawing.
Clear	Deletes selected objects.
Select All	Selects all objects in the current drawing.
Bring to Front	Brings a selected object to the front (top) of a set of overlapping objects.
Send to Back	Sends a selected object to the back (bottom) of a set of overlapping objects.
Edit Object	Changes to read Edit Text, Edit Arc, or Edit Freeform to enable editing of selected objects of these types.

(continued)

continued

The View Menu — *for viewing a drawing at any of the magnifications listed below*

25 percent, 50 percent, 75 percent, full size, 200 percent, 400 percent, and 800 percent	Use the View menu for detail work or to see how a drawing will look if you shrink or enlarge it.

The Text Menu — *for controlling the alignment, attributes, font, and size of text characters*

Plain, Bold, Italic, and Underline	Produces plain text (the default) or characters with bold, italic, or underlined attributes. You can combine attributes if you want.
Left, Center, and Right	Aligns text as you type it, to the left, center, or right of a position marked by the blinking insertion point.
Font and Size	Specifies the font and size of text characters.

Note: You can change text, even after typing and positioning it, by selecting the text and choosing the command or commands you want to apply.

The Draw Menu — *for manipulating objects as you work with them*

Group	Groups selected objects so you can work with them as a unit.
Ungroup	Reverses a Group command.
Framed	Creates a border around objects.
Filled	Creates objects that can be filled with colors or patterns.
Pattern	Displays a set of possible fill patterns, such as horizontal, vertical, and diagonal lines.
Line Style	Produces a list of possible line styles for object frames, including dotted and dashed lines, and lines of different thicknesses (measured in points).
Snap to Grid	Causes objects to "stick" to an invisible grid. When turned on, Snap to Grid provides 12 grid lines per inch. Drawn, moved, or resized objects automatically snap to the nearest grid intersection.
Show Guides	Produces movable guidelines to help with positioning and aligning objects. Objects snap to guides as they do to grid intersections.
Rotate/Flip	Rotates objects 90 degrees left or right, or flips objects horizontally or vertically.

(continued)

continued

The Colors Menu — for using and defining the colors in your drawings

Show Palette	Turns the Line and Fill palettes at the bottom of the window on and off.
Edit Palette	Modifies the color palette by adding, changing, or deleting colors. To change or add colors, you "mix" your own by choosing different degrees of hue, saturation, and luminosity, as well as different combinations of red, green, and blue. You mix colors by choosing from options in a dialog box displayed by this command.
Add Colors from Selection	Adds new colors from selected objects to the color palette.
Get Palette	Changes to a different color palette. Draw is shipped with several palettes. View or use them with this command.
Save Palette	Saves a palette. You can, for example, save a palette that you've modified for a particular use.

The Help Menu — for help and tips on using Draw

To request help from the keyboard, press F1. To close Help, click anywhere outside the Help window. Choose How to when you want to learn more about putting Draw to work.

6

Special Features

Chapters 4 and 5 showed you the Works word processor and its graphics cousin, Microsoft Draw. Most of the word processing you'll do with Works will involve the commands and features introduced in those chapters. There are, however, a number of additional features, which you'll encounter in this chapter: You'll learn how to check your spelling, refine page layouts, print, annotate a long document, search for and replace text, and even save formats for use with other documents.

PAGE LAYOUTS

The layout of a printed page is governed by more than the alignment, spacing, and indentation of the paragraphs on it. You've no doubt encountered form letters or handouts on which the text literally covered the paper, marching down the page in rank after closely spaced rank of small, dark blots of ink.

Such printing might initially save a few dollars, but the money saved can actually be money wasted if no one wants to read what the writer has to say. A better method by far — even in the age of conservation — is to use a little more (recyclable) paper and reach your audience. Conventional wisdom, not to mention countless teachers and professors, maintains that adequate margins, indents, and paragraph spacing enhance the readability of any document. So, too, do less obvious elements, such as page numbers, running heads that identify a document, and controlled breaks that avoid awkward interruptions in words, lines, and paragraphs.

You've already seen how to control the spacing within paragraphs, as well as any extra spacing above and below them. Now you'll see how to control the sizes of the margins at the top, bottom, left, and right edges. To add to the value of your document, you'll also find out how to

- Number pages
- Include running heads at the top and bottom of some or all pages
- Break lines and pages at a specified place

- Hyphenate words as necessary

- Keep certain words together on the same line

- Keep all lines of a particular paragraph on the same page

This chapter won't present a detailed example for you to build, but it will offer sample exercises for you to try. If you want to try these, start Works and open a new word processor document. As usual, maximize the application and document windows to take advantage of the full screen.

Margins

Works automatically sets reasonable margins for a printed page. To check them, open the File menu. The Page Setup & Margins command, which controls overall page layout, is toward the bottom of the menu:

□ Click on Page Setup & Margins to see its dialog box.

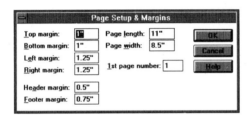

The first four boxes on the left show the current settings for the top, bottom, left, and right margins. They are displayed in whatever unit of measurement you specified in the Works Settings dialog box. If your setting is in inches, you see top and bottom margins of 1 inch and left and right margins of 1.25 inches. To change any of these, type a new measurement (whole or decimal number). You can omit the unit of measure, unless you want to specify a different one. (For example, you can type *5 cm* even though Works displays all other measurements in inches.)

Left and right margins of 1.25 inches are standard for letters and similar documents, but you might want to change one or both to suit a particular layout. For example, if you're planning to print and bind a report, increase the left margin to 1.5 inches, or more, to allow for the binding. If you're preparing a manuscript or a draft document for review, increase both side margins to allow adequate room for editing or review notes.

The default top and bottom margins, on the other hand, might be a little tight for your purposes. Business documents, especially letters, tend to leave plenty of space at the top and a bit less at the bottom, so a top margin of 1.5 inches might be more appropriate.

Header Margins

Increasing the default top and bottom margins can be especially important if you plan to include running heads on the printed pages. Works prints running heads within the top and bottom margins. If you use the defaults, it will print a top running head, or *header,* 0.5 inch from the top of the page and a bottom running head, or *footer,* 0.75 inch from the bottom. To see an example, try this:

☐ Choose Headers & Footers from the Edit menu.

☐ Type *header* in the Header portion of the dialog box that appears and click OK. (You'll see more of this dialog box a little later.)

Nothing appears on your screen, but don't worry. Works is now prepared to print the word *header* at the top of every page. To see this header in relation to some text,

☐ Center the blank paragraph mark on your screen and type *This is a sample line of text I'm typing to see how close it will be to my new header.*

☐ Now click on the Print Preview button in the Toolbar. To see a close-up, click the Zoom In button.

☐ To see how the preview page corresponds to a printout, check that your printer is on and click the Print button.

☐ Click OK in the Print dialog box that appears.

To change the spacing between the header and the text, either specify a larger top margin or type a smaller value for the header margin so that it prints closer to the top of the page.

NOTE: *On some printers, such as the LaserJet, headers and footers don't print exactly where the margin settings indicate they will. This happens because the printer has small "unprintable" regions at the top and bottom of the page. Check your printer manual or experiment a little to determine how close your printer comes to the actual edge of the page.*

Page Numbers and Page Sizes

Before you move on, look at the other options in the dialog box:

☐ Choose Page Setup & Margins once more.

The boxes labeled Page length and Page width allow you to specify different paper sizes, for example, legal size paper (8 ½ by 14 inches). If you use different paper sizes, adjust the measurements in these boxes and in the Paper Size section of the dialog box displayed by the Printer Setup command (also on the File menu). Otherwise, you might wonder why your text doesn't fit on the paper. It's a small item that is easily overlooked, but potentially frustrating.

Finally, notice that you use this command to specify the starting number Works uses when it numbers the pages of the document. (This is discussed further in "Special Characters" later in this chapter.) On a report, for example, you might print a title page before the first actual page of text. To include the title page in the total page count, but start numbering with the first page of text, you would type *2* in the 1st page number box. (To skip a page number on the first page, use the Headers & Footers command, described next.)

 TIP If your printer has the capability, print sideways on a page by transposing the length and width measurements in the Page length and Page width boxes. For example, to print sideways on 8 ½ by 11 inch paper, specify the length as 8.5 inches and the width as 11 inches. If you do this, also use the Printer Setup command to specify the Landscape orientation.

Headers and Footers

A header is any text that repeats at the top of the pages in your document. Likewise, a footer is text that prints at the bottom of the pages. You can create two different types of headers and footers: *standard* or *paragraph*. Both are controlled by the same command:

□ Choose the Headers & Footers command from the Edit menu.

To create standard running heads, you use the Header and Footer boxes. To create paragraph running heads, you click the box next to Use header and footer paragraphs. When you don't want a running head on the first page, you click the boxes next to No header (footer) on 1st page.

Standard Headers and Footers

Standard running heads are single paragraphs that you create as you did in the preceding example: by typing text in the Headers & Footers dialog box. You don't see standard headers and footers as you work, but Works does display them in Print Preview and, of course, it prints them on your documents.

By default, standard headers and footers are centered horizontally on the page. You can, however, use the following codes, each beginning with an ampersand (&), to alter their alignment and to add special elements, such as the page number or the date.

Code	Meaning
&L	Align left
&R	Align right
&C	Center
&P	Print page number
&D	Print short date (1/01/92)
&N	Print long date (January 1, 1992)
&T	Print time (01:01 PM)
&F	Print filename
&&	Print an ampersand

You can include more than one code in a single header or footer. Even though they might strike you as cryptic to begin with, the codes offer you a considerable amount of flexibility. Alignment codes affect all text that follows, until you type another code. Try this:

☐ If necessary, choose the Headers & Footers command from the Edit menu.

☐ Type the following (using either uppercase or lowercase) in the Header box: *&LMY DOCUMENT: &F&C&P&R&D &T.* Click OK.

This is what you've told Works to do to your header: Left align (&L) the characters MY DOCUMENT: on the page; leave a space and print the filename (&F); center (&C) and insert the page number (&P); and right align (&R) the date (&D) and time (&T). To see the result,

☐ Click the Print Preview button in the Toolbar and zoom in.

You should see something like this:

Paragraph Headers and Footers

Standard headers and footers are limited to a single line of text. If you want a multiline running head, or if you simply prefer to see your running heads onscreen, create paragraph headers, footers, or both instead.

☐ Choose the Headers & Footers command.

☐ Click the checkbox next to Use header and footer paragraphs in the dialog box that appears. Click OK.

This time, Works displays two special paragraphs at the top of the document:

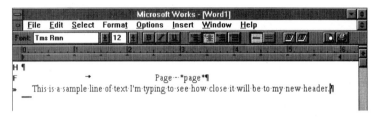

To answer your first question: No, you don't have to include both headers and footers simply because Works displays a paragraph for each. You can't delete a header or footer paragraph, but if you don't want one of these elements, simply leave the paragraph blank or delete any text that appears there.

Header and footer paragraphs are formatted by default with left alignment and two tab stops: one centered in the middle of the page and another right-aligned at the right margin. You can add others if you want.

You can't press Enter to create multiple-line running heads. You can, however, produce multiple-line running heads by pressing Shift-Enter, a key combination that tells Works to start a new line within an existing paragraph.

Try creating a multple-line header paragraph:

☐ If necessary, move the insertion point to the header paragraph by clicking in front of its paragraph mark.

☐ Type *Memo: To all staff,* and press Shift-Enter to start a new line.

☐ Type *From: Regional office/Midwest,* and press Shift-Enter again.

☐ Type *Re: Voluntary overtime.*

☐ Click the Print Preview button on the Toolbar.

Wrong move. Works displays the following complaint:

Nothing's broken, but Works is telling you it can't fit the new header into the available top margin. This is one of the many "fail-safe" features in Works that guarantee both ease of use and the integrity of your documents. The solution:

□ Click No to close the dialog box.

□ Choose Page Setup & Margins from the File menu and change the top margin to 1.5 inches.

□ Click the Print Preview button again and zoom in.

This time, your top margin is large enough to hold a three-line header:

One final difference between standard running heads and paragraph running heads: You don't use the special codes, such as &P, in a paragraph header or footer. If you try, Works simply prints the characters. There's another way to format a paragraph header or footer, though. It's easier than using codes, and it leads right into the next topic.

Special Characters

Page numbers, the date and time, and filenames are useful items of information for a running head (or for other parts of a document, for that matter). Works has special internal codes for these items, which you can add to a document whenever you choose:

□ Choose the Special Character command from the Insert menu.

This dialog box appears:

To insert any of these special characters in a running head, or elsewhere in a document, click the character you want and click OK. The following table lists the characters and describes what they do; later examples show some in use.

Character	Meaning
End-of-line	Start a new line; displayed as ⏎ if Show All Characters is on (Keyboard: Press Shift-Enter)
Optional hyphen	Hyphenates a word if it must be broken at the end of a line; displayed as a hyphen; appears if Show All Characters is on (Keyboard: Press Ctrl-Hyphen)
Non-breaking hyphen	Prevents a hyphenated word from breaking at the end of a line; displayed the same as the optional hyphen (Keyboard: Press Ctrl-Shift-Hyphen)
Non-breaking space	Prevents related words from being broken at the end of a line (Keyboard: Press Ctrl-Shift-Spacebar)
Print page number	Inserts the current page number in a document; displayed as *page*; always shown onscreen
Print filename	Inserts document's filename; displayed as *filename*; always shown onscreen
Print date	Inserts the date, in short form (for example, 1/01/92), that the document is printed; displayed as *date*; always shown onscreen
Print long date	Inserts the date, in long form (for example, January 1, 1992), that the document is printed; displayed as *longdate*; always shown onscreen
Print time	Inserts the time of printing; displayed as *time*; always shown onscreen

(continued)

126

continued

Character	Meaning
Current date	Inserts current date in short form (Keyboard: Press Ctrl-Semicolon)
Current time	Inserts current time (Keyboard: Press Ctrl-Shift-Semicolon)

It would be nice to add the date and page number to the header paragraph you created earlier. If it's still on your screen, return to the first line of the header. Click between the word *staff* and the end-of-line character (a bent-left arrow).

Remember that header and footer paragraphs have two built-in tab stops. You'll use the right-aligned one:

□ Press the Tab key twice.

□ Type *Page* and a space.

□ Choose Special Character from the Insert menu.

□ Click on Print page number, and then click on OK.

□ Move the insertion point to the end of the second line, and press Tab twice.

□ Choose Special Character.

□ Click on Print date and click OK.

Zoom in on Print Preview again to see what your header looks like now. Very professional . . . and easy.

Of Hyphens and Spaces

Before you leave the topic of special characters, there's one more area to consider: line breaks. In particular, you should know about the hyphens and spaces you can insert in a document to control line endings.

Normally, if Works cannot fit an entire word at the end of a line, it simply moves the word to the next line. Sometimes, however, you want to hyphenate words at the end of a line to make the line endings less ragged or to decrease extra space between words in a justified paragraph. Chances are you won't need to do this type of fine-tuning on a day-to-day basis, because most documents look fine without such niceties, but a little tinkering can be useful when an important document — a proposal, a business plan, or a prospectus — must look as good as possible.

Hyphens

A hyphen by any name might seem like a hyphen but, as you can see from the table of special characters, Works actually recognizes three types of hyphens:

- Those you normally type, as in the word *double-click*

- Those you want to use only if a word cannot fit at the end of a line

- Those you want to use at all times to prevent a hyphenated word from being broken at the end of a line

To see how these hyphens work, set your current font and font size to Tms Rmn 12. Check that the right margin is at 6 inches and verify that Show All Characters in the Options menu is turned on. Now type the paragraph you see in the following illustration:

It was a dark and stormy night. The wind howled through the bleak bones of the willow trees. Hollow branches clicked in frantic rhythm, the long, skeletal fingers of departed misers clutching for their lost gold. Sad and tired, Mrs. Haversham-Bavisham hurried, bent and bundled, along the winding road while will-of-the-wisp ghost lights danced madly in the fog rising from the slough.¶

NOTE: *If the text on your screen doesn't break in the same places as the example, you should change the right paragraph indents with the mouse or change the margins with the Page Setup and Margins command from the File menu.*

Now to fiddle with the line endings. Suppose you decide that Haversham-Bavisham, being a hyphenated name, should not break at the end of a line, as it does now:

- Select the hyphen, delete it, and replace it by inserting a non-breaking hyphen from the Special Character list.

The non-breaking hyphen tells Works to keep the name together, which it does by moving the entire name to the next line. Now, however, you've got a considerable gap to fill at the end of one line. One way to do this is by hyphenating words:

- Move the insertion point between the two *l*'s in *willow*.

- Insert an optional hyphen from the Special Character list.

- Insert another optional hyphen so that *departed* becomes *de-parted*.

That did it. Two hyphens in a row are not ideal, but at least now you don't have any major gaps at the ends of lines. To see how optional hyphens differ from normal and non-breaking hyphens, insert an optional hyphen in *frantic*.

Notice that Works displays the word as *fran-tic* and rebreaks the lines. Turn off Show All Characters. The optional hyphen disappears because it is a special character, and the lines are once again arranged neatly on the screen.

NOTE: *As you saw in this example, displaying special characters can produce inaccurate line breaks on the screen. If you insert a lot of optional hyphens in a document, check the finished layout before printing by turning off Show All Characters or by using Print Preview.*

Tables

Although you'll find the Works spreadsheet much easier for creating tables, you might want to use the word processor for simple tables or for those in which one column contains multiple lines of text.

To create columns in a table, set tabs where you want them. Depending on the type of table you create, you can make each line a separate paragraph, or for ease of handling, you can make the body of the table a single paragraph, ending each line with an end-of-line character. Here are two short examples.

To create a simple table in which headings form one paragraph and the body forms another,

- ☐ Move the insertion point to an open area of the screen and press Enter to create a new paragraph.

- ☐ Insert left-aligned tab stops at 2 inches and at 4 inches.

- ☐ Now type the following table. (Press Shift-Enter where you see the bent left arrow.)

To create a table in which one column contains more lines than the others, make each line of the table a separate paragraph and use paragraph indents to align the lines of one column correctly.

- ☐ Create a new table with the same tab stops as in the preceding example.

- ☐ To allow for a multiple-line column, choose Indents & Spacing from the Format menu; give the body paragraph a left indent of 4 inches and a first-line indent of – 4 inches (minus 4).

□ Type the following table:

Breed	→	Price	→	Description¶
German·Shepherd	→	$300	→	Active,·alert,·protective·yet· gentle·with·its·family¶
Collie	→	$250	→	Quiet,·devoted;·needs· considerable·grooming¶
Boxer	→	$275	→	Easy·to·care·for,·active,· good·playmate¶

NOTE: *In some tables, you'll probably want to create headings as separate paragraphs. By doing this, you can center or otherwise align them separately above the columns.*

VIEWING AND PRINTING

Unless you and your computer form a closed society, printing is *the* objective when you create a document of any type. Because Works is an integrated program, the printing process is consistent throughout the three Works applications. Once you've defined the margins, formatting, running heads, and other elements of a document, only two steps remain: previewing and printing.

Print Preview

You've seen a great deal of Print Preview and its Zoom feature by now, so neither needs much explanation. One preview aspect you haven't seen, however, is controlled by two buttons on the Preview screen: Previous and Next. So far, you've previewed single-page documents. On a multiple-page document, you use the Previous and Next buttons to "scroll" from page to page. Previous takes you back one page (if there is one); Next takes you forward one page. Use these buttons freely on long documents, especially when you're checking the following elements:

- Tables, to be sure they're aligned correctly and don't break over pages

- Headers and footers, to verify their placement on the printed page

- Paragraph borders and formats, to ensure they work to enhance the document

- Character formatting, to ensure that you haven't overlooked anything that you meant to add and didn't or — as often happens — left something you meant to remove

- Internal headings, to verify that the fonts, font sizes, and alignment you chose work well with the rest of the document

- Graphics and charts, to be sure that they are sized and positioned correctly

Previewing a document, as you've already seen, saves time. More importantly, it can also reduce the waste associated with printouts that don't turn out quite right. Checking formatting and layout is particularly useful if you use Works to work on a document created with another program, such as Microsoft Word, Word for Windows, Windows Write, or WordPerfect.

Page Breaks

When you create a multiple-page document, Works keeps track of the document's length. Works also shows you where page breaks occur as you're typing by displaying a new-page character (») at the left edge of the screen. Sometimes, pages will break where you don't want them to (for example, at the end of a letter, between the closing and your signature). You can correct such unfortunate breaks in one of two ways:

- By inserting a manual page break

- By stipulating that certain paragraphs must appear together on the same page

Inserting a Manual Page Break

To insert a manual page break, you move the insertion point to the place you want a new page to begin and press Ctrl-Enter. Works then displays a dotted line showing the page break:

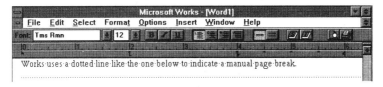

After you insert a manual page break, you don't have to go back and recheck your other pages. Works adjusts the others to fit. To see how your other pages are affected, choose Paginate Now from the Options menu and either scroll through the document or view them in Print Preview. If you later decide you don't want a manual page break you've inserted, place the insertion point in front of the first character following the page break, and press the Backspace key.

Keeping Paragraphs Together

There are two ways you can keep a page break from interrupting paragraphs in a document:

- By keeping a multiline paragraph, such as a list, on one page

- By keeping related paragraphs together on a single page

In either situation, you use the Indents & Spacing command on the Format menu:

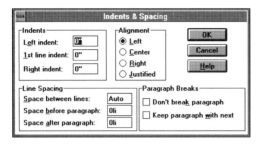

To keep all lines of a paragraph on the same page, click the box next to Don't break paragraph. To keep related paragraphs together, click next to Keep paragraph with next. Here are two examples.

Suppose you've created a list like the one shown in the following illustration, using end-of-line characters (Shift-Enter) to break each line. That way, you would double-space the lines, but could add extra space above and below the list without formatting more than one paragraph:

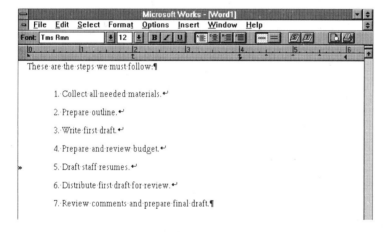

If a page break occurs within the list, you can print the entire list on a single page by selecting the paragraph and choosing Don't break paragraph in the Indents & Spacing dialog box. When you carry out the command, Works will repaginate the document, moving the new-page marker up to the beginning of the list.

Note, however, that Works moves the page break up, not down. If you have a long paragraph, and the page break occurs near the end, it's visually better to add some extra text before the paragraph or (if appropriate) adjust top or bottom margins, rather than break off at a point unnaturally high on the page.

On the other hand, letters often seem to have minds of their own and end like this:

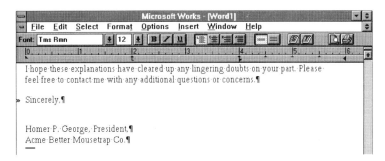

In this situation, you would select the final, short paragraph, and then choose Keep paragraph with next in the Indents & Spacing dialog box. Works would then move the page break up so that the paragraph and closing appear on the next page of the document.

Setting Up for Printing

Before you can print a document, Works must be able to use your printer. In most cases, you needn't worry about this because you should have set up your printer when you installed Windows. Because Works is a Windows application, it can use the printer setup you defined to Windows. You don't have to redefine your printer, fonts, and print capabilities; once you tell Windows about your printer, printing becomes a simple matter of using the Print command in any Windows application.

If you choose the Printer Setup command on the Works File menu, you actually go out to the Printer Setup command in Windows. Use the Printer Setup command when you are changing printers, adding or deleting fonts, or switching to a different printer port, page orientation (portrait or landscape), or paper size. Printer Setup walks you through the process with the aid of a detailed dialog box that is customized for your printer. If you need explanations of any of the options, click the Help button in the dialog box for details.

Printing

After you've set up your printer and your document looks exactly the way you want it to, printing is a snap. All you need is one of the three print commands on the File menu:

- Print, to print a document such as a letter or report

- Print Form Letters, to create letters for mass mailings

- Print Labels, to print names and addresses on mailing labels

The Form Letters and Labels commands give you another way to create the letters and labels described briefly in Chapter 3 on the WorksWizards and in more detail in Chapter 13.

The plain Print command produces this dialog box:

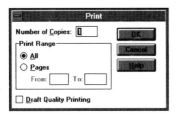

Works proposes to print one copy of the current document. If you want more, type the number you want in the Number of Copies box. If you want to print part of a multiple-page document, click Pages in the Print Range box and fill in the From and To boxes with the starting and ending page numbers.

TIP If you want to print a single page in the middle of a document, type the same page number in both the From and To boxes. If you want to print from a specific page to the end of a document, but you can't remember the number of the last page, simply type a number that you know is greater than the final page, such as 100, in the To box. Works will simply continue printing until it reaches the last page, no matter what the last page number is.

To produce a draft copy quickly, check the Draft Quality Print box. Remember, however, that this option does not print graphics.

NOTES AND FOOTNOTES

Besides its formatting, graphics, and layout capabilities, the word processor offers a number of make-life-easy options. To finish coverage of this application, we'll take a look at these options. Some, such as the spelling checker, might become regular parts of your word processing routine. Others, such as the thesaurus or search and replace, might become occasional assistants you'll appreciate in special circumstances.

Bookmarks

Unless you've got a photographic memory, you'll probably find yourself scrolling up and down in long documents, searching for information you want to refer to as you write about some other topic. One way to give your mouse-clicking finger a rest is to use the split box at the top of the vertical scroll bar to split the document window and display different parts of the document in each "pane."

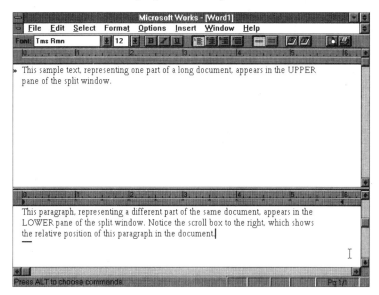

Another method, which can save you a lot of time when you're working on a long document, is to insert *bookmarks* at appropriate sections of the document, for example, at each heading in a proposal or a report, at the top of a price list, or even at the beginning of a graphic.

Bookmarks are your computer equivalent of paper clips, dog-eared pages, marking pens, and highlighters. Although your RAINGEAR.WPS document isn't very long, use it in this exercise to see how easily you can create and use bookmarks:

☐ Open RAINGEAR.WPS.

☐ Scroll down to the bordered paragraphs containing your list of rainwear.

You can place bookmarks anywhere in a document, but you'll probably want most of them at or near the beginning of a topic.

☐ Place the insertion point at the beginning of the list.

□ Choose Bookmark Name from the Insert menu. The following
dialog box appears:

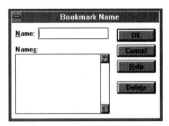

This is where you assign a name to the bookmark. After you've assigned a
name, Works will associate the name with the location you've marked, and you can
return to that exact part of the document whenever you want. For this example,

□ Type *product* in the Name box, and click OK.

Works displays the names of all assigned bookmarks in the Names portion
of this dialog box, so when you assign names, try to make them descriptive and
easy to tell apart. You can include spaces in a bookmark name, but don't try to
make it longer than 15 characters. If you do, Works will truncate the name — but
you can still use it to jump to the part of the document you marked.

When you return to the document, there's no visible indication of a bookmark.

□ Scroll to the top of the document.

□ Choose Go To from the Select menu or press F5. The following
dialog box appears:

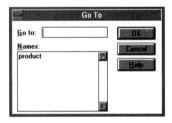

This dialog box lists the names of all bookmarks you've assigned to a
particular document. To go to a particular bookmark,

□ Double-click on the bookmark name, *product.*

Almost instantly, Works jumps to the part of the document you marked.

If you create a bookmark and later decide you no longer need it, choose
Bookmark Name from the Insert menu, select the bookmark name in the dialog

box, click Delete, and then click Close (not OK). If you decide to rename a bookmark, go to the bookmarked place in the document, choose Bookmark Name, and type a new name. When Works asks if you want to replace the existing bookmark, click OK. Once you've assigned a bookmark name, you cannot use it again in the same document.

Footnotes

Footnotes are clearly necessary in professional papers and academic publications, but they can often be useful in off-campus documents too. Reports that include statistics, citations from other sources, and plain facts that you want to document outside the body of your text can all benefit from footnotes. Typing and numbering footnotes can be a chore without a computer. Works makes the process much easier by taking over the drudgery of referencing them. When you print, Works places them all neatly at the end of the document. Footnotes are more easily seen than described, so try creating one:

◻ Clear the screen or open a new word processor document and type the following:

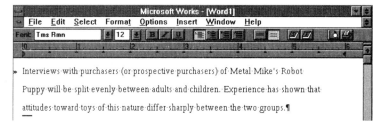

◻ To add a footnote at the end, choose Footnote from the Insert menu. The following dialog box appears:

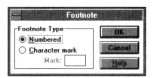

Works lets you mark footnotes with either numbers or special symbols. For this example, choose numbered footnotes:

◻ Numbered is the default footnote type, so simply click OK.

Your screen immediately changes to this display:

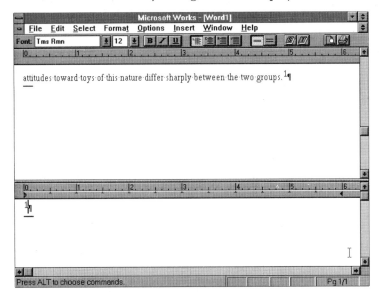

The new window at the bottom is a *footnote window.* Works displays footnotes in their own window, keeping them completely separate from the text. You can make the window larger or smaller by dragging the split bar at the top of the footnote window. You can also make the window disappear altogether by dragging it off the screen or by turning off Show Footnotes on the Options menu. For this example, leave the window as it is.

Notice, too, that Works has inserted a superscripted 1 in the text and in the footnote window. Works keeps track of the numbering, so if you had already inserted four footnotes, a superscripted 5 would have appeared here.

Works applies the font and font size you've chosen for the body of your document to both footnote reference marks and footnote text. To conserve space and to minimize the visual impact of footnote reference marks in text, you might want to print all footnote-related material in a smaller size. To do this,

- Select the footnote reference mark in your text. Change it to a smaller size, such as 10.

- Click in the footnote window, or press F6 to jump quickly to and from the two windows.

□ Select the superscripted 1 in the footnote window, and change its size.

□ Next, type this footnote text: *Based on prior surveys for Super-Fantastic, Inc., manufacturers of the MechanoMiracle line of 25th Century Action Toys.*

After you've created footnotes, you can edit them in the footnote window and move references by cutting and pasting as you do normal text. If you add or delete footnote references in the body of your text, Works renumbers the remaining footnotes for you.

 If you want to use symbols in place of numbers as footnote reference marks, hold down the Alt key and type the number corresponding to an extended character on the numeric keypad. You'll find these characters in Appendix B.

Because Works prints all footnotes at the end of a document, you'll probably want to preview your finished work and insert a manual page break to start all footnotes on a separate page. You can also add and format a heading, such as "References" or "Citations," at the top of the first footnote page to further distinguish the notes from your text.

SAVING TIME

The tasks of creating, formatting, and laying out a document are yours, but Works can help you save time when you're grasping for a word that's just out of reach, when you want to check your spelling, when you want to find or replace specific text, and when you want to save formats so you don't have to duplicate your efforts again and again.

Finding Synonyms

The Works Thesaurus is a large and nicely cross-referenced collection of synonyms for most common (and some uncommon) words. To try it out:

□ Type the following text in an open area of the document window: *Don't desert me now, luck. Serendipity is my middle name.*

☐ Place the insertion point in the word *desert,* and click the Thesaurus button in the Toolbar. This is what you see:

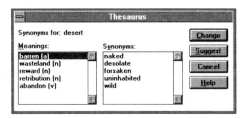

The box entitled Meanings lists various definitions for *desert,* along with the part of speech (noun, verb, adjective) each represents. The highlighted definition shows that the Synonyms box is displaying a list of words, all meaning *barren.* To see a list of synonyms for *desert,* in the sense of "leave behind,"

☐ Click on *abandon* in the Meanings box. The list changes immediately.

At the right of the dialog box are four buttons labeled Change, Suggest, Cancel, and Help. These buttons perform the following functions:

■ Change replaces the selected word in your document with the highlighted word in either the Meanings box or the Synonyms box, whichever is surrounded by a dotted line.

■ Suggest causes the Thesaurus to produce a new list of possible synonyms for the highlighted word. You can have some fun with this by going farther and farther astray from the meaning of the original word you selected. Requesting suggestions for *abandon,* for example, produces: *wantonness, spontaneity, impetuosity,* and *enthusiasm.*

■ Cancel quits the Thesaurus.

■ Help, as usual, provides on-line help.

To finish up with the Thesaurus,

☐ Highlight *forsake* in the list of synonyms for *desert.*

☐ Click Change. The word in your document changes from *desert* to *forsake.*

There are limits to the Thesaurus, however:

☐ Place the insertion point in the word *Serendipity,* and click the Thesaurus button.

Works responds with the following dialog box:

Oh, well.

Checking Spelling

Most people have trouble spelling certain words. Does *parallel* have one *r* or two? Does *embarrassment* really have all those double letters? Does *broccoli* have one *c* and two *l*'s?

Works has a dictionary of *120,000* words it can use to check the spelling in your documents. You can check an entire document, or you can limit the operation by selecting only the section you want to check.

Add some deliberately misspelled words to a sentence on your screen:

☐ Type *Let us go now, yoo and eye, where the sunlight drapes the sky. All the way to microsoft.*

☐ Place the insertion point at the beginning of the sentence, and click the Spelling button.

The following illustration shows the first misspelling found by Works:

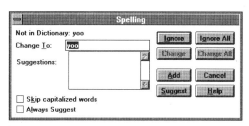

To see a list of possible spellings,

☐ Click the Suggest button.

A list of possibilities appears, among them the correct spelling, *you.* To correct the spelling in your document,

☐ Highlight *you.*

☐ Click the Change button.

Spell then goes on to another problem, this time telling you it has found some *Irregular capitalization:*

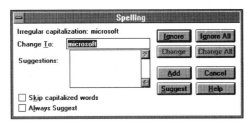

Notice, by the way, that Spell skipped over *eye,* even though it should have been *I.* Works cannot check for correct usage, so remember to give your documents a quick sweep of your own if there's a possibility you've made mistakes like this one.

The occurrence of *microsoft* is the last misspelling in your document, so before you take care of it, take a moment to look at the remainder of Spell's dialog box. The eight buttons along the right side let you do the following:

- Ignore: Disregard the spelling currently highlighted. (You'll probably want to do this with proper names.)

- Ignore All: Disregard all instances of that spelling.

- Change: Change the word in the document to the one highlighted in the Suggestions box.

- Change All: Change all occurrences of the highlighted spelling throughout the document.

- Add: Add the highlighted word to the Works dictionary. (You can do this with the names of people and companies that occur often in your documents.)

- Cancel: Quit the Spelling checker.

- Suggest: Display a list of variant spellings.

- Help: Display help.

At the bottom of the dialog box, you can also choose to:

- Skip: Ignore capitalized words (again, proper names).

- Always Suggest: Provide alternatives without waiting for you to press the Suggest button.

As you can see, Spell is both powerful and flexible. To finish up your example,

- ☐ Click the Suggest button and choose the correct spelling of *Microsoft.*

- ☐ Click OK when Works tells you the spelling check is complete.

NOTE: *The inclusion of* Microsoft *in Spell's dictionary isn't rampant ego-mania. You'll find* IBM *in the dictionary too.*

Find and Replace

Works has two search commands: Find and Replace. Like bookmarks, Find can be useful when you need to search a document for specific text or for special characters, such as tabs and page breaks. Replace works like the Find command, except that it both finds text and special characters and replaces it with other text or special characters.

When you use Find, Works takes you to the first occurrence of the text you specify following the current position of the insertion point. If it is not the occurrence you seek, you can press the F7 key to repeat the search.

When you use Replace, Works also takes you to the first occurrence following the insertion point. It then asks if you want to replace the text and, after following your instructions, goes on to the next occurrence, and the next, until it reaches the end of the document.

Unlike Spell, which asks if you want to continue checking from the beginning when it reaches the end of the document, Find and Replace go only to the end of the document and then stop. To search an entire document, be sure to first place the insertion point at the beginning. It's a small matter, but one that can mean the difference between a complete and an incomplete search or replace operation. To search part of a document, highlight the portion to be searched before choosing the command.

Try out the Find command:

- ☐ Select all the text on your screen.

- ☐ Copy the text to the Clipboard, move the insertion point to the end, and then paste the copied text back in several times to ensure that you have several occurrences of the same text in your document.

- ☐ Place the insertion point at the beginning of the document, and choose Find from the Select menu.

Works displays this dialog box:

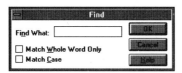

You type the text you want to find in the Find What box. The box is relatively small, but you can type more than it holds. For example, you could type *Don't forsake me now, luck. Serendipity is my middle name,* and Find would search for the entire set of characters.

If you want to limit a search to whole words, check the Match Whole Word Only box. Doing this will eliminate those occurrences in which your search text is part of a larger word, for example, the *works* in *fireworks* and *gasworks.* To search only for exact matches of uppercase and lowercase letters, click the Match Case box. Doing this finds *Works,* but not *WORKS* or *works.*

Tell Works to find the word *sunlight:*

☐ Type *sunlight* in the Find What box, and click OK.

☐ When Works highlights the first *sunlight* it finds, press F7 to go on to the next occurrence.

☐ Continue until Works reaches the end of the document, and then click OK when it tells you No match found.

Now try the Replace command:

☐ Move the insertion point back to the beginning of the document and choose Replace from the Select menu.

The Replace dialog box is almost identical to the Find dialog box. Replace, however, includes a Replace With box where you type the text that is to replace the text in the Find What box. It also includes a Replace All button that you can click to replace, in one step, every occurrence of the specified text in the document. Use this option with care, because all replacements happen quickly. You can reverse all changes with the Undo command, but that will leave you right back where you started.

Notice that Works remembers your last search. Here, for example, *sunlight* is displayed in the Find What box because that is the last text you searched for. Replace *sunlight drapes* with *clouds cover:*

☐ Type *sunlight drapes* in the Find What box, and type *clouds cover* in the Replace With box. Click Replace.

- ☐ Works quickly finds the first occurrence and asks if you want to make the replacement. Click Yes for the first occurrence and No for all others.

- ☐ Click OK when Works reports No more occurrences.

Now try replacing all occurrences in one step:

- ☐ Choose the Replace command again. This time click Replace All.

A few seconds later it's over, and Works tells you how many replacements it made.

Refining Your Search

If you're not certain about the spelling of a word you want to find, you can use a wildcard character, the question mark (?), to take the place of any other character. For example, if you want to find *pin, pan,* and *pun,* you can type the search (or replace) text as *p?n.* Similarly, to find both *soon* and *seen,* you can type the search text as *s??n.*

To search for, or replace, special characters, specify them with the codes in the following table.

Code	*Character*
^T	Tabs
^P	Paragraph marks
^N	End-of-line characters
^D	Manual page breaks
^S	Non-breaking spaces
^^	Caret marks
^?	Question marks
^W	White Space (combination of tabs, spaces, and non-breaking spaces, or non-breaking spaces alone)

You can put these special characters to good use when jumping from page to page of a document with a lot of manual page breaks. You can also use them to clean up files (such as those that are transferred over phone lines) that contain unneeded paragraph marks or that contain blank spaces instead of tabs. For example, if a document contains two paragraph marks between paragraphs, type *^p^p* in the Find What box and *^p* in the Replace With box. To delete unwanted characters, leave the Replace With box empty.

Document Templates

After you've spent a long time formatting a document and making it look exactly the way you want it to, you may want to use the same layout and formatting for other documents. Business letters, bid proposals, reports, and many other types of documents tend to take on the same appearance and, often, the same organization. The content might change, but the overall appearance remains the same. In the rest of this chapter, you'll see how to save formatting for future use. This feature alone can be a tremendous timesaver, especially because you can put the same capability to work in the spreadsheet and the database.

By now, you're familiar with the various types of formatting Works can apply to a document, so the following example will simply show you how to save such formats as a word processing *template*. Essentially, a template is a blank or near-blank document with preformatted paragraphs.

The following example shows a template for a business letter. Brief explanations are included for each paragraph. These brief explanations are particularly useful if the template will be used by people unfamiliar with Works:

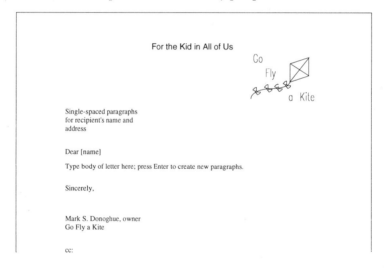

Following are a few items you might want to note for your own use:

- The slogan at the top of the letterhead is part of a centered header paragraph with a centered tab stop at 3 inches. The logo, also part of the header, is separated from the slogan by an end-of-line character and is positioned at the right edge by a tab. This formatting prevents these two elements from extending too far down the page. The top margin has been increased to accommodate such a deep header.

- The salutation is formatted as a single-spaced paragraph with 2 lines before it.

- The body paragraph is double spaced with 1 line after it.

- The closing is a plain double-spaced paragraph.

- The signature line is a single-spaced paragraph with 3 lines before it to allow for the person's signature. An end-of-line character after *owner* breaks the paragraph to a new line for the name of the company.

- The cc: line is single spaced with 2 lines before it and a left-aligned tab stop at 0.37 inches. Additional lines can be created and aligned by pressing Shift-Enter at the end of each line and pressing Tab before beginning the new line.

To save this formatting, you can save the document as a template or as a normal file. If you save formatting as a template, and you check Word Processor in the Use Templates for box of the Works Settings command, Works will automatically open the template whenever you start the word processor. If you save formatting as a normal document, you'll open the template yourself in order to use it.

There are advantages and disadvantages to each method. If you save formatting as a template, it is easy to open, but it is also the only template Works will recognize for the word processor. Works saves the template as TEMPLATE.PS.

If you save formatting as a document, you must open the file yourself, but you can save as many different types of formatting as you want, under different filenames, such as LETTERHD, REPORT, and so on. To make them readily identifiable, you can adopt a convention such as starting each template file with T (for example, TLETTER and TREPORT).

To save formatting as a template,

☐ Choose the Save As command, and click WP Template in the drop-down list displayed in the Save File as Type box.

To save formatting as a normal document, simply choose Save As and assign a filename as you would any other word processing file. Open and use your templates whenever you want, but remember to give different names to the documents you create with them. If you don't assign new names, you'll "overwrite" the template with data.

REFERENCE TO WORD PROCESSOR COMMANDS

Here is a quick reference to Works menus and commands. The following table should serve as a refresher if you can't remember which command to use or what it does. As always, refer to Help if you need more information.

The File Menu — for manipulating entire files in the word processor

Create New File	Opens a new, blank document.
Open Existing File	Opens a previously saved document.
Close	Closes an open document.
Save	Saves a document under its existing name. Use this command to update an existing file.
Save As	Saves a document under a new name, on a different disk, or in a different directory. Use this to save a new file or an existing file that you want to duplicate elsewhere.
Save Workspace	Saves your Works "desktop" as is. If Use saved workspace is checked in the Works Settings dialog box, Works will start with the saved workspace at the beginning of your next session.
Print Preview	Takes you to preview mode, where you can view whole pages of a document.
Print	Prints a document, letting you specify draft mode and page ranges, if desired.
Print Form Letters	Uses a previously created database of names and addresses to create a form letter for mass mailings. (See Chapter 13.)
Print Labels	Uses a previously created database to print mailing labels. (See Chapter 13.)
Page Setup & Margins	Sets up page layout — margins, header position, beginning page number, and page size.
Printer Setup	Adds or modifies information about your printer.
Exit Works	Quits Works.

The Edit Menu — for editing a document

Undo	Reverses the last edit.
Cut	Removes selected text from the document and places it on the Clipboard.

(continued)

continued

Copy	Copies selected text to the Clipboard.
Paste	Inserts the contents of the Clipboard into a document at the current location of the insertion point.
Paste Special	Inserts character or paragraph formats, rather than text, from the contents of the Clipboard. Paste Special also inserts information copied to the Clipboard from other applications. (See Chapter 12.)
Delete	Deletes selected text; does not place it on the Clipboard.
Object	Opens the application in which you created an object, such as a drawing or a spreadsheet chart, so you can make changes to the object. The command name changes, depending on the application used to create the object. For example, it changes to Edit Microsoft Drawing Object if a Draw object is selected. (See Chapter 12.)
Links	Adjusts or changes links between information in a document and in the original version created with a different application. Links enables you to update information when it changes in the source document. (See Chapter 12.)
Headers & Footers	Creates headers and footers in a document.

The Select Menu — *for different ways of selecting text and navigating in a document*

Text	Turns on extended selection to allow highlighting quantities of text.
All	Selects the entire document.
Go To	Jumps to a specified bookmark in the document.
Find	Finds the first occurrence of specified text. Press F7 to repeat the search.
Replace	Replaces individual or all occurrences of specified text with new text.

The Format Menu — *for formatting text and scaling imported graphics*

Font & Style	Applies character formats.
Indents & Spacing	Applies paragraph indents and line spacing.
Tabs	Inserts and deletes tab stops.
Border	Adds or deletes borders around paragraphs.
Picture	Scales imported graphics.

(continued)

continued

The Options Menu — *for turning on or starting various options that refine the way Works works*

Works Settings	Customizes Works.
Dial This Number	Dials a highlighted phone number in a document to enable a voice call (not computer communications).
Show Toolbar	Turns the Toolbar on or off.
Show Ruler	Turns the ruler on or off.
Show All Characters	Turns the display of special characters, such as paragraph marks, on or off.
Show Footnotes	Opens the footnote window for viewing and editing footnotes.
Draft View	Displays documents in a quick-to-display screen font; reserves space for, but does not display, imported graphics.
Wrap for Window	Wraps lines to fit in available window space.
Typing Replaces Selection	Replaces selected text with typed text.
Overtype	Replaces existing characters with typed characters, rather than inserting new characters.
Check Spelling	Starts the Spelling checker.
Thesaurus	Starts the Thesaurus.
Word Count	Provides a count of the words in a document.
Paginate Now	Repaginates a document.

The Insert Menu — *for inserting special elements in a document*

Special Character	Inserts special hyphens, date, time, and other elements.
Page Break	Inserts a page break at the insertion point.
Footnote	Adds a footnote reference mark and opens the footnote window.
Bookmark Name	Marks selected text with a bookmark name.
Database Field	Inserts a placeholder for information held in a database field; used in documents such as form letters. (See Chapter 13.)
Chart	Inserts a chart from the spreadsheet.
Drawing	Starts Microsoft Draw so you can create a drawing to insert at the location of the insertion point.
Note-It	Starts Microsoft Note-It to create a "stick-on" type of note at the insertion point. (See Chapter 12.)
Object	Starts any application that can create a Windows object for inserting into the document.

(continued)

continued

The Window Menu — *for managing the Works window*

Cascade	Overlaps open document windows.
Tile	Arranges open windows side by side.
Arrange Icons	Arranges icons for open, but minimized, documents in the lower left corner of the application window.
Split	Splits a document window into separate "panes" for viewing different parts of a document.

The Help Menu — *for activating Works Help*

Use Help for specific information or as a means of accessing the Works tutorial.

7

The Spreadsheet

From the time you're small, you communicate with both words and numbers. Eventually, words become your primary vehicle for communicating thoughts and ideas, and numbers satisfy the need to organize, understand, and communicate data. In business, at home, and at school, the Works spreadsheet can help you manage the increasing quantity of numbers that seem to define and sometimes dominate life. With the Works spreadsheet, you'll know that your calculations are accurate.

This chapter takes you into the world of spreadsheets — computerized ledger sheets that you can build, organize, alter, format, and print without resorting to pencils and erasers. You'll find the basics here. In Chapter 8, you'll see how to turn data into charts, and in Part III, you'll see how to link related spreadsheets and move information from a spreadsheet to a document in the word processor.

TOURING THE SPREADSHEET

Because Works is an integrated application, you've already seen and used many of the procedures, such as copying and moving data, that you'll use in working with spreadsheets. You no longer have to step through extended how-to examples to see how Works runs, so succeeding examples are shorter and focus on how particular features work. To try out the spreadsheet examples,

- ☐ Start Works, if necessary.

- ☐ Use the Spreadsheet button in the Startup dialog box or the Create New File command to start the spreadsheet with a blank workspace.

- ☐ Maximize the application and document windows.

Works displays a blank spreadsheet:

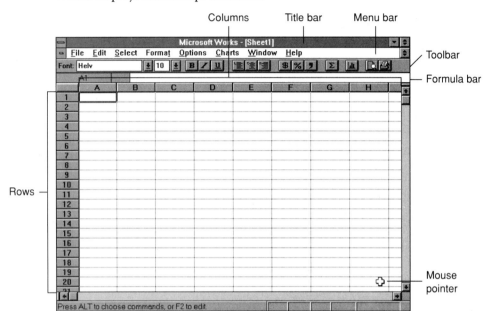

Spreadsheet Cells

At first glance, the spreadsheet window is a lot busier than the word processor's, primarily because the spreadsheet displays a grid of cells. Each cell is capable of holding text, a numeric value, a date, or a formula for calculating new values.

Each cell in a spreadsheet has a unique address, formed by its column letter and row number (For example, A1, A2, B1, B2, and so on). Altogether, a single Works spreadsheet contains 256 columns and 16,384 rows, for a total of 4,194,304 cells. The first 26 columns are lettered A through Z; succeeding columns are lettered AA through AZ, BA through BZ, and so on, ending with column IV at the extreme right edge of the sheet. Rows are numbered sequentially, so the last row is 16384, and the last cell in a sheet, in the bottom right corner, is cell IV16384, which is at the junction of column IV and row 16384.

The Toolbar

Many window elements in the spreadsheet — scroll bars, the title bar, control buttons, and the status bar at the bottom of the window — are identical to the window elements in the word processor.

The spreadsheet Toolbar is similar to the word processor Toolbar, but some of the buttons differ to give you easy access to often-used spreadsheet features:

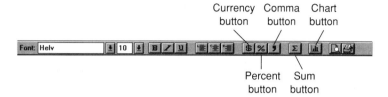

As you saw in Chapter 2, the Currency button formats values as dollar amounts, the Sum button adds rows or columns of figures, and the Chart button creates a chart of selected values.

All of the buttons are easy to use, but as you build your own spreadsheets, remind yourself to stop and think before using the Percent button. To see why,

☐ Type *123* and press Enter.

☐ Click the Percent button.

The number becomes 12300.00%. This happens because whenever you format a number as a percent, Works *multiplies* it by 100. For some values, such as interest rates, you'll want to divide by 100 or convert the number to a decimal before calculating or formatting a percentage. If you forget, which is easy to do, your calculations might be grossly inaccurate. Click the Percent button again to undo the formatting.

The Formula Bar

Below the Toolbar is a reference area. This reference area consists primarily of a *formula bar* where Works displays whatever text, value, or mathematical formula will be inserted into the currently highlighted cell in the spreadsheet. You can both view and edit cell contents in the formula bar. To the left of the formula bar are several related elements:

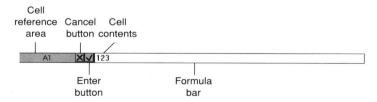

The cell reference area displays the address of the current cell. The Cancel and Enter buttons let you use the mouse in place of Esc or Enter to cancel or accept what you've typed into the cell.

To see how the formula bar and the Cancel and Enter buttons work,

☐ Click on a blank cell. (It doesn't matter where you click, because you'll clear away these experiments later.)

☐ Type *this is a sample of text.*

As you type, notice that the characters in the cell "scroll" to make room for additional typing. Works will remember everything you type and assign it to the proper cell, but the cell is often too narrow to display all your typing at one time. The formula bar, however, can display all or most of a cell's contents.

Cancel the entry:

☐ Click the X on the Cancel button.

The text disappears. Now try the Enter button, and at the same time, see what happens to an entry that's too long to display completely in a cell:

☐ Type *this is a new sample of text.*

☐ Click the checkmarked Enter button to complete the entry.

Works displays your text in both the highlighted cell and the cell to its right. You can see all of a cell's contents if the adjoining cells are vacant, as they are now. Now try this:

☐ Click in the cell to the right of the one in which you entered text.

☐ Type *12345*, and click the Enter button.

The text now appears only in its own cell. You haven't lost any text, though:

☐ Click the cell containing your sample text.

The formula bar displays the entire contents, even though the cell displays only a small portion of it.

Editing Cell Contents

When you're using the spreadsheet, you edit cell contents only in the formula bar, not in the cells themselves. You can clear a cell, or you can replace or edit its contents as follows:

■ To clear a cell, select it and press Del.

■ To replace cell contents, select the cell and type the new entry.

■ To edit cell contents, select the cell and click in the formula bar or press F2.

When you're editing cell contents, you can position the insertion point simply by pointing to the location you want and clicking. Drag the mouse to highlight one or more characters for deletion or replacement. You can also use the keys in the following table to control the insertion point and to highlight characters in the formula bar.

Key	*Effect*
Home	Move to beginning of entry
End	Move to end of entry
Left and Right arrow keys	Move the insertion point one character left or right
Ctrl-Left arrow and Ctrl-Right arrow	Move the insertion point to the beginning or end of a word
Shift-Left arrow and Shift-Right arrow	Extend highlight over one or more characters
Del	Delete selected characters, or (if no characters are selected) delete the next character to the right

NOTE: *A single cell can hold up to 255 characters, so even the formula bar isn't wide enough to display the entire contents in some circumstances. When that happens, you can jump back and forth in the formula bar with the Home and End keys, plus the Left arrow and Right arrow keys.*

Now it's time to move on to the spreadsheet itself. To clear the screen,

□ Drag the mouse until the dark highlight covers all the cells containing what you've typed so far.

□ Choose Clear from the Edit menu.

□ Click on cell A1 to reduce the highlight to a single cell.

Cell Ranges

Building a spreadsheet lets you see your data organized in a way that makes it easy to compare, contrast, summarize, and calculate information. That means you often work with values in groups of cells. A group of cells is called a *range* and can encompass from two cells to all cells in the spreadsheet:

□ Choose All from the Select menu.

Even though you can't see it all, Works is highlighting the entire spreadsheet. In the cell reference area, you see the notation A1:IV16384. When a range of cells is selected, Works identifies the range by displaying the address of the top left-hand cell, a colon, and the address of the bottom right-hand cell. Because the entire spreadsheet is selected here, Works displays the range as A1 through (:) IV16384. You can also highlight the entire spreadsheet by clicking on the unlabeled box to the left of the A-column header.

A range is any group of cells that forms a rectangle. Each cell in the range must share at least one border with another cell; you cannot try to highlight cells in a diamond shape, an L shape, or any other non-rectangular shape. A range can be as small as two adjoining cells or, as you see now, as large as all cells in the spreadsheet.

☐ Press Esc or click on cell A1 to reduce the selection to a single cell.

You'll use ranges for many tasks, including adding columns of numbers, applying formatting, choosing values to chart, and especially, creating formulas that perform calculations.

To begin putting Works to work, build a sample spreadsheet by entering the headings and numbers shown in the following illustration. Use the Tab and arrow keys as an easy way to move from cell to cell. Press Enter when you've finished the last entry:

TEXT VERSUS NUMBERS

Your sample spreadsheet, like most others, includes two types of information: text and values. The distinction between the two is simple: Text is non-numeric information that cannot be used in calculations; values are numeric data and always begin with a numeral (0 through 9), a plus sign (+), a minus sign (−), or a currency symbol. Cells containing dates and times actually contain numeric values, but can be displayed in standard date or time formats.

Most text is easily distinguished from numbers, but on occasion you might include numeric information, such as years (1991, 1992, and so on) or ID numbers, as headings or descriptive text. If the spreadsheet is complex, you can ensure that Works treats these numbers as text by beginning each with a quotation mark. Because Works treats a number preceded by a quotation mark as text, the number won't inadvertently become mixed with cells you calculate.

Formatting Text

Formatting text in the spreadsheet is about the same as it is in the word processor. The only real differences are that you select cells instead of words or paragraphs, and when you choose to align text, you do so in relation to the cell borders, not the margins of the page. To see how this works, boldface and underline the column headings in cells A1 through E1:

   □ Drag the mouse to select the cells.

   □ Click the B and U buttons in the Toolbar.

To repeat the last formatting change (in this case, underline), you can select one or more different cells and use a keyboard shortcut:

   □ Select *Price* in cell A9.

   □ Press Shift-F7.

   □ Click the B button in the Toolbar.

Normally, Works aligns text at the left edge of a cell. You can change this with the alignment buttons on the Toolbar. Right-align the headings in cells B1 through E1, as follows:

   □ Select the cells.

   □ Click the Right button in the Toolbar.

When you apply formats to cells, those formats remain even if you delete the contents of the cell. To "unformat" the cell, select it and remove the formatting.

Numbers

Numbers are at the heart of any spreadsheet. Works always right-aligns numbers in cells, unless you specify otherwise. You can type in numbers with the row of keys at the top of the main part of the keyboard or, when the Num Lock key is turned on, with the calculator-style keypad at the right of the keyboard. You cannot, however, use the keypad keys or the keys at the top of the keyboard to perform "on-the-fly" calculations, such as 123*456. Works will simply treat such an entry as text.

Works normally displays fractional values as decimals and, if the cell is wide enough, displays up to eight decimal places. You can type a number as a fraction less than 1.0 by typing a 0, pressing the Spacebar, and then typing the fraction. Works will still display the result as a decimal, however.

You can type in and calculate both positive and negative values, indicating negative numbers either by preceding them with a minus sign (–) or by enclosing them in parentheses, for example, ($500.00). Works displays negative values in both forms, depending on the format you choose (currency, percent, and so on).

Number Formats

Because numbers can represent so many different types of values — quantities, currency, percentages, and so on — Works offers many different formats for numbers. When you apply number formats, you don't format the number itself. As with text, you format one or more selected cells to display numbers in a specific format. The distinction explains why formatting "sticks" to a cell even after you've changed or deleted the number it contains.

> **NOTE:** *This book assumes you have set up Windows to run with the default numeric settings for the United States. If you have selected International from the Windows Control Panel and made any changes, Works will display different formats in the following examples.*

To see the available number formats, use the Save As command on the File menu to save the current spreadsheet as PIZZA in the WKSBOOK directory. Open a new spreadsheet with the Create New File command and type in the headings and numbers shown in the following illustration:

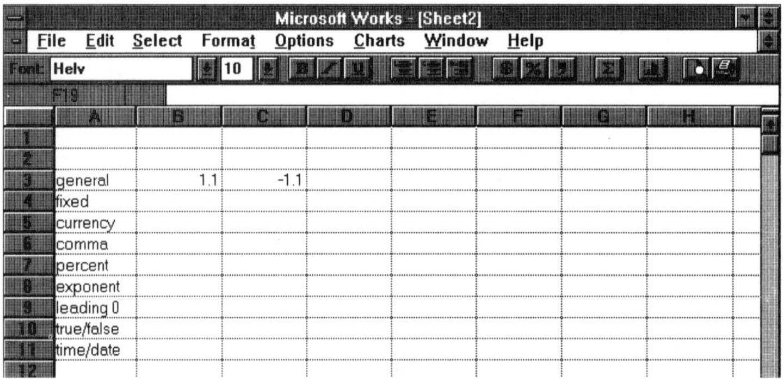

Now use the Fill Down command to duplicate the numbers in both columns.

☐ Select cells B3 through C11.

☐ Choose the Fill Down command from the Edit menu.

The Fill Down command duplicates information by copying it down into selected cells. You'll find the Fill Down command and the complementary Fill Right command particularly useful in repeating formulas for calculating similar values. Now, however, you want to look at the number formats. The first two, next to *general,* show the default format (the format Works uses unless you specify otherwise) for numbers. To see the other formats,

▫ Select the pair of cells, B4 and C4, next to the description *fixed.*

▫ Choose Fixed from the Format menu.

Works now displays a dialog box requesting the number of decimals you want. Notice that the dialog box proposes to use two decimal places:

▫ Click OK to accept the proposed number.

▫ Select the next pair of cells, B5 and C5, and use the Toolbar to apply the currency (U.S.) format.

▫ Use the same procedures, relying on the Format menu or the Toolbar, to apply the formats described in column A to succeeding pairs of cells. When you see a dialog box for the Time/Date format, choose either Month, day or Hour, minute.

	Microsoft Works - [Sheet2]							
File Edit Select Format Options Charts Window Help								
Font: Helv		10	B I U		$ % ,	Σ		
	F19							
	A	B	C	D	E	F	G	H
1								
2								
3	general	1.1	-1.1					
4	fixed	1.10	-1.10					
5	currency	$1.10	($1.10)					
6	comma	1.10	(1.10)					
7	percent	110.00%	-110.00%					
8	exponent	1.10E+00	-1.10E+00					
9	leading 0	00001	-00001					
10	true/false	TRUE	TRUE					
11	time/date	01/01	########					
12								

General formats cells to display numbers as integers (whole numbers) or as decimals. If a number is too long to be displayed in a cell, Works uses the exponential, or scientific, notation (described later in this section). A minus sign indicates a negative number.

Fixed formats cells to display numbers with the number of decimal places you specify. If a number must be truncated, this format rounds the decimal portion up or down accordingly, but Works remembers the actual value. For example, 3.456 formatted for two decimal places would be displayed as 3.46, whereas 3.454 would be displayed as 3.45. A minus sign indicates a negative number.

Currency formats cells to display numbers as currency values. If you type a currency symbol with the number, Works automatically assumes the currency format. Negative amounts are enclosed in parentheses.

Comma formats cells to display numbers with comma separators. For example, 111111 would be displayed as 111,111. As with the currency format, negative numbers are shown in parentheses.

Percent formats cells to display numbers as percents. As you know, this format multiplies a number by 100 and displays it as a percentage to the number of decimals you specify. A minus sign indicates a negative percentage.

Exponential notation, often used in science and engineering, formats cells to display numbers as a "root," such as 1.10, plus the power of 10 by which the number is multiplied to create its "long" form. In the example, the E indicates exponential notation, 1.10 is the number to two decimals, and +00 shows that the number (originally 1.1) is not multiplied by any power of 10.

Leading Zeros formats cells to pad numbers with zeros on the left to fill them out to the required number of digits (five in the example). If the number already consists of the required number of digits, no leading zeros are added.

True/False formats cells to display numbers as logical values in which any nonzero number produces TRUE, and 0 produces FALSE. The true/false format is useful when you want to check spreadsheet cells for 0 and nonzero values, without regard to what the actual values are. For example, you would use the true/false format to see if calculations that depend on other calculations work as expected — that they do, in fact, calculate sample values correctly, for instance, or that you didn't inadvertently reference text or other unworkable values. In the example, both 1.1 and –1.1 produce TRUE, because neither number is 0.

Time/Date formats cells to display numbers as times or dates in any of the forms listed in the Time/Date dialog box:

The long date format would display the first day of January 1992 as January 1, 1992; the short format would display the same date as 1/1/92. Times can be in either 24-hour format (00:00 through 23:59 for midnight through 11:59 P.M.) or the 12-hour A.M./P.M. format that is more typical in everyday life.

The Time/Date format is useful in several different situations. You can use it for entering a series of times or dates and for "stamping" spreadsheets with the time and date of creation. You can also use the format to calculate elapsed times. Works can calculate with dates between January 1, 1900, and June 3, 2079. Dates outside this range are displayed as text.

You won't normally type a decimal number and later turn it into a date as you did here, but the example serves to show the format. It also shows a set of symbols you're likely to see fairly often: a set of number signs (#########). Here, you see these symbols because Works was unable to display −1.1 as a date; it simply didn't compute.

The Too-Small Cell

Most often when you see a set of number signs, Works is telling you a number is too large to be displayed completely in a cell. The solution is simple: Widen the column with the mouse (the easy way) or with the Column Width command on the Format menu. To try this,

◻ Select a blank cell, and give it the Fixed format with two decimal places.

◻ Type *1234567890.*

◻ Press Enter or click the Enter button. Works displays #########.

◻ Place the mouse pointer on the boundary at the right edge of the column header in which you typed the number. The mouse pointer turns into a vertical bar with a double-headed arrow through the middle:

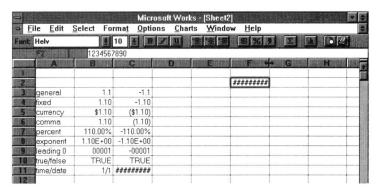

◻ To widen the cell, press the left mouse button and drag to the right.

That's all there is to it. To see the alternative method of widening a cell,

☐ Choose the Column Width command on the Format menu. Works displays this dialog box:

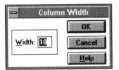

The default width for spreadsheet columns is 10 characters. To change the width, type the value you want and click OK. Try not to be too generous, though. The wider the column, the smaller the area for the remaining columns, which means fewer columns will show onscreen and print on a single sheet of paper. To finish up,

☐ Click Cancel to close the dialog box.

Now on to formulas and the real work you'll do with spreadsheets.

WORKING WITH FORMULAS

A formula is a representation of any set of calculations you want Works to perform. You can use two types of formulas: those you build yourself and those that are essentially plug-in-the-numbers equations that perform useful tasks, such as calculating averages, depreciation, and loan payments.

When referring to cells containing formulas, you can specify a single cell or a range of cells. Even better, you can refer to a cell by its usual address, or you can give it a descriptive name and use the name in your formulas.

> **NOTE:** *When building related formulas in a spreadsheet, be careful not to create a circular reference, that is, one in which a set of formulas refer to one another, like people in a circle pointing to one another. A circular reference has no start and no end, so Works cannot calculate it correctly. If you see the notation CIRC in the status bar at the bottom of the screen, check your formulas for a circular reference.*

Operators

When you build a formula, you use mathematical operators, such as + and −, to tell Works what to calculate, and how. You can use these operators, shown in the table at the top of the next page, in both the spreadsheet and the database.

Operator	Meaning
∧	Exponent, as in 2^3 for 2^3
+ and −	Positive and negative
* and /	Multiplication and division, as in 2*3 and 6/2
+ and −	Addition, as in 2+2, and subtraction, as in 2−1
= and < >	Equal, as in PROFIT = INCOME, and not equal, as in PROFIT < > LOSS
< and >	Less than, as in COST < PRICE, and greater than, as in PRICE > COST
<= and >=	Less than or equal to, as in SUPPLIES <= BUDGET, and greater than or equal to, as in INCOME >= EXPENSE
~	Not, as in ~(PROFIT < INCOME)
¦	Or, as in FIXED COST ¦ VARIABLE COST
&	And, as in ADS & BROCHURES

Some of these operators perform arithmetic calculations and are equally applicable to both the spreadsheet and the database. Others, such as the tilde (~), the pipe (¦), and the ampersand (&), are known as logical operators because they help with comparisons and searches. Depending on the types of spreadsheets you build, you might find that you use the logical operators more in the database than in the spreadsheet.

Controlling the Order of Calculation

Formulas often perform several calculations to achieve a desired result. Calculating an average, for example, requires totaling a group of items and then dividing by the number of items. If you include more than one operator, Works follows the standard *order of evaluation* shown in this table:

Order	Operator
First	∧
Second	+ and − (positive and negative)
Third	* and /
Fourth	+ and − (addition and subtraction)
Fifth	= and < >, < and >, <= and >=
Sixth	~
Seventh	¦ and &

If more than one operator with the same "rank" in the order appears in a formula, Works evaluates them from left to right.

To see how this order of evaluation can affect a formula, select an empty cell on your practice spreadsheet:

☐ Type an equal sign. You must always start a formula in this way.

☐ Now type the formula *8+8/4*3^3.*

☐ Click the Enter button.

Works calculates the result as 62 because it followed its internal rules for evaluating mathematical operators. These are the steps it followed:

1. It evaluated the exponent: 3^3, or 27.

2. It evaluated the division and multiplication operators from left to right: 8/4, or 2, followed by 2*27, or 54.

3. It evaluated the addition operator: 8+54, or 62.

But this formula is extremely vague; you might have been looking for an entirely different calculation, such as 8 plus 8, divided by 4, times 3, with the result then taken to the third power.

To override the normal order of evaluation, enclose sets of values in parentheses. If you want to control more than one calculation, you can nest one set of parentheses within another to determine the order in which their contents are calculated. Works evaluates sets of parentheses before it does any other calculating, and it works out from the innermost set.

Using the same formula as before, you can produce an entirely different result by enclosing values in parentheses. Select an empty cell and try this instead:

☐ Type the formula *=(8+(8/4)*3)^3,* and click the Enter button.

This time the parentheses control the order of evaluation, so the result is 2744:

1. The inner set of parentheses produces 8/4, or 2.

2. The multiplication operator takes precedence over the addition operator in the outer set of parentheses to produce 2*3, or 6, followed by 6+8, or 14.

3. The exponent is evaluated to produce 14^3, or 2744.

Building a Formula

You tell Works that you are building a formula by typing an equal sign (=). If you don't type an equal sign, Works will interpret a combination of cell references, operators, and numbers as text.

To build some sample formulas, close and discard the current worksheet by choosing Close from the File menu. Click No when Works asks if you want to save the changes you made. If necessary, open the PIZZA worksheet:

	A	B	C	D	E	F	G	H
1	Pizza	Small	Medium	Large	Total			
2								
3	Cheese	57	32	29				
4	Sausage	97	143	168				
5	Pepperoni	102	169	185				
6	Anchovy	23	17	9				
7	Vegetarian	49	73	53				
8								
9	Price:							
10	Small	$7.95						
11	Medium	$9.95						
12	Large	$12.95						
13								

Your sample spreadsheet includes a number of values that would provide useful totals, so start off by building a simple formula that adds the number of small, medium, and large cheese pizzas.

Although this first example is comparable to walking around the block to go next door, it's included here for two reasons: to explain the basics of putting formulas together and to explain, by contrast, how useful built-in functions can be. The values you want to add are in cells B3, C3, and D3, so tell Works to total them:

☐ Click on cell E3 to select it.

☐ Type an equal sign to indicate you're starting a formula.

☐ Click on cell B3.

Works immediately displays the cell reference in the formula bar, indicating that it will use the value in B3 in its calculations. Next,

☐ Type a plus sign.

The plus sign appears in the formula bar and in cell E3, the selection jumps back to E3, and Works waits for your next move. Now,

☐ Click on cell C3, type another plus sign, and click on cell D3.

Each of these moves adds another cell reference to the formula:

☐ Click the Enter button, or press Enter to complete the formula.

As soon as you're done, the total for cells B3 through D3 appears in cell E3. Whenever you want to refer to cells in a formula, simply point and click. Works does the rest.

To prepare for the next example,

☐ Select cell E3, if necessary.

☐ Press Del to clear away the cell contents.

☐ Click the Enter button to complete the process.

Using a Built-in Function

Now for the shortcut. The Works SUM function is a more efficient means of totaling values. You can use the SUM function by typing it or by clicking the Sum button in the Toolbar. Here

☐ Double-click the Sum button.

The same total appears in cell E3, but a new and rather different formula is displayed in the formula bar.

Double-clicking the Sum button caused a number of sophisticated operations to take place in a very brief time. Works scanned the spreadsheet, "decided" that cells B3, C3, and D3 were the logical cells to total, highlighted those cells, built the formula, calculated the total, and displayed the result in cell E3.

> **NOTE:** *If you want to verify the cells Works will total, click the Sum button once. After highlighting the cells and building the formula, Works will wait for you to click the Sum button again to confirm that it chose the correct cells.*

Before going on, take a moment to dissect the formula that Works is displaying in the formula bar. Although the calculations are the same, the formula itself looks considerably different from the previous example. That's because it is built to specification for the SUM function. Built-in functions follow the same basic design, regardless of the calculations they perform. The SUM function can be broken down as follows:

- The formula starts with an equal sign, as do all Works formulas.

- The word SUM names the function. Works built the SUM function here, but when you enter other functions of your own, remember to start them with the function name.

- A set of parentheses surrounds the cells that Works is proposing to total. Whenever you use a function, you must enclose values or cell references within parentheses.

- The cells chosen by Works are displayed as a range beginning with B3 and ending with D3. Ranges are the easiest method of specifying continuous groups of cells in a formula or a function.

The Sum button is a great tool when you've built a spreadsheet, and the cells you want to total are grouped in an obvious set (either down a column or across a row). Sometimes, however, you'll want to add values from cells scattered around the sheet. Works is not smart enough to pick individual cells for the formula, so in those cases, type in the SUM function, using the same format Works used here. Appendix C shows the correct format for this and the rest of the built-in functions.

Duplicating Formulas

When you work with spreadsheets, you'll often need to perform the same calculation on different groups of cells. In the sample, for instance, you need totals for the other types of pizza, and it wouldn't hurt to see totals for the different sizes, too. Start off by using the Sum button to total all the small pizzas in cell B8:

☐ Select cell B8.

☐ Double-click the Sum button.

Now to duplicate the formulas. Earlier, you used the Fill Down command to copy information to selected cells. You can use this command with formulas as well. To see the results more clearly,

☐ Choose Show Formulas from the Options menu.

The Show Formulas command tells Works to display formulas in those cells that contain them. To accommodate the command, the columns suddenly expand until your Total column is almost off the screen. Don't worry about it. Scroll to the right so you can see columns B through E. Now,

☐ Select cells E3 through E7.

☐ Choose Fill Down from the Edit menu.

☐ Select cells B8 through D8.

☐ Choose Fill Right from the Edit menu.

Notice the formulas that now appear in cells C8 and D8, and in cells E4 through E7. In each, Works has adjusted the cell references so they refer not to the cells in the original formula, but to cells in the same position relative to the new formula. The formula in E4 refers to the cells in B4 through D4, the formula in E5 refers to B5 through D5, and so on. Works modifies cell references in this way, so you don't have to adjust them manually.

Of course, you won't always want cell references to change. You might, for example, want each formula to refer to a value in one particular cell. You do this by using *absolute* or *mixed* cell references, rather than the relative cell references you've been using.

Relative, Absolute, and Mixed References

Relative cell references refer to a cell's position relative to another cell. A relative reference is comparable to saying, "Go one block east and three blocks north." When you build a formula using relative references, you're telling Works to use the value in the cell that is X columns and Y rows away from the current cell. That's what happened when Works created the Sum formulas with the Fill Down and Fill Right commands.

Absolute cell references refer to a specific cell in a spreadsheet. An absolute reference is comparable to saying, "Go to the intersection of State and Main." No matter what the starting point, there is only one intersection of State and Main.

To distinguish an absolute cell reference from a relative cell reference, insert a dollar sign ($) before the column letter and row number. For example, the notation A5 in a formula would tell Works to use the value in cell A5, regardless of that cell's location relative to the formula cell. Typing dollar signs could become tedious with a large spreadsheet, however, so Works gives you a simple alternative: Press the F4 key to change any cell reference from relative to absolute.

Absolute cell references are particularly useful in spreadsheets where a single value, such as a price or a loan rate, is used in multiple formulas scattered throughout the spreadsheet, or when you move or copy formulas to new locations but want to retain a reference to a particular cell. Depending on how your spreadsheet is constructed, you can also create mixed cell references by inserting a dollar sign before the absolute portion (either the column or the row) of the reference. For example, you could type *$A1* when the column is always A, but the row number can be any row, or you could type *A$1* when the column is not necessarily A, but the row is always row 1.

The next example uses absolute references and the built-in PMT function to calculate monthly payments on a loan of $50,000 taken over 15, 25, and 30 years:

☐ Select Show Formulas from the Options menu to deselect that option.

☐ Save the PIZZA spreadsheet, and open a new spreadsheet with the Create New File command.

☐ Type in the entries shown in the following illustration:

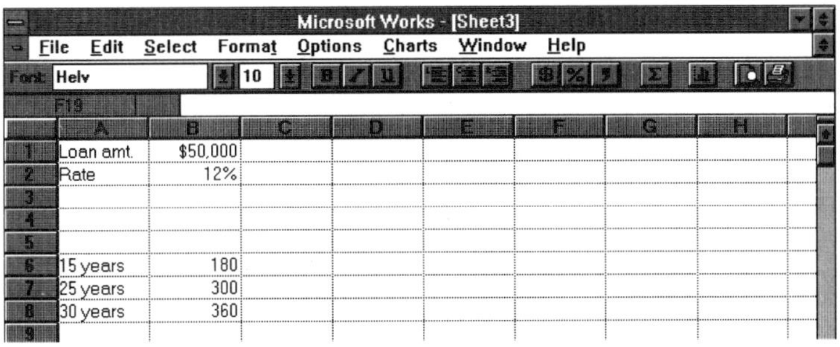

The PMT function uses a loan amount, interest rate, and term to calculate the periodic payment on a fixed-rate loan or investment. The format of the PMT function is

=PMT(*amount, rate, term*)

where *amount* is the amount of the loan, *rate* is the interest rate, and *term* is the length of the loan.

You'll use three formulas to calculate payments for the three terms. Each formula, however, will refer to cells B1 and B2, so by using absolute references for the first formula you can then use the Fill Down command to copy the formulas to the remaining cells. To simulate a real-life loan, this example uses an annual rate of interest but assumes payments will be made monthly. To avoid inaccurate results, you must divide the rate by 12 and enter the term in months:

☐ Select cell C6.

☐ Type =PMT(

☐ Click on cell B1. Works displays the address as a relative cell reference, so press F4 to change it to an absolute cell reference.

☐ Type a comma, and click on cell B2 to enter the rate. Press F4 to change this reference too.

- Because this is an annual rate, divide it by 12 to get the monthly rate. Type */12* and another comma.

- Finally, click on cell B6 to enter the term, in months, into the function.

- Type a closing parenthesis and click the Enter button. The result appears in cell C6.

NOTE: *If you type the function name in lowercase, Works will convert it to uppercase when you click the Enter button.*

Now to copy the function to the remaining two formula cells,

- Select cells C6 through C8.

- Choose the Fill Down command from the Edit menu.

- When the results appear in cells C7 and C8, select each cell in turn, and check the formula bar to see the cell references. B1 and B2 remain the same in each formula because they are absolute references. The references to the cells containing the terms, however, change from one formula to the next because they are relative references.

- To polish up this small spreadsheet, use the Toolbar or the Format menu to format cells C6 through C8 as currency values with two decimal places.

Inserting and Deleting Rows and Columns

A spreadsheet doesn't spring into being at the click of a mouse button. It takes time, patience, and often, experimentation before you get it right. But suppose you've been entering data and building formulas, and you suddenly realize you forgot to allow an extra column or row for some needed element.

Chances are this will happen to you more than once because you'll be concentrating on what you want the spreadsheet to do, rather than on how you want it to look. As the spreadsheet takes shape, you'll find places where you could use an extra row or column for displaying information you hadn't originally thought about including. Conversely, you'll sometimes want to delete extra rows or columns that you allowed for but don't need. You might also want to select and delete rows or columns to "erase" information or cell formatting.

When you feel the need to add or delete rows or columns, you can do so with the Insert Row/Column and Delete Row/Column commands on the Edit menu. You can use these commands at any time, and you don't have to worry about adjusting relative cell references in the formulas you've built: Works does it for you, changing any affected formulas to match the new spreadsheet layout.

To select the row or column to insert or delete, you can simply select any cell in the area. An even quicker way to do this is to select the entire row or column before choosing the command:

- To select an entire row, point to the row number and click. Works highlights the row (or as much of it as you can see onscreen).

- To select an entire column, point to the column letter and click. Again, Works highlights that section of the spreadsheet.

To try inserting and deleting columns, return to the PIZZA spreadsheet:

- □ If the file is still open, choose its name from the Window menu.

- □ If you've closed the file or quit Works after saving the file, either choose its name from the bottom of the File menu (if displayed there), or open it with the Open Existing File command.

	A	B	C	D	E	F	G	H
1	Pizza	Small	Medium	Large	Total			
2								
3	Cheese	57	32	29	118			
4	Sausage	97	143	168	408			
5	Pepperoni	102	169	185	456			
6	Anchovy	23	17	9	49			
7	Vegetarian	49	73	53	175			
8		328	434	444				
9	Price:							
10	Small	$7.95						
11	Medium	$9.95						
12	Large	$12.95						
13								

In the section titled "Using a Built-in Function," you used the Sum button to total the sales of small, medium, and large pizzas. To find out the total sales, in dollars, of each type of pizza, you could multiply the group total by the price. An obvious location for these sales amounts would be directly below each of the group totals, but, unfortunately, you didn't leave any room. Insert Row/Column comes to the rescue:

- □ Point to row number 9 at the left edge of the spreadsheet, and click to select the row.

- □ Choose Insert Row/Column from the Edit menu.

Notice that Works adds the new row *above* the row you selected, and it renumbers the rows below, so there is no break in the numbering sequence. For the sake of appearance,

- ☐ Add another row above the row you added to give the spreadsheet a less cramped feel.

- ☐ As long as you're at it, insert a new column between D and E to separate the totals from the numbers of pizzas sold. Point to the column E header, and click to select the entire column.

- ☐ Choose Insert Row/Column from the Edit menu.

Notice that Works inserts the new column to the *left* of the column you selected. Inserted rows always appear above the selected row, and inserted columns always appear to the left of the selected column. When you use the Delete Row/Column command, however, Works deletes the row or column you've selected.

> **NOTE:** *If you had selected a cell rather than an entire row or column, the end result would have been the same, but because Works would not know whether you meant to insert a row or a column, it would have displayed a dialog box to ask which you wanted. Selecting the entire row or column doesn't take any longer than selecting a cell, but it can make these particular commands much faster to use.*

Naming Cell Ranges

As long as you're on the subject of pizzas, you can use this spreadsheet to experiment with naming cells and cell ranges. Even though cell references become second nature and are easier to interpret after you gain a little experience with Works, they're still somewhat cryptic at first glance. Names, which you can assign to any cell or range of cells, are much easier to decipher, if only because they are closer to "real" language and can more clearly describe the cell contents they refer to.

Cell and range names are particularly useful in the following types of spreadsheets:

- Large or complex spreadsheets containing specific information that you want to refer back to

- Spreadsheets you want to extract or link information from for use in another document such as a word-processed document

- Spreadsheets in which descriptive formulas would be a real help to yourself or to other people

Naming cells and ranges is easy and one of the more entertaining features of the spreadsheet. To see how many ways you can assign and use names,

☐ Begin by highlighting cells A3 through D7, the pizza names and number of sales by size.

☐ Choose the Range Name command from the Edit menu. Works displays a dialog box like this:

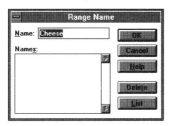

Notice that Works is proposing the name Cheese, which corresponds to the text in the top left-hand corner of the selected range. That's not terribly appropriate, so to change the name,

☐ Be sure the highlight is in the Name box.

☐ Type *Pizza sales* and click OK.

Now for some fun:

☐ Click on any cell outside the Pizza sales range.

☐ Choose Go To from the Select menu. (Press F5 for the keyboard shortcut.) Works displays a new dialog box similar to the one it uses for assigning names:

The name Pizza sales is listed in the Names box.

☐ Double-click the name.

Works immediately highlights the range you named Pizza sales.

Even though you've assigned a name to cells A3 through D7, those cells are not off-limits as far as other names are concerned. You can assign different names to sets of cells within the named range, as well as to sets of cells partly in and partly out of the range:

☐ Select cells B3 through B7 and assign them the name *Small*.

☐ Assign the name *Medium* to cells C3 through C7, and assign the name *Large* to cells D3 through D7.

☐ Assign the name *Price-small* to the price in cell B12, *Price-med* to the price in B13, and *Price-lge* to the price in B14.

☐ Assign the name *Total-small* to the total in cell B8, *Total-med* to the total in C8, and *Total-lge* in D8.

TIP Choose the Range Name command again and look at the list of names displayed in the Names box. Notice that Works alphabetizes them. When you assign related names to different cells, as you did in naming prices and totals, it helps to start them off the same way. Works will group the names together in its lists, and you'll be able to see more clearly which names are related.

All these names are overkill for such a small spreadsheet, but there's a point to this exercise: In your own spreadsheets you might find that you've named so many groups of cells that you're beginning to lose track of what's what. To refresh your memory, use the List button in the Range Name dialog box:

☐ First — and this is very important — find an empty group of cells below or to the right of any cells containing text or data. In this case, select cell G11.

☐ Choose the Range Name command, and click the List button in the dialog box.

Works inserts a list of names and the cells they represent, beginning the list in the cell you selected before choosing the command. Notice that Works requires two adjoining columns and the number of rows that correspond to the number of names you've assigned. If you had not moved the selection,

Works would have overwritten existing data with the list of names. This is why it's so important to find a vacant area of the spreadsheet that is large enough for listing names.

If you want to insert the list well away from your working area, yet be able to consult it freely, scroll to an empty part of the spreadsheet, select a cell, and request the list. Next select the list and assign it a name before scrolling back to your workspace. When you want to consult the list, use the Go To command from the Select menu. Before you print the spreadsheet, however, be sure to check for the list and either delete it (with the Clear command) or omit it from the print area (with the Set Print Area command, which is described in "Printing Part of a Spreadsheet," later in this chapter).

Range Names and Formulas

Now that you've named some cells and cell ranges, you can see how descriptive formulas can be:

☐ Select cell B8. (This is the cell in which you created a formula that totals the cells you just named *Small*.)

Notice the formula in the formula bar. Without prompting, Works has replaced the original cell designation (B3:B7) with the name you assigned those cells. You'll see this happen whenever you assign a name to a cell or a range of cells incorporated in a formula. If you select cells C8 and D8, you'll see that they now contain formulas showing range names, instead of range references.

You can use assigned names in creating formulas too:

☐ Select cell B9 and type an equal sign to begin a formula.

☐ Click on cell B8 (named *Total-small*) to tell Works you want that cell in the formula.

☐ Type the multiplication operator (*), and click on cell B12 (the price).

☐ Click the Enter button to complete the command.

If you hadn't assigned names to these cells, your formula would be =B8*B12. Useful, but not very descriptive. Instead, the formula bar reads = '*Total-small*'*'*Price-small*'. Much better. (The single quotation marks enclosing the names are added by Works.)

Create similar formulas for medium and large pizzas:

☐ Select cells B9 through D9, and choose the Fill Right command.

It looks like you've made a blunder here. Works displays 0 as the totals for medium and large pizzas.

□ Select cell C9, and look at the formula bar.

□ Check the formula for cell D9 as well.

There's the problem: Works treats names as relative references. It found the totals for each size pizza because the original formula simply referenced the cell directly above the formula cell. However, Works expected to find the price for medium pizzas in cell C12, and the price for large in cell D12 — the cells in the same relative position as the price for small pizza in the original formula.

You've actually done yourself a favor and saved some work here by doing the "wrong" thing. You can edit the formulas, as follows:

□ Select cell C9.

□ Select the cell reference C12 in the formula bar.

□ Click the price for medium pizzas.

Works replaces the highlighted portion of the formula with the cell reference you clicked. The formula is now correct, so do the following:

□ Click the Enter button to finish.

□ Edit the formula for totaling large pizzas in the same way.

As a final touch,

□ Select cell F9 and use the Sum button to total the amounts in cells B9 through D9.

□ Use the Sum button again to total the number of pizzas sold in cell F8.

□ Format cells B9 through F9 for currency.

□ Insert a blank row above row 8.

□ Use the Border command in the Format menu to create an outline around cells B9 through F10.

This is the result in Print Preview:

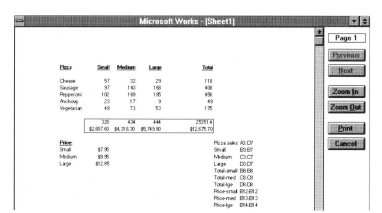

NOTE: *Notice that Works includes a blank cell in the formula calculating total sales (cell F10 in the finished spreadsheet). It doesn't matter here, because you won't be inserting any data or a formula into the blank cell. In your own spreadsheets, watch for such potential problem makers. A good solution, both here and in other spreadsheets, would be to edit the formula immediately, changing the reference to exclude the blank cell.*

Creating a Series

One element common to many, if not most, spreadsheets is repetition. Because of its columnar format, a spreadsheet is ideal for laying out sequential sets of data: sales by month, salaries by week, operating expenses by quarter, and so on. You've seen how to use the Fill Down and Fill Right commands to build a spreadsheet. A related command, Fill Series, can also help you organize a spreadsheet quickly and with minimal fuss.

The Fill Series command is particularly useful in creating headings. It can take a starting value and generate a series of numbers or dates in selected cells, increasing them by whatever intervals you specify. To see how this works,

☐ Open a new spreadsheet and maximize the document window.

□ Type the text shown in the following illustration:

□ Select cells A5 through A12. You must include A5 in the selection because it contains the "seed" number that Works will use to start the series. Without a starting point, Works cannot carry out the Fill Series command.

□ Choose Fill Series from the Edit menu. Works presents this dialog box:

You use this dialog box to choose a numeric series or a series of dates. The Step by box lets you choose the intervals within the series. For example, stepping by two would create the series 1, 3, 5, 7, and so on.

For this example, the only series choice available is Number, because your starting value, 1, can only be part of a numeric series. To create the series,

□ Click OK.

Now create the second series you need, the days of the week, across the top of this small spreadsheet:

□ Select the seven cells B3 through H3.

□ Choose Fill Series again.

This time, Works suggests Day — the most likely choice, and the one you want — so click OK.

You could have chosen Weekday if you wanted to skip Saturdays and Sundays. The other possible choices for a date are Month, which fills the series with monthly intervals, and Year, which steps through the series by year. Before you close this example, you might want to have a little fun with it:

☐ Type the following numbers in cells B5 through B12: *5, 12, 9, 15, 22, 3, 11,* and *7.*

☐ Fill cells C5 through H12 with numbers by using the Fill Series command. Specify different step intervals, such as *3* and *7,* to make the entries seem somewhat random.

☐ Type *Total* in cell A14.

☐ Select cell B14, and use the Sum button to total the numbers in column B.

☐ Use the Fill Right command to copy the formula from cell B14 into cells C14 through H14.

☐ Select cells B12 through H12.

☐ Choose the Border command from the Format menu, and click Bottom to create a border line along the bottom of each cell. Click OK to carry out the command.

☐ Select cells A1 through A14, and click the B button on the Toolbar to boldface all entries.

☐ Select cells B3 through H3, and boldface them.

☐ Select the word *Total,* and italicize it.

☐ Click the Print Preview button in the Toolbar to see what you have created.

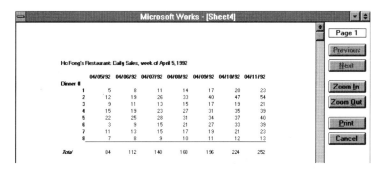

WHAT IF

Far and away, the most valued feature of a spreadsheet program is its ability to test different values to see what impact they will have on your calculations. Using the built-in function called IF, you can create a formula that tailors the result to conditions you define: *If* we sell 10,000 gizmos, *Then* our profit will be X, *Else* our profit will be Y. IF produces one of two results, depending on whether the condition you specify (If we sell 10,000 gizmos) is true (our profit will be X) or false (our profit will be Y). The following examples show you the basics of using the IF function.

The format of the IF function is

IF(*Condition, TrueValue, FalseValue*)

where *Condition* is a value or the result of a calculation, *TrueValue* is the result produced if the condition is true, and *FalseValue* is the result if the condition is false.

The following example uses the sales from four Gizmo, Inc. stores to determine how much of the total for each month represents profit. The example assumes that gizmos sell for $0.99 each and that Gizmo, Inc. makes 18 percent per gizmo on sales over 10,000, and 14 percent per gizmo on sales of 10,000 or less. To create the example,

☐ Start a new spreadsheet with the Create New File command. If necessary, maximize the window as usual.

☐ Create the spreadsheet shown in the following illustration:

	A	B	C	D	E	F	G	H
1	Gizmo sales: January-June							
2								
3		January	February	March	April	May	June	
4	Store 1	2500	1983	3345	4121	1398	2765	
5	Store 2	1750	2576	1522	1893	2175	3021	
6	Store 3	3456	3602	2043	1087	2890	2998	
7	Store 4	2892	1923	2980	3056	2901	2795	
8								
9	Total sales							
10	$$ Volume							
11								
12	Profit							
13								
14								

☐ Format cells B10 through G10 and cells B12 through G13 for currency and two decimal places.

□ Use the Sum button to create a total in cell B9, and use the Fill Right command to copy the formula through cell G9.

□ To derive the income values, enter the formula *=0.99*B9* in cell B10. Use the Fill Right command to copy the formula through cell G10.

Now that you've finished the preparation, enter an IF function in cell B12:

□ Select cell B12.

□ Type *=IF(*

□ Click on cell B9 to add it to the function.

□ Type *10000,*

□ Click on cell B10 to add it to the function.

□ Type **18%,*

□ Click on cell B10 again to add it to the function.

□ Type **14%)*

□ The formula is complete, and it should look like this:

```
=IF(B9>10000,B10*18%,B10*14%)
```

□ Click the Enter button.

□ Use the Fill Right command to copy the formula through cell G12.

Notice that in the formula bar Works converts the numbers you typed as percentages into their decimal equivalents: 0.18 for 18% and 0.14 for 14%.

What Does It Mean?

An IF function isn't the easiest set of characters to interpret. This is what your formula means, piece by piece:

■ *=IF(B9>10000* is the conditional part of the formula. This is the part Works evaluates to check whether the condition is true or false. Here, the condition tells Works to find out if the value in cell B9 is greater than 10,000.

■ *B10*0.18* is the result if the condition is true. If sales are greater than 10,000 for the month, Gizmo, Inc. makes a profit of 18 percent per gizmo, so if the condition is true, Works calculates 18 percent of the income shown in cell B10.

■ *B10*0.14* is the result if the condition is *not* true. If sales are 10,000 or less for the month, Gizmo, Inc. makes only 14 percent profit, so if the condition is false, Works calculates 14 percent of the income shown in cell B10.

IFs Within IFs

Sometimes you'll want to evaluate conditions that can have more than one true/false outcome. When this happens, you can place one IF function inside another, in the same way you place sets of parentheses inside others when controlling the order of calculation.

In this example, for instance, Gizmo, Inc. might find that profits are 18 percent for sales of 10,500 or more, 14 percent for sales between 10,001 and 10,500, and 12 percent for sales of 10,000 and less. To calculate profits for all three situations,

❑ Type the following formula in cell B13:

```
=IF(B9>10500,B10*.18,IF(B9>10000,B10*.14,B10*.12))
```

❑ Again, use the Fill Right command to copy the formula through cell G13.

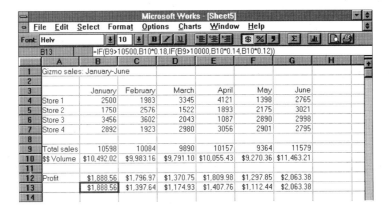

Now your formula translates as follows: If the value in cell B9 is greater than 10,500, multiply the income in cell B10 by 0.18. If the condition is false, but the value in cell B9 is greater than 10,000, multiply the income in cell B10 by 0.14. Otherwise, multiply the value in cell B9 (now down to any value of 10,000 or less) by 0.12.

To check that your IF functions are working as expected, try calculating the profits for January (18 percent), February (14 percent), and March (12 percent). You should get the same results you now see in row 13.

Calculating with Dates and Times

Although numeric values are, by far, the most common entries in spreadsheets, dates and times can be valuable too. Date and time values can be used for "stamping" spreadsheets, tracking progress, and calculating elapsed times. Works gives you two ways to use dates and times: as fixed values or as entries that are updated when you open the spreadsheet.

To display the date or time, Works starts with a serial number based on your computer's internal clock and calculates the appropriate result. Dates are formatted in long (spelled out) or short form, and times are formatted on the basis of a 12-hour or a 24-hour clock. The following tables show each of these formats:

Time	12-Hour	24-Hour
Hour, minute, second	02:26:31 P.M.	14:26:31
Hour, minute	02:26 P.M.	14:26

Date	Long Format	Short Format
Month, day, year	January 1, 1992	1/1/92
Month, year	January 1992	1/92
Month, day	January 1	1/1
Month only	January	No short form

Open a new spreadsheet and try entering the time and date in each of these formats.

Entering Any Date or Time

One way to enter times and dates is to simply type them in. Use this method when you want one or more entries that do not represent the current time or date. You can follow one of the formats shown in the preceding table, or you can type the time or date in one form and then use the Time/Date command on the Format menu to change the format:

- ☐ Select a cell, and widen it to accommodate about 15 characters.

- ☐ Type 1/1/92, and click the Enter button.

- ☐ You entered the date in its short month/day/year form. To change it to the long form, choose Time/Date from the Format menu, and click Long in the Date box.

- ☐ Click OK to carry out the command. As soon as you finish, the date changes to January 1, 1992.

Entering the Current Date or Time

There are two other methods you can use to enter the current date or time. One method, which makes use of the NOW function, inserts a serial number in the cell. When you use the NOW function, Works updates the serial number whenever you reopen the spreadsheet and, in doing so, recalculates and updates the time or date as well. After you use the NOW function, you can use the Time/Date command to convert the serial number to either a time or a date, in whatever format you want. You can also switch the format from time to date, or vice versa. To try the NOW function,

- □ Select an empty cell, and type *=NOW()*.

- □ Works inserts a number, such as 33604.629, in the cell.

- □ Choose the Time/Date command from the Format menu, and format the serial number for the date or the time in the format you prefer.

Another way to enter the current date or time is to use the keyboard shortcuts Ctrl-semicolon for the date and Ctrl-Shift-semicolon for the time. When you use this method, Works inserts the date or time as a fixed entry that will not be updated, unless you specifically change it. To enter the current date and time,

- □ Select a cell, and press Ctrl-semicolon.

- □ Press Enter to insert the current date.

- □ Use the Time/Date command to format the date if you want. (If a set of number signs (#) appears because you chose the long format, remember that you can widen the column simply by pointing to the boundary between column labels and dragging to the right.)

- □ Select another cell, and press Shift-Ctrl-semicolon.

- □ Press Enter to insert the current time. Use the Time/Date command to format the time if you want.

Using Dates and Times in Formulas

A truly multipurpose application, the Works spreadsheet can even stretch its wings a bit and pretend to be a project-management program of sorts. Because Works can use dates and times in calculations, you can use the spreadsheet to track elapsed times. When you use dates and times as part of a formula, you can either refer to the cells that contain them, or you can type the dates or times as part of the formula. If you choose the latter approach, however, enter dates in short form. Also, be sure to enclose the date or time in single quotation marks, for example, '1/1/92'. If you don't, Works won't recognize the entry as a valid date or time. The following example shows a simple tracking spreadsheet:

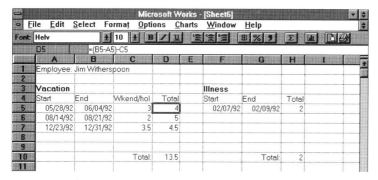

If you want to create this spreadsheet or a similar one, keep the following points in mind:

- The formula for calculating days elapsed subtracts the *start* date from the *end* date, not vice versa. Because Works does not compute weekends and holidays in its calculations, column C gives the number of weekends and holidays to subtract from the total. (The complete formula is shown in the formula bar.)

- The word *Total* is right-aligned.

- A SUM function totals the number of vacation and sick days in columns D and H.

- Extra cells are left blank for additional entries. Entering additional formulas would be a simple matter of filling the extra cells. If you wanted, you could omit the extra columns and add new ones as needed with the Insert Row/Column command.

All other parts of this spreadsheet should be old news to you by now.

MANAGING A SPREADSHEET

There's a lot to learn about using a spreadsheet, but you're coming into the homestretch now. In the rest of this chapter, you'll learn how to manage the spreadsheets you build.

Moving Around

Many spreadsheets are too large to display on a single screen. When you learned about range names, you encountered one easy way to move from place to place in a large spreadsheet: the Go To command. Go To is a natural with named cells, but it can also be used to jump to specific cells or cell ranges. Instead of typing a name, you simply type the cell reference, like this:

When you carry out the command, Works will jump to the cell or cells you specified and highlight them.

As you're working with a spreadsheet, you'll also want to scroll or move from place to place. The scroll bars are obvious mechanisms for moving quickly, but you can use the keyboard too. The following table lists useful keys for moving around in a spreadsheet:

Key	*Result*
Left arrow and Right arrow	Left or right one cell
Up arrow and Down arrow	Up or down one row
Home	First cell in current row
End	Last column containing data in any row
Ctrl-Home	Top left corner of the spreadsheet
Ctrl-End	Last cell in the bottom right corner. This cell is in the last row and the last column that contain data or formatting. The cell itself does not necessarily contain data or formatting
PgUp and PgDown	Up and down one screenful
Ctrl-PgUp and Ctrl-PgDown	Left and right one screenful
Ctrl-Left arrow and Ctrl-Right arrow	Left and right to the beginning or end of the current or next block of cells
Ctrl-Up arrow and Ctrl-Down arrow	Up and down to the beginning or end of the current or next block of cells

Moving and Copying

Moving information on a spreadsheet is generally synonymous with organizing or reorganizing a spreadsheet. Although copying is as easy as moving information, it is a little harder to define because there are several ways to copy spreadsheet information. You might want to *enter* the same data or formula in a number of cells, you might want to *copy* cell contents to another part of the same spreadsheet, or you might want to copy all or part of one spreadsheet to another.

Entering Data in Multiple Cells

You've seen how the Fill commands can quickly duplicate information in adjoining cells. There's another way to fill cells with the same information: the keyboard shortcut Ctrl-Enter. You can use this key combination to enter either data or formulas. For example, suppose you want to fill a set of cells with the number 123:

☐ Open a new spreadsheet.

☐ Select cells A1 through D7.

☐ Type *123* but don't click the Enter button or press a key. Instead, press Ctrl-Enter.

Works immediately fills the selected cells with the same data:

	A	B	C	D	E	F	G	H
1	123	123	123	123				
2	123	123	123	123				
3	123	123	123	123				
4	123	123	123	123				
5	123	123	123	123				
6	123	123	123	123				
7	123	123	123	123				
8								

Microsoft Works - [Sheet7]
File Edit Select Format Options Charts Window Help
Font: Helv   10

Moving and Copying Values

You can move and copy values to any area in the same or a different spreadsheet. It doesn't matter if the values are those you've entered as data or those you've calculated with formulas.

To move or copy data to the Clipboard, you use the Cut and Copy commands, which work exactly as they do in the word processor. You can copy cells or cell ranges in either rows or columns, but you cannot alter the orientation of a range: If the cells you copy are in a column, you can't duplicate them in a row, nor can you reorient a row to become a column. Works isn't quite that flexible. Try copying values, using the data you just entered:

☐ Select cells A1 through A7.

☐ Copy the selected cells to the Clipboard with the Copy command.

☐ Select cell E1 and choose Paste from the Edit menu.

Works copies the contents of the Clipboard to column E, placing the first of the copied cells in E1. When you copy or move a range of cells, remember that Works uses the selected destination cell as the top left corner of the incoming range. Be sure that there are no cells containing data or formulas within the area to be filled by the copy. If there are cells in this area, the information they hold will be overwritten by the contents of the copied cells.

To move or copy values calculated by formulas, start with the same Cut/Copy process, but use the Paste Special command to insert the contents of the Clipboard. To try this,

□ Select cells A8 through E8, and double-click the Sum button to enter a formula in each cell.

□ Copy the contents of these cells to the Clipboard.

□ Select cell A9, and use the Paste command to insert the contents of the Clipboard. The regular Paste command copies formulas as well as values, so each cell now holds a new copy of the Sum formula.

□ To insert the values (not the formulas) of the cells you copied to the Clipboard, select cell A10 and choose Paste Special from the Edit menu. Works displays this dialog box:

The Paste Special command lets you insert values from cut or copied cells that contain formulas. You can choose to insert the values (with the Values only option), add the incoming values to those already in the selected cells (Add values), or subtract the incoming values (Subtract values). In this case, use the proposed response, Values only:

□ Click OK. The cells in row 10 fill with the same values calculated by the formulas in row 8.

Moving and Copying Formulas

Works lets you copy and move formulas as well as data, but you must be careful when you do this. Works does the best it can, but both moving and copying formulas can produce inaccurate, sometimes bizarre, results. In general, Works does the following when you move or copy a range of cells containing one or more formulas that refer to cells outside the range:

- In a *move,* Works keeps the original references to non-moved cells. The references to moved cells reflect their new location.

- In a *copy,* either within the same spreadsheet or from one spreadsheet to another, Works alters all relative references to reflect the new location of the copied cells.

Here are some experiments to help you visualize what happens:

☐ Select all the filled cells in the current worksheet.

☐ Delete the contents of the filled cells with the Clear command.

☐ Type *1* in cell A1, *2* in cell A2, and *3* in cell A3.

☐ Use the Sum button to total the three values in cell A4. Notice that the formula displays *=SUM(A1:A3).*

☐ Enter the formula *=A4*2* in cell A5, and enter the formula *=A5*3* in cell A6.

☐ Select cells A4 through A6, and copy them to the Clipboard with the Copy command on the Edit menu.

☐ Select cell D6, and choose Paste from the Edit menu.

Notice that the formula bar tells you cell D6 contains the formula =SUM(D3:D5). Works has adjusted all references to reflect the cells' position after the copy. Now see what happens during a move:

☐ Select cells A4 through A6, and choose Cut from the Edit menu.

☐ Select cell C6, and choose Paste. For comparison, also paste the cut cells back into cells A4 through A6.

☐ Select cell C6 so you can see its contents in the formula bar.

This time Works retained the original cell references in the SUM function, the first of the three formulas you moved. If you select cell C7, however, the formula bar displays *C6*2.* Works has altered this formula so that the cell reference is relative to the formula's new location. If you check cell C8, you'll find an altered reference there, too. Finally, see what happens when you paste cut or copied formulas into a new spreadsheet:

☐ Open a new spreadsheet, and paste the contents of the Clipboard into cell A1.

This is where you see some odd, yet logical, results. The formula bar shows the contents of cell A1 as the sum of cells A16382 through 16384. You pasted the formula into the first row of a new spreadsheet, so the only possible reference

Works can make to cells above A1 are the cells in the last three rows of a "preceding" spreadsheet.

The logistics of moving and copying formulas, especially within or between spreadsheets that contain other formulas and data, can make you feel like Hannibal taking elephants across the Alps. If you're not a puzzle fancier, your best bet is to copy or move data, not formulas. If you must move formulas, consider changing cell references from relative or mixed to absolute so you'll know exactly which cells they refer to after the copy or move. You can always use the F4 key to adjust the references quickly and one at a time, if necessary, to verify the calculations. Such precautions are particularly important in spreadsheets with sensitive information, like your annual income taxes. Sometimes reinventing your formulas is preferable to untangling masses of relative cell references.

Controlling a Spreadsheet

You can control the appearance, display, and behavior of your spreadsheets in several ways. By default, Works displays the Toolbar, and it also displays gridlines onscreen, although it doesn't print them unless you choose to do so with the Page Setup & Margins command on the File menu. The following sections describe the commands you use to control Works. Most of these commands are on the Options menu.

Displaying Gridlines

If you find that the dotted gridlines on the screen get in your way, you can turn them off and on at will. Use the spreadsheet currently onscreen and do the following:

- □ Click on Show Gridlines in the Options menu.

- □ Press the Arrow keys, and click on a number of different cells or cell entries.

Even though the gridlines are turned off, the rectangular cell highlight jumps from cell to cell as it does when gridlines are turned on.

Freezing Row and Column Titles

When you're working on or printing a large spreadsheet, you can freeze row and column titles. Doing this keeps the frozen titles onscreen at all times and also causes Works to print them on each page of a multiple-page spreadsheet.

To freeze column titles,

- □ Select a cell in column A, below the titles you want to freeze.

- Choose Freeze Titles from the Options menu. No matter how far down you scroll, the frozen column titles will remain onscreen.

To freeze row titles,

- Select a cell in row 1 to the right of the last title you want to freeze.

- Choose the Freeze Titles command. No matter how far to the right you scroll, the frozen row titles will always be displayed.

To freeze both row and column titles,

- Select a cell below and to the right of the last row and column title you want to freeze.

- Choose the Freeze Titles command. No matter how far down or to the right you scroll, the titles will remain onscreen.

Working with frozen titles can feel awkward at first, because you cannot scroll into or select the titles, although you can use the Go To command to highlight them. Clicking on a frozen title causes Works to scroll to that location and display both the title and its associated data, but outside the frozen area of the screen. The first time you try this, you might develop a momentary sense of seeing double as Works duplicates the frozen area elsewhere on the screen. All told, however, freezing provides a terrific way to view both titles and offscreen data related to them. To see what freezing does,

- Open or return to your GIZMO spreadsheet.

- To freeze the titles in rows 1 through 3, select cell A4 and choose the Freeze Titles command.

- Use the vertical scroll bar to scroll downward. No matter how far you go, the titles remain onscreen.

- To freeze the heading in column A, turn off the Freeze Titles command, select cell B1, and choose the Freeze Titles command again. Now the titles remain onscreen, no matter how far to the right you scroll.

- To freeze both the row and column headings, turn off the Freeze Titles command, select cell B4, and choose the command again. Now both row and column titles remain onscreen.

- Turn off the Freeze Titles command again for now.

Another way to view different parts of a large spreadsheet is to split the window and scroll to the areas you want to view. You've already split a window and scrolled in a document with the word processor. It's the same in the spreadsheet, so there's no need to repeat the procedure. Simply remember that the capability is there and ready to use. (See Chapter 4 if you need to review the procedure.)

Protecting Information

Protecting information is vital in certain spreadsheets. When you protect data or formulas, you ensure that they can't be changed or deleted accidentally. Essentially, protected cells become read-only cells, as opposed to read-and-write cells. To protect information, you use two related commands: Style, on the Format menu, and Protect Data, on the Options menu.

The Style command determines, among other things, whether Works will apply the locked "style" to particular cells of your spreadsheet. Although locking seems a bit unusual compared to alignment and character formats, it is an attribute you apply to the data or format in selected cells. When you first use Works, it assumes that you want the locked attribute for every cell in your spreadsheet.

Aha, you might think, I've been changing data all through this chapter. How could that happen if Works assumed I wanted the cells locked? The reason is you haven't yet told Works to protect your data and formulas. That's the second part of the process. It doesn't matter whether locking is turned on or off. If you don't select the Protect Data command from the Options menu, nothing happens.

The net effect is this: The Protect Data command tells Works to check the locking status of a cell before it updates its contents.

To see how locking works, use the GIZMO spreadsheet:

□ Select the values in cells B4 through F7.

□ Choose the Style command from the Format menu. When Works displays a dialog box, verify that the Locked option at the bottom of the box is checked to indicate it's turned on. (If locking isn't on, click the box to enable it.)

□ Select the values in cells G4 through G7.

□ Choose the Style command again, and turn off the Locked option by clicking the locked box to remove the check.

□ Choose Protect Data from the Options menu.

Now cells B4 through F7 are secure from change, but cells G4 through G7 are not secure from change. To see what happens,

☐ Select locked cell B4 and type *1992.*

☐ Click the Enter button.

Instead of changing the value as it normally would, Works displays this dialog box:

☐ Click OK to eliminate the dialog box.

☐ Select unlocked cell G4, and type *1992.*

☐ Click the Enter button.

As you can see, you can change the last month's data while protecting older data. Before you can make any changes to the data in cells B4 through F7, you must turn off protection:

☐ Choose Protect Data from the Options menu a second time.

That's all it takes. All of the cells are once again open for editing.

Hiding Cells

Another way to protect data and formulas, or at least remove them from open view, is to hide the columns in which the data or formulas appear. Although this approach is less effective than locking, it is useful when you want to temporarily eliminate columns that intervene between two or more sections of a spreadsheet you want to work on or compare on the screen. Even when columns are hidden, Works remains aware of their contents and calculates any formulas accurately.

To hide columns, you simply reduce their width to nothing. To hide a single column, use the mouse:

☐ Use the GIZMO spreadsheet again.

☐ Point to the boundary between columns F and G.

☐ When the mouse pointer changes to a vertical bar with a two-headed arrow running through it, drag the boundary left, all the way to the edge of column E. Release the mouse pointer, and column F is gone.

When you "hide" columns, Works does not change the remaining column letters. Column F is now missing from the column labels. Because of this, hidden columns should not be considered a true security measure. Anyone who knows Works will know how to redisplay the missing columns.

You'll "unhide" column F in a moment, but first try hiding more than a single column:

☐ Select columns D and E on the spreadsheet.

☐ Choose the Column Width command from the Format menu. Works will display this dialog box:

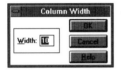

You use this command and dialog box not only to hide columns, but to change their widths whenever you want. Simply type the width (in characters), and click OK. To reduce the column widths to nothing in this example,

☐ Type *0* (zero), and click OK.

To redisplay the columns,

☐ Choose the Go To command on the Select menu.

☐ Type cell references for the columns you want to redisplay — in this case, type *D1:F1*. Click OK.

Although the columns are hidden, Works displays a small, double-thick gridline between cells C1 and G1. This means the hidden columns are now selected, so you can return them to a visible width:

☐ Choose Column Width from the Format menu.

☐ Either click OK to accept the default width of 10, or type a new width and then click OK.

The hidden columns return to the screen.

Keep in mind that if you hide columns D through F, as you did in the previous example, and then use the mouse to highlight columns C and G, you have actually selected all five columns (C, D, E, F, and G). So any action you perform on that highlighted range, such as formatting or clearing, also affects the hidden portion of the range. So be careful!

Controlling Calculation

In the examples you've tried so far, you probably noticed that Works calculated (or recalculated) formulas whenever you changed the spreadsheet. Sometimes, however, you might want to put a hold on the calculations until you've made a series of changes to a spreadsheet. You might also find that this constant recalculation on large spreadsheets can become time-consuming. You can control when Works calculates formulas using two commands on the Options menu: Manual Calculation, which tells Works not to update the spreadsheet each time you make a change that affects a formula, and Calculate Now, which gives Works the go-ahead to recalculate all the formulas in a spreadsheet.

The Manual Calculation command affects only the spreadsheet that's open at the time you choose the command. Thus, if you have three spreadsheets open and specify manual calculation for one of them, Works will still recalculate the other two whenever you make a change that affects a formula. The only time Works overrides manual calculation is when you enter a new formula. In that case, Works calculates the formula whether manual calculation is turned on or off. To try controlling calculation, use the GIZMO spreadsheet again as an example:

- □ Select cells G3 through H13.

- □ Use the Fill Right command to copy column G into column H.

- □ Choose Manual Calculation from the Options menu.

- □ Select cell H7, type *2022,* and click the Enter button. Notice that Works does not recalculate any of the formulas, but it does warn you that the spreadsheet needs to be recalculated by displaying CALC in the status line.

- □ Now select cell H14, and enter the formula *=H13+2.* Works does calculate this formula because it's a new one.

- □ Finally, choose Calculate Now from the Options menu, or press F9, the keyboard shortcut. Works immediately recalculates all formulas and removes the CALC message from the status line.

- □ The cells you copied into column H were useful for comparison, but you don't need them, so select them all and delete the copy with the Clear command on the Edit menu.

- □ Reset the calculation mode to automatic by again choosing the Manual Calculation command on the Options menu.

REFINING A SPREADSHEET

In addition to the different ways Works helps you organize, set up, and calculate spreadsheets, it also offers a number of approaches for refining your work and making the actual use of the spreadsheet as easy as possible.

Formatting Your Work

One highly visual way to enhance or clarify a spreadsheet is, of course, through formatting. As in the word processor, Works gives you a variety of options in terms of fonts, font sizes, alignments, and borders. All of these options should be familiar from your work with the word processor. The only real difference you must note is that changes in font or font size affect *entire* spreadsheets, not just selected cells. You cannot, for example, use Helv 14 for a title and Courier 12 for the data.

When it's time to print your spreadsheet, be sure to use the Print Preview command to see how much information fits on a page. To improve the overall layout, remember that you can juggle column widths, fonts, and font sizes to open up a cramped spreadsheet or condense one that sprawls a little too much. Simple as it sounds, sometimes a small change in font or font size can make a dramatic difference in your printed documents. This is especially true when you change from a monospace font such as Courier, in which a lowercase *i* requires as much space as a capital *W,* to a proportional font such as Helv, in which characters take up only as much linear space as they need. This chapter won't walk you through an example of text formatting, but you might want to try using different fonts, font sizes, alignments, and borders on one of your sample spreadsheets to see their effects on a document.

Sorting Rows

Like the database, which you'll encounter in Chapter 9, the Works spreadsheet has the ability to sort information, arranging rows of entries you've selected in alphabetic or numeric order. Works sorts based on the information in a column (A, B, C, and so on), and you can specify up to three columns, in order of importance, for it to consider. During the sort, Works checks the contents of the first, most important column and arranges the rows to match the sort you specified (ascending or descending). If you've specified a second and, possibly, a third column, Works turns to them in order to refine the result by sorting entries that are duplicated in the previous column(s). The following example sorts a list of expenses alphabetically in column A, and then by amount in column B:

☐ Open a new spreadsheet and enter the text and values shown in the following illustration:

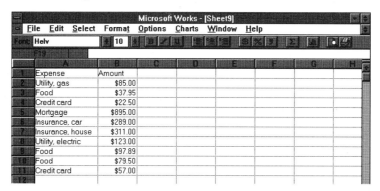

☐ First, you must tell Works which rows you want to sort. You don't want to include the column titles, so select cells A2 through B11.

☐ Now choose the Sort Rows command from the Select menu. Works displays this dialog box:

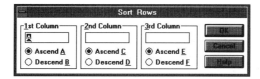

This is where you tell Works which columns to use for the sort and the order in which to sort them. For the first column, Works always proposes to use the first column in your selection. In this case, it's column A. Notice, too, that Works proposes to sort in ascending order: A to Z or lowest to highest. For this example, the proposed responses for the first column are correct. If they were not, you would type the column letter and choose the type of sort you wanted.

You also want Works to consider column B if it finds duplicates in the sort:

☐ Click in the box headed 2nd Column, and type *B*. Once again, ascending order is fine, so click OK to begin the sort.

Almost instantly, Works rearranges the entries like this:

	A	B	C	D	E	F	G	H
1	Expense	Amount						
2	Credit card	$22.50						
3	Credit card	$57.00						
4	Food	$37.95						
5	Food	$79.50						
6	Food	$97.89						
7	Insurance, car	$289.00						
8	Insurance, house	$311.00						
9	Mortgage	$895.00						
10	Utility, electric	$123.00						
11	Utility, gas	$85.00						
12								

Sorting is fast and useful for arranging any type of alphabetic or numeric information. If you want to preserve both the original and the sorted versions, save the original under one name and the sorted spreadsheet under another. Use some type of "key" in naming the files so you'll be able to tell that they are related and that they represent sorted and unsorted data. The preceding example, for instance, could be saved in its original form as EXP.WKS and in sorted form as EXPSORT.WKS.

Searching for Information

The Go To command provides a quick way to jump to a specific cell, regardless of what it contains. But what do you do if you know the value you want, but don't know where the cell is? You use the Find command on the Select menu.

Find in the spreadsheet works much like Find in the word processor with one exception: The word processor lets you refine a document search by limiting the command to whole words or case, but the spreadsheet lets you refine a search by specifying direction (left to right by row, or top to bottom by column). If you're searching a large spreadsheet, specifying a horizontal or vertical scan can speed the process by accommodating the search to the orientation or layout of the spreadsheet.

You can select columns, rows, or cell ranges to limit the search to a particular part of the spreadsheet, or you can select any cell and have Works search the entire spreadsheet. To see how simple it is, use the GIZMO spreadsheet as an example:

☐ Choose the Find command from the Select menu.

☐ Type *10157* in the Find What box.

□ Works proposes to search by rows, rather than columns. Your spreadsheet is small enough that the search direction doesn't matter, so click OK.

Almost immediately, Works selects cell E9, where it found the value 10157.

PRINTING A SPREADSHEET

NOTE: *Because printing in Works is uniform throughout the three applications, this section deals only with features unique to the spreadsheet. If you need more information about headers, footers, or other topics, refer to the longer discussions in Chapter 6.*

When it comes to printing, a spreadsheet can differ from a word-processed document in one important aspect: Although it is a single document, the spreadsheet can be either too wide or too long to fit on a single page. This means you might find yourself doing some fine-tuning before you print.

If you create a document that is both too wide and too long to print on one page, Works breaks up the spreadsheet and prints it on separate pages, in this order: upper left section first, lower left second, upper right third, and lower left fourth.

To control page breaks at the bottom, you can use the Insert Page Break command on the Edit menu. To control page breaks from side to side, you can insert a page break between columns with the Insert Page Break command, but you can also adjust column widths or insert a blank column wide enough to force the column to its right onto a new page.

As in the word processor, you can add headers, footers, and page numbers to a printed spreadsheet. You can also adjust page and header margins and, of course, preview the spreadsheet before printing. If your printer can print sideways (landscape orientation), you can reverse page length and width in the Page Setup & Margins dialog box. Use this option to fit a wide, but short, spreadsheet on one page.

Printing Part of a Spreadsheet

You can choose to print all or only part of a spreadsheet. This is one area in which the spreadsheet differs significantly from the word processor. To print part of a word-processed document, you specify the starting and ending pages in the Print dialog box. To print part of a spreadsheet, you specify the area to print with the Set Print Area command on the File menu. Using the command is simple: Select the cells you want to print, and then choose the Set Print Area command. For example,

- □ Display the GIZMO spreadsheet, and select cells A1 through G7.
- □ Choose the Set Print Area command from the File menu.
- □ To see the cells before printing, click the Print Preview button on the Toolbar. Only the print area you specified appears.

To deselect a print area, select the entire spreadsheet, and choose Set Print Area again. (To select the entire spreadsheet quickly, either choose All from the Select menu or click on the unlabeled, rectangular box above row 1 and to the left of column A.)

Page Setup and Printing

You can use the Page Setup & Margins command to set the layout of your spreadsheet before printing. When you choose this command, you'll see this dialog box:

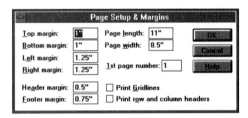

Most of this dialog box is similar to the one in the word processor. Page length and Page width, you'll recall, are the two measurements you can switch (length 8.5, width 11) to print in landscape mode, if your printer is capable of it.

Two elements in this dialog box are unique to the spreadsheet: Print Gridlines, which causes Works to print the same type of grid you see onscreen, and Print row and column headers, which causes Works to include the column labels (A, B, C) and row numbers (1, 2, 3) in the printout. If you choose either or both of these options you can produce a printed version of the spreadsheet that very closely matches the screen display.

> **NOTE:** *Although it sounds as if Print row and column headers should cause Works to print row and column* titles, *remember that it does not. Works always prints the titles that appear on a given page of a spreadsheet, but to repeat titles on consecutive pages, you must use the Freeze Titles command, described in "Freezing Row and Column Titles," earlier in this chapter.*

Once you've laid the groundwork, printing is simply a matter of choosing the Print command.

USING TEMPLATES

Chances are that your spreadsheets will tend to follow certain forms and patterns. When you find yourself repeating layouts and formatting, remember that all of the Works applications let you set up and save templates that can save you from reinventing the wheel time and again. To create a single spreadsheet template that opens whenever you start the Works spreadsheet,

1. Create the layout you want.

2. To save it as a template, choose the Save As command, and then choose SS Template from the Save File As Type box in the Save As dialog box.

3. To ensure that Works starts with the template each time, choose Spreadsheet in the Use Templates For box of the dialog box produced by the Works Settings command on the Options menu.

To save a template for occasional use, save the layout and formatting as a normal spreadsheet file. Open the file whenever you want to use the template. Save the finished spreadsheet under a different name to keep the template unchanged.

REFERENCE TO SPREADSHEET COMMANDS

This final section presents a quick reference to the spreadsheet menus and commands. Use it as a refresher if you can't remember which command to use or what it does. As always, refer to Help if you need further information.

The File Menu — for manipulating entire files

Create New File	Opens a new document.
Open Existing File	Opens a previously saved file.
Close	Closes an open file; prompts if the file contains unsaved changes.
Save	Saves a file under the existing name.
Save As	Saves a file under a new name, in a different directory, on a different disk, with a backup copy, or as a different file type.

(continued)

203

continued

Save Workspace	Causes Works to "memorize" the number, names, and status of open files for redisplay during the next session. The workspace is used only if Use Saved Workspace is checked in the Works Settings dialog box.
Print Preview	Displays a document as it will be printed.
Print	Prints all or part of a document.
Page Setup & Margins	Sets margins and paper size, and determines whether gridlines and row and column heads will be printed.
Set Print Area	Restricts printing to the currently selected range of cells.
Printer Setup	Sets up or modifies the definition of a printer and its capabilities.
Exit Works	Exits the program; prompts if any files contain unsaved changes.

The Edit Menu — *for organizing and refining spreadsheets*

Cut	Removes the contents of selected cells and places them on the Clipboard.
Copy	Copies the contents of selected cells to the Clipboard.
Paste	Inserts the contents of the Clipboard into a spreadsheet. Ranges are pasted into selected cells from the top left-hand corner, overwriting any existing cell contents.
Paste Special	Pastes values instead of formulas; also adds or subtracts incoming values to those in the receiving cells.
Clear	Deletes the contents of selected cells.
Delete Row/Column	Deletes one or more selected rows or columns.
Insert Row/Column	Inserts a row above the selected row; inserts a column to the left of the selected column.
Fill Right	Duplicates values or formulas from the leftmost cell in all selected cells to the right; adjusts relative references to reflect new formula locations.
Fill Down	Duplicates values or formulas from the topmost cell in all selected cells below; adjusts relative references to reflect new formula locations.
Fill Series	Fills out a series of numbers or dates, beginning with a value entered in the first selected cell; allows different step intervals to be specified.
Delete/Insert Page Break	Two commands. One deletes a manual (forced) page break, the other inserts a page break above the selected row or to the left of the selected column.
Range Name	Assigns a name of 15 characters or less to the selected cell or group of cells; also lists assigned names on a spreadsheet for reference.

(continued)

continued

Headers & Footers	Adds headers and footers to spreadsheets. Accepts the following codes: &P (page number), &F (filename), &D (date), &T (time), && (ampersand), &L (align left), &R (align right), &C (center). Does not allow header and footer paragraphs, as in the word processor.

The Select Menu — for navigating in a spreadsheet

Cells	Anchors the selection to enable extending the highlight. Primarily a keyboard command; shortcut key, F8.
Row	Extends the selection to include the entire row containing the currently selected cell or cells.
Column	Extends the selection to include the entire column containing the currently selected cell or cells.
All	Extends the selection to the entire spreadsheet.
Go To	Moves the highlight to a specified range name or cell reference.
Find	Searches the spreadsheet for specified cell contents. Repeat a search by pressing F7. Case is not significant with text.
Sort Rows	Sorts rows alphabetically or numerically, in ascending or descending order, using up to three columns as sort criteria.

The Format Menu — for formatting cells

General	Formats cells for general display: left-aligned text, right-aligned numbers. Numbers are displayed as integers or decimals.
Fixed	Formats cells for a fixed number of decimal places.
Currency	Formats cells to display currency.
Comma	Formats cells to insert a comma separator in numbers of 1,000 or more.
Percent	Formats cells to display values as percentages.
Exponential	Formats cells to display values in exponential (scientific) notation, such as 2.3E+03.
Leading Zeros	Formats cells to pad numbers with leading (left-hand) zeros to fill out a specified number of digit positions.
True/False	Formats cells to display *TRUE* for all nonzero numbers, *FALSE* for zero.
Time/Date	Formats cells to display values as times or dates.
Font	Specifies the font and font size to be used for a spreadsheet.
Style	Specifies alignment and character styles for selected cells; also enables locking for data protection.
Border	Draws a border around selected cells.
Column Width	Adjusts the widths of selected columns.

(continued)

continued

The Options Menu — *for modifying spreadsheet behavior*

Works Settings	Sets Works to run according to individual preferences.
Dial This Number	Dials a selected telephone number on the spreadsheet to enable voice (not computer) communication.
Show Toolbar	Turns the Toolbar on and off.
Show Gridlines	Turns gridlines on and off.
Show Formulas	Turns the display of formulas, rather than values, on and off.
Freeze Titles	Freezes onscreen titles so they are always displayed; also enables printing titles on each page of a multiple-page spreadsheet.
Protect Data	Prevents contents of selected cells from being deleted or changed; effective only if locking is already enabled with the Style command on the Format menu.
Manual Calculation	Turns on manual calculation; prevents recalculation whenever a value that affects a formula is changed.
Calculate Now	Causes recalculation when manual calculation is turned on.

The Charts Menu — *for turning spreadsheets into charts (described in detail in Chapter 8)*

Create New Chart	Creates a chart.
Name	Names or renames a chart.
Delete	Deletes a selected chart.
Duplicate	Duplicates an existing chart.

The Window Menu — *for managing the spreadsheet window*

Cascade	Cascades (overlaps) open document windows.
Tile	Tiles (sets side by side) open document windows.
Arrange Icons	Arranges icons for open, but minimized, documents in rows.
Split	Splits a document window.

The Help Menu — *for requesting Help*

Provides access to Help topics specific to using the spreadsheet.

8

Creating Charts

Do you see a pattern in the numbers 5, 7, 11, and 17 versus 1, 4, 9, and 16? How about now, when you look at this chart?

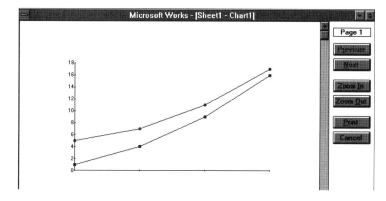

Corresponding numbers in these two sets differ by 4, 3, 2, and 1, and succeeding pairs of numbers come closer and closer together. You probably saw the pattern more quickly in the chart than you did in scanning the numbers themselves because patterns are easier and faster to recognize in graphics than they are in independent sets of numbers, letters, symbols, or other characters.

When you work with numbers, charts can be invaluable in helping yourself and others visualize patterns of any type: trends, comparisons, ranges, or fluctuations. This is especially true in real-life situations because patterns usually aren't clearly defined. One scatter chart can be clearer than pages of data to the scientist trying to figure out how many starfish are on the bottom of the sea, and a set of bar charts or line charts can be more useful than piles of printouts in helping an economist interpret the effects of gasoline prices on the cost of fruit and vegetables.

CREATING A CHART

Works can chart spreadsheet data at the click of a mouse button. The charting program is accessed through the spreadsheet much as the Draw module is accessed through the word processor. All you need is a spreadsheet to provide the values you want charted. You created a number of spreadsheets in Chapter 7, so you can use them as a starting point:

□ Start Works, if necessary, and open the file named PIZZA.

To create a chart, you begin by selecting the range of cells containing the data you want charted. For charting, a range can consist of up to six consecutive rows or columns. Although you can include blank rows or columns of cells in the range, it's best not to because in a bar or line chart Works will plot the "values" of those empty cells or treat text differently from the way you might expect. At best, the chart might look unprofessional; at worst, it could be misleading.

In the PIZZA spreadsheet, you have a made-to-order range of cells to chart: cells A3 through D7, which list sales of five types of pizza in each of three sizes. To turn this data into a chart,

□ Select cells A3 through D7.

□ Click the Chart button on the Toolbar.

Almost immediately, Works opens a new window and displays this chart:

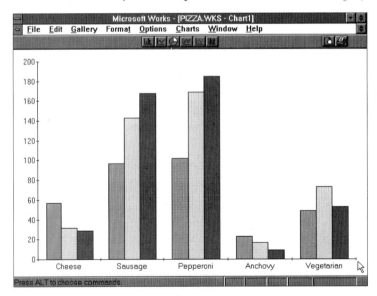

This is a bar chart, the default chart type Works uses when you click the Chart button. Note that Works has turned text into labels along the horizontal axis of the chart. When the first column or top row of a range of cells contains text, Works turns the text into labels like these.

Some Charting Terminology

Even though charting is easy, it helps to know how Works "views" a chart and the data in it so that you can use the charting module with a minimum of backing, filling, and redoing. The best way to develop a feel for the charting process is by displaying the chart and spreadsheet side by side:

☐ Choose Tile from the Window menu.

When you compare the cells you selected with the chart Works produced, you can see that Works rotated the spreadsheet cells 90 degrees. This happens when the selection includes more rows than columns. When the selection includes more columns than rows, Works keeps the original orientation.

Except for circular pie charts, all charts have both a horizontal, or X axis, and a vertical, or Y axis. Works refers to the X axis as the *category axis* and the Y axis as the *value axis*. The category axis identifies the values being charted; the value axis is the measure against which values in a line, bar, or scatter chart are plotted.

The value axis of the chart is divided into units against which Works plots the values in the cells you selected for charting. Works determines the lowest and highest values for you, depending on the smallest and largest values in the range. This scaling takes place automatically, but you can change it, as you'll see in "Changing the Scale of an Axis," later in this chapter. When you chart more than one set of data, as you did here with small, medium, and large pizzas, Works uses a different color or pattern to represent the values in each set.

Finally, note that each series of values is given its own color (or pattern). A *series* is a related group of values from a single row or column in the range selected for charting. Conceptually, a series of values in a chart is comparable to a series of books, movies, or collectible items. The number of small pizzas forms one series in the chart, just as *Glop, Son of Glop,* and *Return of Son of Glop* would form a recognizable (if uninspiring) series of films.

TIP If you create a chart, and you want to be sure you know which cell range is included in each series, choose the Go To command from the chart module's Edit menu. Although the Go To command is intended to help you jump back to selected cells in the spreadsheet (for editing and other work), the dialog box it produces is a handy reference device. It lists the cell ranges Works used for the chart categories and for the series of values charted.

Saving a Chart

Saving a chart can be so simple you literally don't have to think about it. Works links charts to the spreadsheets from which they're created, so saving one or more charts is simply a matter of saving the spreadsheet file. Even if you forget about a new or changed chart and proceed to close the spreadsheet, Works reminds you when you choose the Close command. The following dialog box will appear, asking if you want to save changes.

This step is the only one that could conceivably cause you to lose a chart because Works doesn't remind you that "changes" not only refers to new entries and additions on the spreadsheet, but also refers to any charts you created or updated. If you click No because you want to lose some editing changes, you'll lose your new or changed charts as well.

CHANGING CHART TYPES

Works creates a bar chart by default, but you can choose from several other types of charts, all of which are available through buttons on the charting module's Toolbar or through commands on its Gallery menu. The illustration at the top of the next page shows the charting buttons on the Toolbar; the same names are used in the Gallery menu.

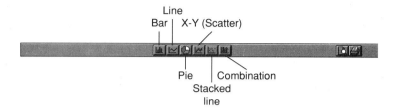

After you've created a basic bar chart from the spreadsheet, you can change chart types at any time to see which type best suits the data you're charting. Before you get more involved in the whys and wherefores of charting, you might like to see what your chart looks like in other formats. To get started,

☐ Click the button for the Line chart.

Works displays this dialog box:

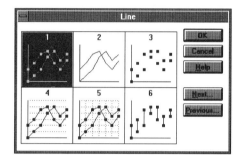

This dialog box expands your choices even further. The button for each chart type produces a dialog box like this with variations of the basic chart you selected. The two buttons at the right, labeled Next and Previous, take you from one chart type to another without having to close the current dialog box and choose a different chart type. In the following sections, you'll transform your chart several times to see how the same data is represented in the different chart types.

Bar Charts

Bar charts, like the one currently on your screen, are often used for comparing values, such as total sales of My Better Mousetrap, by region, for the last four quarters; the U.S. national deficit compared to tax revenues for the years 1980

211

through 1990; consumption of electricity by your household for each of the last 12 months. Works produces five types of bar charts. To see them,

☐ Click Cancel if the Line chart dialog box is still displayed.

☐ Click the Bar chart button.

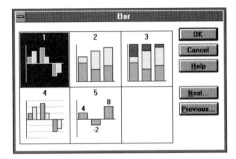

Notice from the examples in the dialog box that Works charts positive values above the X axis and negative values below. To make values easier to interpret, the bar chart can include horizontal gridlines or it can print the actual value above or below each bar.

The stacked bar charts in choices 2 and 3 "add" series values to produce a single bar for each category on the X axis. To see how this works,

☐ Double-click choice 2 to literally stack the series values. This creates a bar equivalent to the sum of its parts for each category.

☐ Click the Bar chart button again, and double-click on option 3 to represent the parts of each bar as a percent of the total for each category.

Line Charts

Line charts are useful for showing trends and fluctuations over time, such as Atlantic and Pacific tuna catches over the last decade; number of travelers per month on three major airlines; ice cream sales in Phoenix and Minneapolis from January through December. There are six types of line charts. To see them again,

☐ Click the Line chart button.

Most of the line charts use markers to indicate individual values. These markers help distinguish one series from another by color or shape. Works uses differently colored circles on a color screen and solid shapes — such as circles, squares, and diamonds — on a black-and-white screen. If you want, you can change the markers with the Patterns & Colors command on the Format menu. (See "Patterns and Colors," later in this chapter.)

If markers are not important to your chart, you can choose option 2 to display lines alone. Conversely, if the lines are not important, you can choose option 3 and display markers only. Options 4 and 5 are standard line charts, but with horizontal or both horizontal and vertical gridlines. To turn the PIZZA chart into a line chart,

□ Double-click on an option you want to see.

NOTE: *Option 6 looks a bit odd for a line chart, but it is well suited for stock prices and similar values in which highs and lows are equally significant to or more significant than trends over time. This chart differs from the others in using markers and a straight line to show the* range *between the lowest and highest values in each set. If you have intermediate values, Works adds markers on the line to show the position of each intermediate value, relative to the lowest and highest.*

Whole and Sliced Pies

Pie charts, familiar to any reader of the local newspaper, show a single set of values as ratios — slices of a pie. Pie charts are commonly used for demographic reports (for example, percent of households in various income ranges that have one or more computers). Both eye-catching and easy to interpret, pie charts are useful in any situation in which the parts need to be seen in relation to the whole, such as poll results, census results, federal spending, state spending, city spending . . . personal spending.

Creating a pie chart is straightforward:

□ Click the Pie chart button.

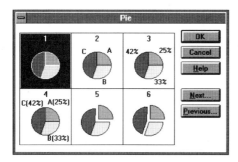

Notice that you can create a pie chart with category labels, percents, or labels and percents.

□ Double-click on option 3 to create a pie chart that shows the percentage each slice represents.

So far, so good. But there's something subtle going on here. When you create a pie chart, Works uses only a *single* set of values — one row or one column of cells. If you choose more than a single row or column, as you did in the PIZZA spreadsheet, Works creates a pie chart from the first value series. This one-series limit applies only to pie charts, and although it isn't apparent on your screen, there's an easy way to check:

- □ Select cells B3 through B7 in the PIZZA spreadsheet.

- □ Click the Chart button to create a chart.

- □ Now click the Pie chart button, and choose option 3 again.

- □ Tile the windows so you can see both pie charts. They're identical because both charts are based on the same cell ranges, even though you might have assumed that the original pie chart represented a compilation of all selected values.

- □ You don't need the duplicate chart anymore, so click in the chart window, and choose Delete from the Charts menu.

- □ When a dialog box appears, click the Del button, and then click OK to complete the command.

- □ Tile the windows again to neaten up the display.

Aside from labels, the biggest difference between types of pie charts is whether, and what part or parts you explode, or separate, from the rest. If you choose option 5 from the dialog box, Works explodes the first value outward. If you choose option 6, Works simulates the Big Bang and explodes the entire pie.

If you don't want to explode the entire pie, but you do want to explode a slice other than the first, create a standard pie and choose the Patterns & Colors command from the Format menu. This dialog box will appear:

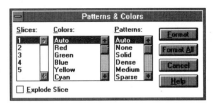

Choose the slice you want to explode from the Slices box, click Explode Slice, and then click the Format button. You can repeat this procedure to explode additional slices. When you have finished, click the Close button. (Here, the Close button is labeled Cancel until you choose some type of formatting or click the Format or Format All button.) The Patterns & Colors command is also used to create an exploded pie chart with labels, percentages, or both — something you cannot do directly from the pie chart dialog box.

Stacked Line Charts

Stacked line charts are line charts with a dash of stacked bar chart tossed in. Instead of plotting values independently, stacked line charts add or subtract the values in each series so that the marker in the topmost line reflects the combined total. Sound confusing? Not really.

☐ Click the Stacked Line chart button.

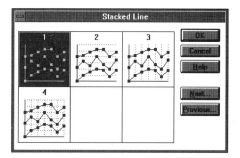

☐ Double-click option 2 to turn your PIZZA chart into a stacked line chart with horizontal gridlines that make it easier to read.

☐ Click in the spreadsheet window, and scroll to the right so you can see the totals in column F.

By comparing the chart with the totals for each type (category) of pizza, you can see that Works has added the values for each series (small, medium, and large) in constructing the line chart, and the markers in the topmost line correspond to the combined total for each category. In contrast, a regular line chart for the same range of cells would plot values independently.

X-Y (Scatter) Charts

Scatter charts show relationships between sets of data by plotting values against both the horizontal and vertical axes of the chart. Whereas bar, line, and stacked line charts use the X axis for categories, scatter charts, by their nature, use both the X and Y axes as scales for numeric values. Typical examples of data used in scatter charts are height versus weight, or education versus income. Other charts might compare age with auto accidents or sick time reported against overtime worked. If you were a scientist, you might use scatter charts to see if there's a relationship between hours of light and flower production for geraniums. Works gives you the following options for scatter charts:

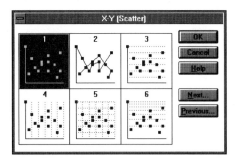

Because both the Y and X axes must be scaled, a scatter chart is the only type of chart you cannot create simply by clicking a button (even though one exists on the Toolbar) or by choosing from a menu. Creating such a chart is not difficult, however. Here's an easy way to create a scatter chart:

- □ Select the data you want to chart on the X axis. (Ignore the Y axis values for now.) Remember that the data must be numeric — no text. Copy the selected data to the Clipboard.

- □ Now select the data you want to chart on the Y axis. Click the Chart button, as usual. Works will produce a bar chart with the values scaled against the Y axis.

- □ Next, select Paste Series from the Edit menu. When a dialog box appears, click Category to indicate that the series you copied to the Clipboard belongs on the category (X) axis. Click OK.

- □ Click the Scatter chart button on the Toolbar, and double-click on the type of scatter chart you want.

Slightly roundabout, but not bad. If necessary, you can fine-tune the scale of the X axis with the Horizontal (X) Axis command on the Format menu. (See "Changing the Scale of an Axis," later in this chapter, for details.)

Your PIZZA spreadsheet doesn't contain any series that are suitable for a scatter chart, but you can create a simple, illustrative example in a few minutes:

□ Open a new spreadsheet, and type the entries shown in the following illustration:

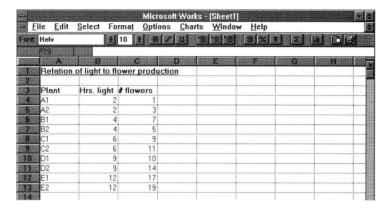

Notice that values are repeated in column B. This is often true of scatter charts, because they plot values for comparison.

□ Select cells B4 through B13, the values you want scaled on the X axis.

□ Copy the selected cells to the Clipboard.

□ Next, select cells C4 through C13.

□ Click the Chart button on the Toolbar.

□ Choose Paste Series from the Edit menu.

□ Click the Category button in the Paste Series dialog box. Click OK.

□ Click the Scatter button on the Toolbar, click OK, and you're done. You can cascade the windows for a better view of the chart.

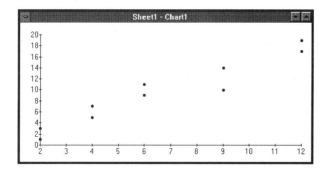

Well, the correlation was pretty obvious from the start, but the chart graphically illustrates that you do get more flowers on plants that receive more light.

Combination Charts

A combination chart is, as its name indicates, a combination of two chart types: bar and line. Because you can include a second vertical axis on the right of a chart, the combination chart is especially useful when you want to chart two differently scaled series. Combination charts are also valuable when you want a clear distinction between two series of values. You might, for example, choose this type of chart when plotting the asking and selling prices for homes, sales volumes for new and used cars, average loan amounts during periods of volatile interest rates, and so on.

You can choose from four types of combination charts:

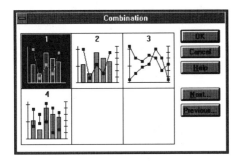

Options 2 and 3 are useful for displaying differently scaled values. Option 4 is a likely candidate for financial data, for example, bars showing stock volumes and range lines showing high, low, and closing prices.

Again, the PIZZA spreadsheet is not particularly well suited to this type of chart. You can, however, use the GIZMO spreadsheet you created in Chapter 7:

☐ Open the GIZMO spreadsheet.

Suppose you want to chart sales at stores 1 and 2 over the last six months:

☐ Select cells A3 through G5. Click the Chart button to create a normal bar chart.

☐ To turn the values for store 1 into bars and the values for store 2 into a line with markers simply click the Combination button.

☐ Volumes for both stores are measured against the same scale, so choose option 1, which is the default.

This is the result:

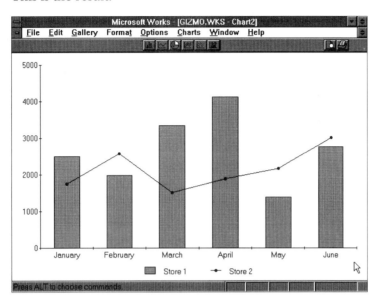

DRESSING UP A CHART

After you've created a chart, there are many ways you might want to dress it up. For the sake of appearance, you can change fonts, add boldfacing and other character styles, choose or change colors and patterns, and even frame the chart in a border. To make charts more informative, you can add titles to them, include legends that identify series within categories, and insert labels that clarify some or all of the data points in the chart. You can also add a second Y axis, as well as define or change the intervals and scales Works uses for both axes of a chart.

Titles

Titles are, no doubt, high on your list of good things to add to a chart. Works lets you add a main title, a subtitle, and titles for the X, Y, and (if you include one) right vertical axis. To include any or all of these on a chart, you use the Titles command on the chart module's Edit menu.

The PIZZA chart will serve the following experiments well. To begin,

□ Clear the screen by closing any other spreadsheets you created or opened.

□ Switch to the PIZZA chart window.

☐ Click the Bar chart button to turn the chart back into a bar chart. If necessary, click the document window's Maximize button to take full advantage of the screen.

Now add a title, a subtitle, and a title for the vertical axis:

☐ Choose the Titles command from the Edit menu.

☐ Fill in the dialog box, as shown in the following illustration:

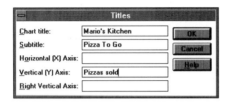

☐ Click OK.

As easily as that, you can add titles to your charts. There's no worrying about spacing or alignment; you simply type in the title you want. To delete a title, reverse the command. Select the Titles command, select the title you don't want, press Del, and then click OK.

When adding titles to a chart, you can simplify the job by using text that already exists on the spreadsheet. Instead of typing the title in the Titles dialog box, simply type the reference of the cell containing the text you want. When it carries out the Titles command, Works will use the text in the cell you specified as a title on your chart.

You can also use range names instead of cell references. If a name refers to more than a single cell, however, Works will use the contents of the first cell in the range as the title. In the PIZZA spreadsheet, you assigned the name Small to cells B3 through B7. If you were to type *small* in the Titles dialog box, Works would use the first value, 57, as the title of the chart.

If you are going to use range names, keep in mind that Works treats them as references to cells. If you want to use a name as text, rather than as a cell reference, precede the name with a double quotation mark ("). For example, the name *Pizza sales* refers to cells A3 through D7 in the spreadsheet. To use the name as the title for the vertical axis, you would type "*pizza sales* in the Titles dialog box. The double quotation mark would tell Works to treat the name as text. This situation is comparable to typing a double quotation mark in front of a number when you want to enter the number in a cell as text, not a value.

Legends

A legend is the key to the color, pattern, or marker used for each series in a category. Like the marks, symbols, and colors on a map, a blueprint, or a diagram, legends help the reader interpret the material correctly and with the least amount of effort. You can include legends on all but pie charts. You identify slices on those charts by choosing the chart option that includes percents, categories, or both when you create the pie chart.

When you select a range of cells to turn into a bar, line, or scatter chart, Works creates the appropriate legends for you if the range includes row or column titles for each series being plotted. Note that this is not the same as creating category labels on the X axis. Category labels (such as *cheese* and *anchovy*) identify the *categories* Works is charting; legends identify the *values* (such as *small, medium,* and *large)* that are plotted. To see the difference, and to create some legends of your own,

    □ Open the Format menu, and verify that a checkmark appears next to Show Legend. Works lets you turn the display of legends on and off; right now, you want it on.

    □ Choose Legend from the chart module's Edit menu.

    □ Type the following cell references in the Legend command's dialog box:

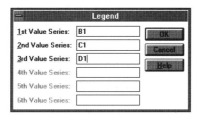

    □ Click OK to create the legends.

At the bottom of the chart, *below* the category labels, Works creates three legends next to three small boxes showing the color or pattern used for the values plotted for small, medium, and large pizzas. If this were a line chart, Works would display markers, rather than colors or patterns, but the result would be the same — a key to understanding the chart.

Notice that in this example you typed cell references in the Legend dialog box. If you tile the windows, you can see that the references refer to cells containing the text for each of the legends. As in creating titles, you can use cell references, rather than typing the text you want. To use text that is also a range name, again precede it with a double quotation mark to indicate that the name is to be treated as text, not a cell reference.

Labels

Titles, legends, and labels form a descending sequence for identifying chart elements. Titles identify all or part of the chart; legends identify key elements; labels identify actual values. You can label values on a bar or line chart, but not a pie chart. For a pie chart, use the labeling options in the dialog box for the chart type.

The easiest and most common way to label data is to include the actual value for each data point. You can also label data with text or other information by using existing entries from the spreadsheet or by typing new entries for use as labels. You cannot insert such labels directly from the chart module.

When you choose the Data Labels command from the chart module's Edit menu, this dialog box appears:

The checkbox at the top, titled Use series data, is all you need to label a chart with the actual values plotted. Simply click in the checkbox, and click OK to carry out the command. Choosing this label option overrides any others you specify in the rest of the dialog box.

The Value (Y) Series box is where you enter the references of cells containing the labels you want to use. To ensure that values are labeled correctly, be sure you understand which values are included in the first, second, and subsequent Y series. If you need to check, cancel this command and choose Go To from the Edit menu. Works will display the cell ranges for each series in the Go To dialog box.

The OK, Cancel, and Help buttons in the dialog box work as you would expect, but the Paste button is new. When you want to use cell contents other than plotted values as data labels, you can copy the information from the spreadsheet to the Clipboard and then use the Paste button to insert the copy in one of the Value (Y) Series boxes.

To experiment with data labels, add the plotted values to the bars in your PIZZA chart:

☐ Choose Data Labels from the chart module's Edit menu.

☐ Click in the Use series data box, and click OK to carry out the command.

Your chart should look like this:

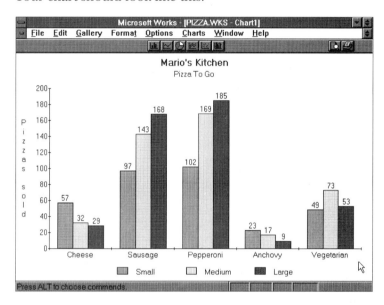

Now try a different type of label:

☐ Return to the spreadsheet. Type *S* in cell B2, *M* in C2, and *L* in D2.

☐ Copy the contents of the three cells to the Clipboard, and return to the chart.

☐ Choose the Data Labels command again, and click the Use series data checkbox to turn the option off.

☐ Type *B2* for the 1st Value (Y) Series, type *C2* for the 2nd, and *D2* for the 3rd. Click OK.

The value labels disappear to be replaced by S, M, and L at the top of the three series bars in the first chart category.

As a final experiment, use the Paste button:

☐ Choose the Data Labels command again.

- ☐ Click Paste to paste the range reference for the cells you copied earlier into the 1st series box.

- ☐ Tab to the remaining series boxes, and press Del to clear them. Click OK.

This time, you defined the labels incorrectly. You pasted three cell references, and thus three labels, into what Works interprets as the first Y series, so it spread the labels over the first three values in the series. Logical, but not what you wanted. When you label data values, especially by pasting cell references, work with one label and one value at a time.

Your chart isn't very presentable right now, so correct the labels:

- ☐ Choose the Data Labels command again.

- ☐ Click the Use series data checkbox, and (for neatness more than anything else) clear the incorrect cell references from the Value (Y) Series box.

- ☐ Click OK to relabel the chart.

Adding a Second Vertical Axis

In bar, line, and scatter charts, Works normally displays a single Y axis. You can add a second vertical axis at the right edge of the chart when it's important to enhance readability or you want to show two different scales. To add a second vertical axis, you use the Two Vertical (Y) Axes command on the Format menu. To use this command to create a second vertical axis on the PIZZA chart,

- ☐ Choose the Two Vertical (Y) Axes command. Works displays this dialog box:

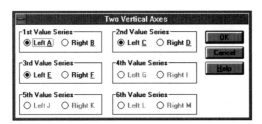

The box might seem a bit cluttered at first, but the contents are typically Works-easy to interpret. There are boxes for six value series, the most Works can handle in a single chart. For each value series, you can choose an axis on the left or on the right. (The letters A through M represent the keys you press to choose each of the options if you don't use a mouse.)

When you have a single vertical axis, as you do now, Works turns on the Left option for each plotted series. To create a right vertical axis scaled to the values in a particular series, you click the Right option in that series box, as follows:

☐ Click the Right option in the 1st Value Series box.

☐ Click OK to create the right vertical axis.

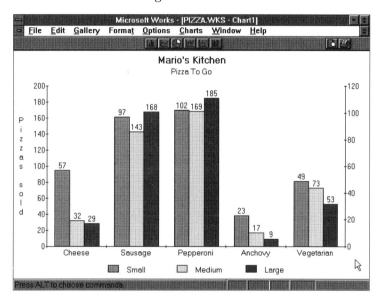

Notice that the new axis has a different maximum value (120), even though it defaults to the same 20-pizza intervals on the left axis. This happened because Works used the maximum and minimum values in the first value series to create the scale. This series, which contains the number of small pizzas sold, has a smaller range (23 to 102) than do the other series, and so Works has created a "smaller" scale. Notice, too, that creating a right axis that is scaled differently from the left one can have some potentially confusing results. The bars for the first value series are no longer proportional to the bars in the other series, even though they all represent the same basic information.

Given the type of values this chart displays, a much better approach would be to create a right axis that is identical to the left one. To create this type of right axis, you click the Right option in *all* series boxes:

☐ Choose the Two Vertical (Y) Axes command again.

☐ Click the Right option for all three series, and then click OK to carry out the command.

Now you have two identical axes. To enhance readability even further, you could click the Bar chart button and choose option 4 to display gridlines.

NOTE: *If you try this and your data labels disappear, choose the Data Labels command, and click the Use series data checkbox. The result, however, might look a little busy.*

Changing the Scale of an Axis

Although Works is excellent at figuring out an appropriate scale for the values it plots, you'll sometimes want to change the scale it uses. (For example, you might want to unclutter the Y axis by leaving larger intervals between measures or change the proportions of the bars in a chart by using a logarithmic scale based on a multiplication factor, rather than a progression of equal values.)

The Vertical (Y) Axis and (if you've added a second axis) the Right Vertical Axis commands on the Format menu let you change the scale of the left and right Y axes on a bar or line chart. The Horizontal (X) Axis and Vertical (Y) Axis commands, again on the Format menu, do the same jobs on a scatter chart. All of these commands produce a dialog box like this:

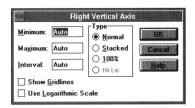

Note the following aspects of this dialog box:

- The Minimum and Maximum boxes let you set the smallest and largest values on the scale. The Auto setting lets Works determine these values.

- Interval lets you specify how large the steps between measurements should be. Again, Auto lets Works do the work.

- The entries in the Type box set the type of scale: Normal for charts like the current one; Stacked for stacked bar or stacked line charts in which each value contributes to a total; 100% for stacked bar charts in which each value is represented as a proportion of 100%; and Hi-Lo for line charts in which you display high and low ranges, as in stock values.

- Show Gridlines is another way (besides chart-type options) of displaying gridlines.

■ Use Logarithmic Scale sets the scale to a logarithmic rather than arithmetic measure.

Suppose you want to unclutter the scale on the vertical axes of your PIZZA chart. You've added data labels, so you really don't need the closely spaced intervals Works has provided.

☐ Choose the Right Vertical Axis command on the Format menu.

☐ Type *50* in the Interval box, and then click OK to carry out the command.

Works immediately changes *both* scales. When you have identical left and right axes, as you do here, use the Right Vertical Axis command to change both at the same time. If you have different scales, use the Vertical (Y) Axis command to change the left axis, and the Right Vertical Axis command to change the right one.

Fonts

The Works charting feature is like the spreadsheet when it comes to fonts: You're limited in the amount of mixing and matching you can do. Unlike the word processor, which lets you change virtually every character in a document, the chart module lets you specify a maximum of two fonts: one for the title of a chart, and one for everything else. You use the Title Font command to change chart titles and the Other Font command to change the rest of the chart. Both of these commands are on the Format menu. Except for the title bar, both commands produce identical dialog boxes:

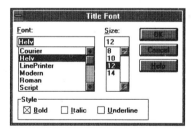

If possible, Works uses the Helv font, or a close approximation, to display its charts. As in the other Works applications, however, the actual fonts and font sizes available to you depend on your computer and, even more so, on your printer, its capabilities, and the way you've defined it to Windows.

227

So far, your chart looks pretty good, but it could use a little sprucing up in the font department:

☐ Choose Title Font from the Format menu.

☐ Choose a font you like, such as Tms Rmn. If necessary, click the Bold checkbox to boldface the title. Click OK.

☐ Choose Other Font from the same menu.

☐ Choose a font for the rest of the chart, and boldface those characters too. Click OK.

When you finish, your chart should look sharper and darker.

Patterns and Colors

The Patterns & Colors command can provide more fun than most others, in or out of the charting module. With this command, you can specify screen and print colors (the latter only if you have a color printer), patterns for different series in bar and pie charts, and markers for data values in line charts. As mentioned earlier, you can also use this command to explode the slice of your choice in a pie chart.

When you choose the Patterns & Colors command, Works displays a dialog box like this:

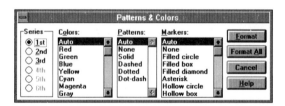

Works tailors the options in the dialog box to suit the type of chart you're working with. For example, the preceding dialog box shows the options available for a line chart. If you're working with a bar chart, you don't see any options in the Markers box because a bar chart doesn't use them. If you're working with a combination chart, Works displays a choice of markers if you select a series (in the Series box) that is represented by a line in the chart.

The following options are included in the dialog box:

■ The Series option lets you choose the value series to format.

■ The Colors option lets you pick a color for the series. Auto tells Works to use a predefined set of colors (red for the first series, green for the second, and blue for the third).

- The Patterns option lets you choose a pattern for the bar or line representing the selected series. If you work in color, but print in black-and-white, Auto tells Works which predefined patterns to use in place of color during printing. (You can see these patterns onscreen by choosing Display as Printed from the Options menu.)

- The Markers option lets you choose the type of marker used for data points in a line chart. Auto again sets the markers for you when you display or print the chart in black-and-white.

- The Format button in the dialog box tells Works to apply the choices you've made to the selected series. Use this button if you want to make additional changes to other series.

- The Format All button applies one or more choices you've made to all series in the chart. Use this button, for example, to change all lines in a line chart from solid to dotted, or to change all bars in a bar chart from multicolored to magenta. (In the latter case, Works changes to a different pattern or marker for each series, so you can still distinguish one bar or line from another. Smart.)

- The Close button is labeled Cancel until you make a formatting change. Cancel, as usual, cancels the command. Close tells Works you've finished formatting. When you click Close, Works updates the chart with the changes you specified.

To experiment with patterns and colors,

☐ Choose Patterns & Colors from the Format menu.

☐ If you have a color screen, choose a new color for the 1st series, and click the Format button. Do the same for the other two series, clicking the Format button for each. Click Close to carry out the command.

☐ Choose the Patterns and Colors command again. This time, select a single color, and click Format All. Click Close to make the changes. Note that Works displays different patterns to distinguish one bar in the chart from the next.

☐ Return the formatting to Auto, unless you prefer the display you've produced.

A more noticeable difference in the dialog box appears when you're working with a pie chart. Works then displays the dialog box you saw earlier:

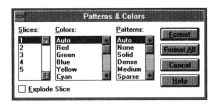

Here, you choose slices, rather than series. You can change colors and patterns as you did in the preceding example, and you can use the Explode Slice checkbox at the bottom of the dialog box to explode whichever piece of the pie you select in the Slices box.

MODIFYING A CHART

After you've created a chart, you don't have to worry about updating it whenever you change data in the spreadsheet. Works does that automatically because the two documents are so closely linked. You might, however, want to change category labels, alter the definition of a series, add a new series, or delete an old one from a chart. Then, too, you might find yourself wanting to create or change a chart by including one or more series from separate (nonadjacent) locations on the spreadsheet. You can do all this with the Series and Paste Series commands on the Edit menu.

Changing Category Labels

Category labels, like data labels, must already exist on a spreadsheet before you can incorporate them in a chart. After you've entered them on your spreadsheet, however, you can simply select them and copy them into place. The orientation of the copied cells doesn't matter, so you can copy a row of labels into a chart whose categories are based on column titles, and vice versa. For example, suppose Mario has developed a political consciousness and has decided to name his pizzas:

□ Switch to the PIZZA spreadsheet, and type the following entries in cells B18 through F18: *Purist, Conservative, Liberal, Independent,* and *Grassroots.* The titles won't show completely in the cells, but that's no problem.

□ Select the titles, and copy them to the Clipboard.

◻ Return to the chart and choose Paste Series.

◻ Click on Category, and click OK.

Your old categories are replaced by the new.

Another way to accomplish the same task is to use the Series command, instead of Paste Series. The Series command produces a dialog box like this:

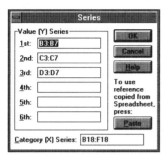

To turn the cell contents you copied into category labels on the X axis, you would click in the Category (X) Series box, click the Paste button to paste the range into the box, and then click OK to complete the command.

Changing Series

Changing the Y series is similar to changing category labels. Once again, you use cell references and either the Paste Series or Series command. For example, suppose Mario adds a giant-sized pizza to the menu and wants to include it in the chart:

◻ Return to the PIZZA spreadsheet.

◻ Type *X-large* in cell E1; boldface and underline the title.

◻ Type *20, 13, 17, 1,* and *15* into cells E3 through E7.

◻ Copy the contents of cells E3 through E7 to the Clipboard.

◻ Return to the chart. You could use Paste Series now, but try the Series command instead. Click in the box next to *4th,* click the Paste button, and click OK to add the new series.

The series appears to be fine, but as often happens when you're working with a computer program, one change affected other parts of your work. The data labels probably look a bit squeezed now, and the new series is controlling the left vertical axis. To adjust these,

- ☐ Choose the Other Font command from the Format menu, and select a smaller font size, such as 8. Click OK to take care of the font situation.

- ☐ Now choose the Two Vertical Axes command from the Format menu.

- ☐ Notice that the Left option is turned on in the 4th Value Series box. Because you created two vertical axes, and this is the only Left option selected, the new series is controlling the left axis. Click the Right option, and click OK to bring everything into line.

Like any other activity, computer work often leads to tinkering and fine-tuning to get everything the way you want.

Charting Nonadjacent Ranges

You can use the Series and Paste Series commands to create a chart from nonadjacent ranges. The ranges don't have to be oriented in the same directions, so these commands can also be useful if you want to chart related values that are laid out horizontally in one range, but vertically in another. The preceding examples illustrated the two commands, so this section will simply outline the procedure you would use:

- ■ If you're creating a new chart, select the first range, and click the spreadsheet's Chart button to create a chart.

- ■ From the new chart, return to the spreadsheet, select the second range to chart, and copy it to the Clipboard.

- ■ Return to the chart, and use the Paste Series or the Series command to turn the references for the copied cells into the second value series. Click OK to update the chart.

- ■ If necessary, return to the spreadsheet and repeat the procedure for additional cell ranges.

That's it. Horizontal, vertical, close together, or widely spaced, you can turn the cell ranges of your choice into the chart you want to see.

SETUP AND PRINTING

Most page setup and printing is the same in the charting module as in the other applications, thanks to the integration of the Works features. There are a few differences, however.

Previewing a Chart

If you work with a color display but print in black-and-white, the colors you see onscreen are replaced by patterns and differently shaped markers in print. There are several ways to see what the printed chart will look like. The easiest method, and the one designed for this purpose, is to choose the Display As Printed command from the Options menu. This, for example, is what the sample chart in this chapter looks like:

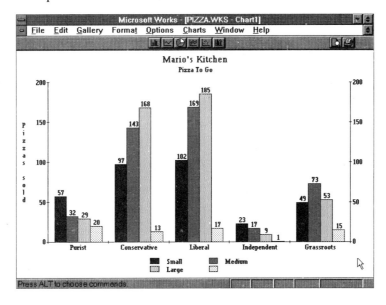

If you don't feel like using this command, click the Print Preview button on the Toolbar. You'll see a smaller, but otherwise identical, "printed" version of your chart. If you don't want to use either of these methods, you can also choose Black as the color for the entire chart in the Patterns & Colors dialog box. This last approach is pretty roundabout, but if you like it, it's there.

Page Setup and Printing

When you're ready to finish up and print a chart, you can add running heads, page numbers, and other information with the Headers & Footers command on the Edit menu. When you create running heads, you can use any of the special characters you use with spreadsheets: &P for the page number, &F for the filename, &D or &N for the date in short or long format, &T for the current time, && for an ampersand, and &L, &C, and &R to left-align, center, or right-align any text that follows.

To set up your margins, you use the Page Setup & Margins command from the File menu. As usual, this command displays a dialog box in which you can set top, bottom, left, and right margins as well as header and footer margins, paper size, and starting page number. Unlike the spreadsheet and word processor, however, the charting module includes three additional options in a Size box:

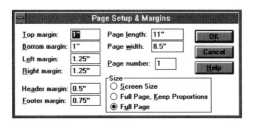

Normally, Works sets up a chart so that it prints on a full page. If you turn on the Screen Size option here, Works reduces the chart to the size one screen would occupy — roughly one-quarter of a page. This is a useful option when you're printing small or uncomplicated charts, but if you use it, be sure to check all text and labels before printing to verify that they will be reproduced completely and without appearing too cramped. If some text disappears or labels overlap, you can try changing to a smaller font size. If that doesn't work, you can export the file to a word processor document, as described in Part III, and scale the chart there.

The two remaining options in the Size box tell Works whether to print the chart within the margins, keeping the original proportions — the ratio of height to width — or expand the chart to fill the page. Keep the original proportions if what the chart "says" is more important than the way it looks, that is, if relative heights of bars or relative placement of lines is critical to the chart's impact. Specify a full page if the overall appearance of the chart is more important than exact ratios of height to width, and you don't mind the chart being shortened or widened to accommodate the page size.

NOTE: *Neither of these size options produces a chart that looks exactly like the one you see onscreen. Charts tend to to be taller and narrower when printed. To match the screen as closely as possible, print in landscape mode if you can, and print the chart as a full page.*

Printing a chart is, as usual, a simple matter of choosing the Print command and specifying the number of copies you want. If you switch between portrait and landscape mode for printing, however, Works might tell you that the printer setup description needs to be modified, even if you've switched the page length and width measurements in the Page Setup & Margins dialog box. If you have to modify your printer setup, check the dialog box that appears for options that let you toggle between portrait and landscape mode. Be sure to reset the printer when you're finished, to avoid surprises when you try to print your next "normal" document.

REFERENCE TO CHARTING COMMANDS

The following table presents a tabular reference to the charting menus and commands.

The File Menu — for manipulating entire files

Create New File	Opens a new document.
Open Existing File	Opens a previously named and saved file.
Close	Closes an open chart and displays either the prior chart (if any) or returns you to the spreadsheet.
Save	Saves an open chart, or more specifically, saves the spreadsheet and adds chart information to it, rather than saving the chart as a separate file.
Save As	Saves an open chart under a new name. Again, saves the spreadsheet with chart information, giving the spreadsheet the name specified.
Save Workspace	Saves the names and positions of open documents so you can restart with the same files.
Print Preview	Displays a chart as it will be printed; shows color charts in black-and-white if the printer is a noncolor printer.
Print	Prints a chart.
Page Setup & Margins	Specifies margin sizes, header and footer margins, page size, starting page number, and chart size (screen size, full page with same proportions, or full page).
Printer Setup	Sets up the printer for use with Works.
Exit Works	Quits Works; prompts if unsaved changes exist.

(continued)

continued

The Edit Menu — for adding to and enhancing charts

Copy	Copies the current chart to the Windows Clipboard; useful when you want to paste a chart into the word processor or another application.
Paste Series	Pastes cell references of a range copied from the spreadsheet to the Clipboard; an easy way to insert or edit a category or value series.
Series	Allows editing, replacement, or deletion of value and category series in a chart; pastes copied cell references into series boxes.
Titles	Adds titles to a chart and to the horizontal and vertical axes.
Legend	Creates a legend identifying colors, patterns, or markers used for value series in a chart.
Data Labels	Adds labels to data values.
Go To	Goes to the specified cells in the "parent" spreadsheet.
Headers & Footers	Adds and modifies running heads.

The Gallery Menu — for selecting chart type

Menu equivalents for the chart buttons on the Toolbar; create Bar, Line, Pie, Stacked Line, X-Y (Scatter), and Combination charts.

The Format Menu — for changing the appearance of a chart

Horizontal (X) Axis	On a bar, or line chart, displays vertical gridlines and sets the frequency at which category labels are displayed — for example, setting the interval to 2 would label every other category (1990, 1992, 1994, and so on, instead of 1990, 1991, 1992). Changing the frequency of labeling can open up the X axis and prevent labels from overlapping. On a scatter chart, sets the scale, minimum and maximum values, and interval of measurements and displays vertical gridlines.
Vertical (Y) Axis	Sets the scale, type of axis (normal, stacked, 100%, or hi-lo), minimum and maximum values, and interval for the left vertical axis; also turns horizontal gridlines on and off.
Right Vertical Axis	Sets same options as the Vertical (Y) Axis command, but for the right vertical axis. Available only if a second axis has been created in a combination chart or by using the Two Vertical (Y) Axes command.
Two Vertical (Y) Axes	Creates and scales a second (right) vertical axis.
Mixed Line & Bar	Sets up a chart so that value series can be displayed as lines and bars; similar to a combination chart, except this command allows you to specify the display format for each series.

(continued)

continued

Patterns & Colors	Sets colors, patterns (for black-and-white), and markers for different charts; explodes specified slices other than the first in a pie chart.
Title Font	Sets the font and font size for the main chart title.
Other Font	Sets the font and font size for all other characters in a chart.
Show Border	Draws a printable border around a chart.
Show Legend	Turns the display of chart legends on and off, both onscreen and in print.

The Options Menu — for customizing the charting module

Works Settings	Sets Works to your preferences.
Show Toolbar	Turns the Toolbar on and off.
Display As Printed	Displays a color chart as it will be printed in black-and-white.

The Charts Menu — for managing charts

Create New Chart	Creates a chart from whatever cells are currently selected in the spreadsheet.
Name	Names a chart. Names can be up to 15 characters long. Click the Rename button to replace the default (such as Chart 1) with the new name. Click OK when naming of one or more charts is complete.
Delete	Deletes a chart. Click the Delete button to delete the chart highlighted in the command's dialog box. Click OK when finished.
Duplicate	Duplicates a chart. In the command's dialog box, choose the chart to duplicate, assign a name, and click the Duplicate button. Click OK when finished.

The Window Menu — for managing the chart window

Menu options cascade windows, tile windows, and arrange minimized windows as icons at the bottom of the screen. Chart windows cannot be split, so that option is grayed out.

The Help Menu — for learning about charting

Menu options provide a charting overview, index, and help, as well as access to the Works tutorial.

9

The Database

The Address Books WorksWizard you used in Chapter 3 created a database of names and addresses. This chapter and Chapter 10 describe ways to use the Works database module to create and manage other types of information, such as inventories, price lists, and catalogs. After you're familiar with this application, you'll probably find many ways to use it. (You can even use it for "word-processed" documents, such as bibliographies and indexes.) After all, data is data; what you can do with data depends on how you view it and choose to manage it.

Database programs require more structure than most other types of applications because they provide what amounts to impromptu access to any fact in a collection of information. Like a librarian who must be able to pinpoint any single book or set of books in a collection of unrelated volumes, a database program must be able to find the one record you seek in an entire collection of related, but independent, entries. Neither the librarian nor the database program can anticipate what you'll request, so both must rely on a consistent structure — a form — to make searching both quick and effective.

Using the database program is a two-step process. First, you design a form for your data and enter the information you want it to hold. Later, you use the program to search, sort, and report on the data you've compiled.

FORMS, RECORDS, AND FIELDS

For its structural underpinnings, the Works database relies on *forms, records*, and *fields*. A form is the onscreen representation of a paper data-entry form, for example, an inventory form for a car lot. A record is one completed form — one set of information about a particular entry in the database — for example, the make, model, year, license number, and price of a particular Toyota Celica. A field is one item of information within a record, such as the price of the Celica.

In this chapter, you'll create two databases, one a simple record of imaginary stock prices and the second a more detailed inventory form that you will experiment with to see how Works operates.

Start Works, if necessary, and click the Database button in the Startup dialog box to create a new database document. Maximize the application and document windows.

When you start the database, Works presents this display:

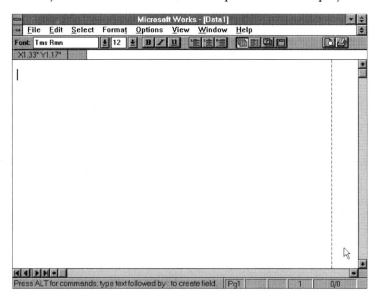

This window shows the Works database in the mode called *form view*.

Database Views

The database is as simple to use as any of the other Works applications, but if you don't quite know what's happening, the program can be somewhat confusing because the database displays and lets you work with data in different *views*.

Using views is comparable to using a set of lenses on a camera. You can point the camera at something, such as a tree, but what you see through the viewfinder changes with the lens you use. One view of the tree can show its entire structure, another can show the leaves in great detail, and yet another can filter the light so you see one particular aspect of the tree, such as different colors corresponding to warm and cool areas. It's the same with the database: Each view shows your data from a different aspect.

Altogether, the Works database operates in three views, plus a reporting mode that — to carry the camera analogy to an extreme — corresponds to developing a picture. The three main views, briefly introduced in Chapter 2, are

- Form view, in which you enter, view, and modify database records one at a time. You generally use form view for creating the form into which you'll enter database records. Because you work with records one at a time, this view is comparable to the close-up lens on your camera.

■ List view, in which you enter, view, and modify database records on a spreadsheet-like grid that shows many entries at the same time. You generally use list view for scanning and editing a database, or for viewing selected records in it. Because list view shows many records at a time, it is comparable to the wide-angle lens on your camera.

■ Query view looks like form view, but you use it for formulating criteria that tell Works which specific records you want to see. Query view doesn't come into play until you've created a form and entered your data. Because you can use it to display selected entries, query view is comparable to a special lens or filter for your camera.

FORM VIEW AND LIST VIEW

When you start the database application with a new "document," Works begins in *form view,* because it assumes you want to create a form to hold the entries in a new database.

In actuality, you can create a form — and a database — in either form view or list view. Of the two, form view is easier to work with when you're creating a complex form or one in which alignment, explanatory text, and other details are important. List view, however, lets you create a simple form or put together a "quick and dirty" outline that you can later modify in form view.

As you work with the database and your own data, you'll develop your own methods of working. In general, however, you can assume that form view is particularly useful when you want to

■ Cut, copy, delete, or insert whole records

■ View or rearrange the form

■ Insert, delete, or modify fields

List view, on the other hand, is valuable when you want to

■ View or select multiple records at the same time

■ Select a field and all the entries in it

■ Copy, clear, or fill fields in multiple entries at the same time

Although form view is the default starting point in Works, you'll start working in list view to see how to create a simple database. After that, you'll switch to form view to develop a feel for modifying and enhancing a database form. Before you get started, however, take a look at the window you'll be working in.

The Database Window

Most of the database window should look familiar, even if you've never worked with a database before. The document window within the database window currently contains a blank "form." Above the window are a Toolbar and a formula bar. The database-specific buttons in the Toolbar are labeled in the following illustration:

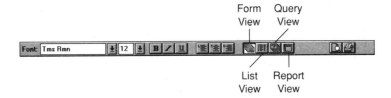

The formula bar is similar to the one you see in the spreadsheet, but instead of a cell reference at the left edge, Works displays the current location of the insertion point along X and Y axes that begin at the top left corner of the page. In form view, you can control the placement of database fields with considerable precision. The location of the insertion point can help you move or insert fields with an accuracy of up to 0.01 inch. Working with the default settings of 1.00 inch for the top margin and 1.25 inches for the left margin, the insertion point in form view starts out slightly below (1.17 inches) and to the right (1.33 inches) of the top and left margins.

The "perforated" line running down the right edge of the screen marks the right margin of the page in form view. If your form extends beyond the margin, Works might not be able to print it all, so this line is useful in helping you see how an evolving form fits the paper size you'll use for printing. To move the margin line left or right, use the Page Setup & Margins command on the File menu.

At the bottom of the window, Works displays a horizontal scroll bar with several buttons that don't appear in other applications or in other database views. Because you work with one record at a time in form view, these buttons help you page through records. The buttons are labeled in the illustration at the top of the next page:

First record
Next record
Previous record
Last record

While you're looking at the database window, notice the status bar at the bottom of the screen. You'll find this bar particularly useful in form view because the two compartments at the far right show the number of the record you're viewing, the number of records that match criteria you've applied (described later), and the total number of records in the database:

Record number
Records shown
Records in database

CREATING A FORM

In form view, you can design a form in any way you want, even matching the layout of a preprinted form. Although Works lets you rearrange fields, add new ones, and delete unneeded ones with little effort, you should plan your form ahead of time. Deleting fields after you've entered data deletes the data in those fields. This can mean extra work recovering or redistributing information in each existing record.

The fields you create will eventually be your means of searching for and sorting your data, so you want to create as many fields as you need, but not so many that searching your database becomes a chore. For example, you can create a single field for area code, exchange, and telephone number, or you can create separate fields for each. If you create a single field, you'll only be able to search for, or sort, entire phone numbers, such as 206-555-1000. If you create separate fields for each, you will be able to search your database by area code, exchange, or phone number. But think about how often you'll want to find exchanges only. In the end, a compromise would probably be the best choice: area code in one field, exchange and number in a second.

Creating a Form in List View

To start off in a familiar environment, create your first database in list view. You'll see how it relates to forms in a minute or two:

☐ Click the List View button on the Toolbar.

List view, in many respects, resembles the spreadsheet. You have labels with row numbers down the left side and a (currently blank) set of column labels across the top. To create a field in a new document in list view, you select a "cell" and use the Field Name command on the Edit menu:

☐ With the selection in the first cell in row 1, choose the Field Name command from the Edit menu. Works displays a dialog box like this:

☐ To create the first field, type *Stock* and click OK.

Notice that the field name appears at the head of the column, even though you selected a cell within the column. When you create or rename fields in list view, the field names always appear as column labels.

☐ To create the next field, select a cell in the second column, and choose the Field Name command again. Name this field *Day 1*.

☐ Repeat the process to create fields named *Day 2* through *Day 5*.

☐ Now add the data shown in the following illustration:

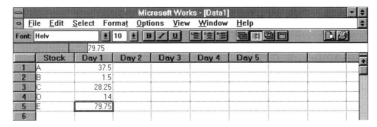

You can now use a familiar command, Fill Series on the Edit menu, to fill in the remaining stock prices for days *2* through *5:*

☐ For stock A, select the fields Day 1 through Day 5, and choose the Fill Series command from the Edit menu. Change the interval in the Step by box from 1 to 1.25 and click OK.

☐ Do the same for stocks B through E, varying the intervals by using *–.25* for B, *–.75* for C, *1.5* for D (good performer), and *.5* for E.

Now your database should look like this:

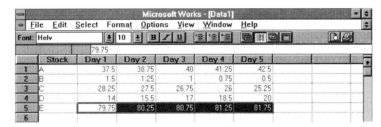

You've completed two steps: creating a form (though you might not have thought so) and filling it in.

Now it's time to see what you've got in form view:

☐ Click the Form View button on the Toolbar.

Works responds with this display:

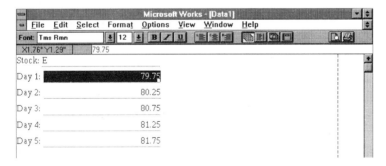

When you're in form view, notice that you see one complete record at a time. To see other records, use the scroll buttons at the left of the horizontal scroll bar.

Back Again to Form View

Most of the functions in list view carry over into form view, and vice versa — but not all of them. As you can see, you can create fields in list view and see them in form view, and you can enter data in list view and see it in form view. You can also format fields for currency or some other format and see the same in either view. You can't, however, assume that the same field width will carry over into both views, nor, as you'll see, can you specify a particular font and size for one and assume the same for the other.

Notice the default font and font size (Tms Rmn 12 in the preceding illustration) and the field width (20 characters) Works uses in form view. If you contrast this with list view by clicking the List View button, you'll see that the defaults change. In this case, the font and size changed to Helv 10 and the column (field) width changed to 10 characters.

This disparity between list view and form view might strike you as odd or unsettling, but it isn't really — at least not any more odd than discovering that one camera lens can take a picture of a tree and another can take a picture of a whole forest. The following rules generally hold true:

- Additions, deletions, and changes that affect the information or structure of the database carry over from one view to the next.

- Characteristics that are not integral to the form or data differ from view to view.

You're finished with the stock database for the time being, so save it under the name STOCK, close the file, and open a new database document.

Working in Form View

Now that you've seen how easily you can create a form and a database in list view, it's time to go where the "action" is — form view. This is where you can visualize, organize, and modify a form to your heart's content.

Creating a Form

You can create a field anywhere in the form view window simply by pointing to the location you want and clicking the mouse button. The sensitivity of Works is remarkable; you can move the insertion point with an accuracy of a hundredth of an inch. This type of mobility is valuable in some situations, but when you want to line up fields either horizontally or vertically, you'll want more control. Works provides an invisible grid like the one you used in Draw. With the grid turned on, Works "snaps" your fields to the gridlines, creating even spacing above and below, and identical alignment from side to side.

Before you begin the second database example, an inventory form for tracking used cars, check that the grid is turned on:

□ Open the Options menu, and verify that a checkmark appears next to Snap To Grid.

To create a field in form view, you type a field name and end the name with a colon (:). The same way the equal sign at the beginning of a formula tells Works you're entering a formula, the colon at the end of a field — in this view — sends a signal to Works indicating that the text is a field name. A field name in the database can be up to 15 characters long. You can include up to 256 fields in a single form. You won't create anything quite so elaborate here, however:

□ Leave the insertion point where it is, in the top left corner of the document window, and type *Make:* (including the colon). Notice that the formula bar shows the field name, exactly as the spreadsheet's formula bar displays cell entries.

□ Press Enter, or click the Enter button. Works displays a dialog box requesting the size of the field:

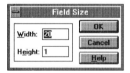

In form view, by default, Works proposes 1-line, 20-character fields. You can specify a different height (for multiple-line fields) and width in this dialog box, but for now, accept the proposed field size:

□ Click OK. A dotted line appears next to the field name, and the insertion point jumps down to the next line.

□ Type in the fields *Model:*, *Year:*, *License:*, and *Price:*, one below the other. Accept the default width for each.

When you finish, your form should look like this:

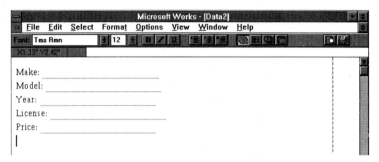

Before you move on, note how the mouse pointer changes when you're working in form view:

☐ Press Shift-Tab to move the highlight to the Price field.

☐ Move the mouse pointer into the highlight. As you do, the mouse pointer changes to a small hand. When the mouse pointer is shaped like a hand, you can use the mouse to drag a field to another location when you're reorganizing a form. (Don't do it right now.)

☐ Next move the mouse pointer to the small, light box in the lower right corner of the highlight. The mouse pointer changes to a slanting double-headed arrow because it is on a size box like the ones you use in Draw. You can use the size box to change field widths quickly.

> **TIP** Until you're accustomed to them, the highly sensitive mouse actions can cause you to inadvertently move fields as you click on them. If alignment is important in your form, and you don't want to take a chance on moving fields even slightly, use the Tab key to move forward in the form from field to field, and Shift-Tab to move backward.

Formatting a Form

When you create a form, you can specify a particular font and font size. Font formatting in the database works as it does in the charting module: A single font and font size affects the entire form and all the records in it. You cannot specify different fonts or sizes for individual fields, but you can specify a different font when you switch to list view. For this form,

□ Use the Toolbar to choose a font and font size, such as Helv 10.

You can format individual fields in a form with commands from the Format menu, so format the Price field for currency and two decimals:

□ Choose Currency from the Format menu, and click OK to accept two decimal places.

 If you create a field for numeric values that begin with zero, such as inventory or serial numbers, be sure to format the field for leading zeros. If you don't, Works will eliminate the zeros and display only the nonzero digits.

ENTERING AND EDITING DATA

Now it's time to enter some data. To do this in form view, you move the highlight to the dotted line next to the field name you want and simply fill out the form for each record you want to create. To move to the first field, either click on the dotted line next to the field name *Make*, or use Shift-Tab to move backward in the form. To create the database,

□ Fill out the form as shown in the following illustration:

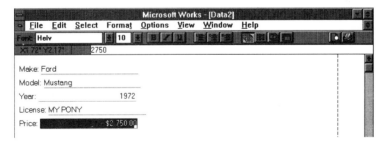

- □ Press Tab to move to the start of a new record.

- □ Create a record for each of the following entries. Press Enter when you finish the last record.

Porsche	914	1975	KATES	$4,500.00
BMW	2002	1974	BCY 608	$2,350.00
Honda	Civic	1989	932 ABC	$6,800.00
Lincoln	Mark V	1978	DEC 184	$5,000.00
Lincoln	Continental	1990	038 MAR	$17,500.00
Lincoln	Continental	1986	814 AUG	$9,000.00
Lincoln	Town Car	1988	500 DOS	$17,500.00
Lincoln	Mark VII	1990	KAY 124	$18,000.00
Toyota	Celica	1988	NINJA	$7,500.00

Changing Field Widths

As you typed you probably noticed that Works left-aligns text and right-aligns numbers the same way it does in the spreadsheet. Most of the fields in your sample now contain left-aligned numbers in some records and right-aligned text in others. Change the field widths so the entries have less room to sprawl. There are two ways to do this:

- □ Move the highlight to the dotted line in the Model field.

- □ Choose Field Size from the Format menu. When Works displays the Field Size dialog box, type *8* for the width, and click OK.

Now try a faster, but less precise method:

- □ Move the highlight to the dotted line after the Year field.

- □ Point to the size box in the lower right-hand corner of the highlight, as shown in the following illustration:

You can drag the box left or right to resize the width of a field, and you can drag it up or down to change the number of lines in a field. Here, change the width:

☐ Drag the box to the left until it's slightly wider than the four digits needed for the year. If your hand slips and drags the corner downward, slide the mouse pointer up again to keep this a one-line field.

☐ Move the highlight to the License field. Use the size box again to narrow the field to seven characters. (If you want to double-check, choose the Field Width command from the Format menu and check the width displayed in the dialog box.)

☐ Do the same to narrow the Price field to eight characters.

Your form should look a little neater now. For consistency, also narrow the Make field, to about half its current width.

Switching to List View

When you're working in form view, you can use the buttons on the horizontal scroll bar to move back and forth among records. This could get tiring, however, because Works can accept as many as 32,000 records in a single database. An easier way to view multiple records is to switch to list view:

☐ Click the List View button on the Toolbar.

Now your database looks like this:

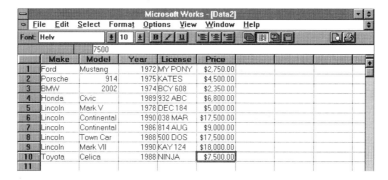

Much easier. Notice again, however, that the Field widths in list view don't match the field widths in form view. The Year field, for example, is ten characters (the default) in list view, even though you narrowed it to four characters in form view.

You can change the field (column) width in list view whenever you want by using the Field Width command on the Format menu or by dragging the column boundary left or right as you did in the spreadsheet. If you widen or narrow columns in list view for printing, Works will use the widths you specified for the view from which you print. A database in any view remains the same database, but Works is flexible enough to let you mold the fields to match the type of view you want to see and print. Remember, too, that Works can display and print a database in one font and size in form view, and a different font and size in list view. To see this,

▫ Choose a different font, font size, or both for list view. For example, if you chose Helv 10 in form view, choose something considerably different, such as Script 16, if it's available.

▫ Click the Print Preview button on the Toolbar. Zoom in once or twice to see what Works will print in this view.

If your printer works with a variety of fonts, you should see something like this:

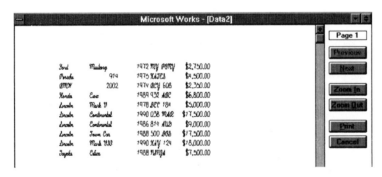

▫ Cancel preview mode, and change back to the previous font and size.

▫ Now click the Form View button.

▫ Click the Print Preview button again to see how one record in the same database would print from form view.

Now your Preview screen should look like this:

Even if you never opt for such drastic alterations between form view and list view, it's nice to know you can do it. It's even better to know that switching from one view to another doesn't change your database or its contents.

Splitting the Screen

Your sample database isn't long enough to require more than one screen to display it all, but the database, like the spreadsheet, lets you split the screen and scroll independently in two or four "panes" to view different parts of a large database. For practice,

□ Switch back to list view.

□ Drag the split box at the top of the vertical scroll bar, and release the mouse button when the bar is about two-thirds of the way down the screen.

□ Drag the split box at the left edge of the horizontal scroll bar, and release the mouse button when the bar is about halfway across the screen.

□ Clicking in one pane and then another, scroll through your database to see different parts of the same "document." As you do, notice that the top and bottom panes on each side show the same fields, but can show different records; the left and right panes can show different fields, but the same records. You don't have totally independent scrolling in each pane when you split a window four ways.

□ When you finish viewing the panes, drag the split boxes out of the document window to eliminate the splits, and scroll to the beginning of the database.

EDITING A DATABASE

Databases are rarely static. Even one as simple as an address book grows, shrinks, and is modified as you add new names, cross out old ones, and pencil in new addresses. The databases on your computer won't be any different, and you'll have to update them periodically, too. It's easy to put off updating your database, but you'll like Works a lot more if you don't end up frantically typing at the last minute or losing track of which databases you last updated, and when.

Editing Data in Fields

Whether you're working in form view or list view, replacing data in a field is simple: Select the data and start typing. When you select a field entry and press a key, Works takes that keystroke as a signal to overtype whatever information is currently in that field. To see how this works,

☐ In either list view or form view, move to the first record and click on the price for the Ford Mustang.

☐ This car isn't selling, so lower the price a bit. Type *2250*, and click the Enter button.

As easily as that, one entry replaces another. If you want to delete and not replace the contents of a field, select the data, and choose the Clear Field Entry command from the Edit menu:

☐ Switch to list view, if necessary, and click on the Year field for the Ford Mustang.

☐ Choose Clear Field Entry from the Edit menu. As soon as you click the mouse, the year number disappears.

☐ You can't undo a Clear command, so restore the year by typing *1972* and clicking the Enter button.

You can also edit field contents in the formula bar, much as you do in the spreadsheet. The usual mouse movements and keystrokes apply in the database:

■ Drag the mouse, or press Shift and an arrow key to highlight one or more characters.

■ Click anywhere in an entry to position the insertion point at that location. With the keyboard, move the insertion point one character at a time with the arrow keys. Move the insertion point to the beginning of the entry by pressing Home, or move it to the end by pressing End.

■ Press Del to delete characters you've highlighted.

When you're making scattered changes to different fields in many records, you'll probably find list view preferable to form view. List view is also better when, as you saw with the STOCK database, you want to use the Fill commands to add the same type of information to a group of records.

Adding New Records

After you've created a database, you can add records in either form view or list view. Your screen should be showing the database in list view right now, so start there. To add a new record at the end of the database,

☐ Click in the Make field of row 11, and type *Ford*.

☐ Using the Tab key to move from field to field, type *Tbird* in the Model field, *1990* in the Year field, *XYZ 123* in the License field, and *17000* in the Price field. Press Enter when you're finished.

To add a record *within* a database, select the row above which you want to add the record. Use the Insert Record/Field command to insert a blank record, and then type the entries:

☐ Click on the 8 to the left of row number 8 to select the entire row, as shown in the following illustration:

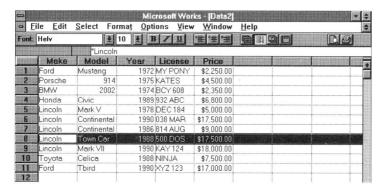

☐ Choose the Insert Record/Field command from the Edit menu. Works inserts a new row above row 8 and renumbers all of the records below the new one.

☐ Add the following data to the new record: *VW* for Make, *bug* for Model, *1973* for Year, *JKL 001* for License, and *400* for Price.

You can create records in form view and display them in list view, and conversely, you can create them in list view and see them, in the same order, in form view:

▫ Click the Form View button, and scroll through the database. The VW record should be number 8, and the Ford Thunderbird should be record number 12.

TIP Works will insert a new record if you select a single field cell instead of an entire row, but because it cannot tell whether you want to insert a record or a field, it will display a dialog box asking which you want. Selecting an entire row or column in the database is much simpler because it bypasses the dialog box.

Adding records in form view is similar to doing so in list view, so you won't go through the motions here. For reference, however, follow these steps when adding a record in form view:

■ Click the Last record button at the left edge of the horizontal scroll bar to move to an empty form at the end of the database. Add whatever records you want, and Works will add them after the existing records.

■ Scroll to the record before which you want to add a new record. Choose Insert Record from the Edit menu, and Works will add a blank form at that location. All succeeding records will be renumbered.

Deleting Records

The process of removing whole records is similar to adding them. To delete a record use one of these methods:

■ In form view, scroll to each record you want to delete, and choose the Delete Record command from the Edit menu.

■ In list view, click on the row number to select the entire record, and then choose Delete Record/Field from the Edit menu.

You should be in form view now. To try deleting a record,

❑ Use the buttons in the horizontal scroll bar to find the record for the BMW.

❑ Choose Delete Record from the Edit menu. The record is gone, and the succeeding records are renumbered so no gap is left behind.

 To select a group of adjacent records for deletion in list view, click on the row number of the first record, hold down the Shift key, point to the row number of the last record, and click. The highlight will extend to cover all of the records. Then choose Delete Record/Field from the Edit menu.

Cutting and Pasting

Deleting is easy, but when you're removing records, remember that there's a big difference between deleting them and cutting them. The Works database does not include an Undo command, so a deletion is irreversible. The only way you can retrieve inadvertently deleted material is by quitting Works and telling it you don't want to save any changes you made to the database. This is a drastic step in some cases, however, because even though you get back the deleted information, you also lose any other changes that you hadn't yet saved on disk.

A better choice, especially if you're experimenting with a new feature or you aren't sure how your work will turn out, is to cut, rather than delete outright. Cutting, as in other Works applications, removes the record from the database, but it also gives the record temporary sanctuary on the Clipboard. If you want to restore a record, you can paste it back in — as long as you haven't replaced it with any other cut or copied material in the meantime. The following examples use cut and paste as a means of reorganizing and deleting records in a database.

NOTE: *Cut and paste are also used for moving information within and among the Works applications and other Windows programs. This chapter is about working with a single document and application. Part III covers ways to move your data from place to place.*

Deleting with Cut and Paste

Suppose the Toyota and the Lincoln Mark V don't belong on this list. To cut a record in form view,

 □ Scroll to the record for the Toyota, and choose Cut Record from the Edit menu.

Now switch to list view and try cutting there:

 □ Click the List View button on the Toolbar.

 □ The Lincoln Mark V should be record number 4, so click on the row number (not on a field) to select the entire record.

 □ Choose Cut from the Edit menu.

The record for the Toyota no longer exists because it's been replaced on the Clipboard by the record for the Lincoln Mark V. You can reinstate the record for the Lincoln, however, and place it anywhere in the database you want:

 □ Click on row number 1, and select Paste from the Edit menu.

The Lincoln is back, though in a different place. Notice that you didn't have to insert a blank record to hold the incoming information. Works makes room in both list view and form view, so you don't have to worry about overwriting an existing record with information you paste in.

Reorganizing Fields in List View

Cutting is a useful alternative to deleting whenever you think you might want to retrieve records you've taken out of a database. Cutting and pasting can also be an effective means of reorganizing fields in list view.

 Remember, however, that you work with separate views when you work with a database: Reorganizing fields in list view does not carry over to the layout in form view, and vice versa. Try cutting and pasting to see what happens:

 □ In list view, click on the field name License to select the entire field.

 □ Choose Cut from the Edit menu. The field, and all its contents, disappear to the Clipboard.

 □ Now click on the blank column to the right of the Price field. You can click anywhere in the column, but for consistency you might want to form the habit of clicking the column head.

□ Choose Paste from the Edit menu; Works immediately fills the selected column with the field and entries you cut.

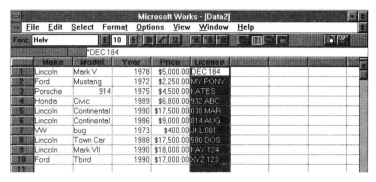

□ Click the Form View button. Notice that the License field remains in its original position in this view.

NOTE: *You've done quite a bit of work by now and should save this file if you haven't already. The following examples will assume the file has been saved under the name CARLOT.WDB.*

Reorganizing Fields in Form View

In the next example, you'll move the Model field to the right and the Make field down, to make room at the top of the form for some descriptive text you'll soon add. You can move a field in form view with the Position Field command on the Edit menu or — faster, but otherwise the same — with the mouse alone:

□ To make alignment easy, verify that Snap to Grid is turned on in the Options menu.

□ Point to any part of the Model field, either the field name or the entry portion, and click the left mouse button.

□ When the hand pointer appears, drag the entire field to the right, to about the center of the page.

□ Point to and click on the Make field. Drag it down. As you move the field, notice that an outline of the field "snaps" into place when you reach the same position on the Y axis that the Model field occupies. If Snap to Grid were not turned on, you could maneuver the outline up, down, and sideways in smaller increments. Here, however, such mobility would be a handicap, so Snap to Grid is preferable.

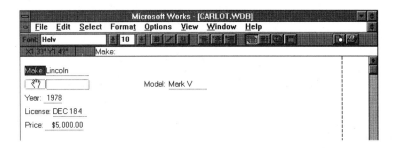

Adding and Deleting Fields

You can add and delete fields in either list view or form view, and the deletion process is basically the same in either view. Be careful when you delete fields, however. When you delete a field, you also delete the data in it, for *every* record in the database.

You can add new fields anywhere in a form — at the end, at the beginning, or between existing fields — and then edit the records to include whatever additional information you want. You can work in either list view or form view, but the best choice depends to some extent on which view you used in creating the form.

Adding Fields to Forms Created in List View

If you created a form in *list* view, you can add fields to the end of the form or insert fields within the form in either list view or form view. Works always displays (and prints) the new fields to the right of previously existing fields in list view and at the bottom of the form in form view.

Adding fields in list view, however, has two slight disadvantages:

- If you're adding a new field between existing fields in list view, you must first insert a blank field, and then assign the field a name with the Field Name command. In form view, you insert and name the field at the same time.

- In list view you can specify the width, but not the height, of a new field. This means you can add only single-line fields in list view. To change them to multiple-line fields, you must use the Field Size command in form view.

Adding Fields to Forms Created in Form View

If you created a form in *form* view, you should probably add new fields in form view for one main reason: Adding new fields in list view causes Works to insert them at the top of the screen in form view, sometimes partially obscuring (though not erasing) existing fields. When you add fields this way, you'll have to move them to new locations anyway, so you might as well start out in form view and simplify matters.

In the following examples, you will add new fields in both list view and form view, so you can see how each works. Start by adding a field in list view:

☐ In list view, click on the Price field name.

☐ Choose Insert Record/Field from the Edit menu. Immediately, a new, blank field appears between Year and Price.

☐ To name the field, choose Field Name from the Edit menu, and type *Color* (no colon) in the dialog box that appears.

☐ Click OK to name the new field.

Now switch to form view to see where the new field appears. Your screen should look something like this:

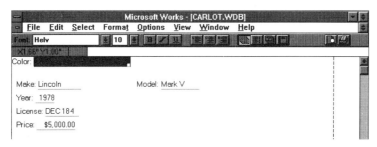

☐ Drag the new field into position, placing it to the right of the Year field.

☐ To make it look better, narrow the Color field to about eight characters.

Reorganizing a Form in Form View

When you add a field in form view, you use the same procedure you used to create the form in the first place: Click on the position you want, type a field name, and set the field size. Where you click to insert the field doesn't really matter, so you don't have to worry about aligning the field perfectly before you create it. You can always nudge the field into position after you've named and sized it.

You created a number of fields in the CARLOT form, so you don't have to step through a detailed example on adding another field. Instead, try modifying your form on your own, working in form view so you can hone your skills where they'll be needed most in your own work:

☐ Move the License field to the right of the Color field, placing it under Model.

☐ Now add the new fields shown in the following illustration:

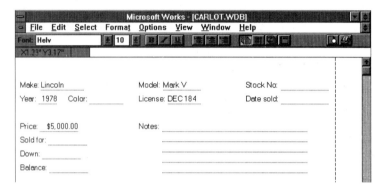

For reference, the following table lists the new fields, their positions, and sizes:

Field to Add	*Position*	*Size*
Stock No:	Top line, near right margin	10 characters
Date sold:	Below Stock No	10 characters
Sold for:	Below Price	8 characters
Down:	Below Sold for	8 characters
Balance:	Below Down	8 characters
Notes:	Below License, and to the right of Price	30 characters by 5 lines

☐ When you've finished adding the new fields, switch to list view. Scroll to see how Works has added all of the new fields to the right of the existing fields.

☐ Finally, try a quick way to format several fields at the same time. In list view, click on the field name Sold for, and drag the highlight until it covers the Balance field.

☐ All three selected fields need formatting for currency values, so do them all at the same time. Choose Currency from the Format menu, and click OK when Works proposes two decimals. It's finished: one command, three formatted fields.

You've made some extensive additions to the form now, so its organization in form view and list view no longer matches. To avoid such mismatches, remember to think your forms through before creating them. Even though you can add, delete, and rearrange your forms, doing it right the first time will save work later.

Adding Numbers and Dates

The database, like the spreadsheet, includes three Fill commands: Fill Right, Fill Down, and Fill Series. These commands are available only in list view, because only there can you make entries to multiple records. The Fill commands work exactly as they do in the spreadsheet, so a quick example should be enough:

☐ In list view, click on the first cell in the Stock No field.

☐ Type *1*, and click the Enter button.

☐ Extend the highlight so that it covers the cells for all records in the database (through row 10).

☐ Choose the Fill Series command from the Edit menu; Click OK.

☐ Now for some fun. With the entries still selected, format the field for leading zeros, and specify the number of digits as 8.

You've now added "instant" stock numbers for the cars, with plenty of room for future additions. When car number 11 arrives, the data-entry person need only type 11 and tab to the next field. Works will take care of all the extra zeros.

Adding Labels and Descriptions

There are only three differences between a label and a field name: a colon, the number of characters you can use, and the fact that a label cannot be displayed in list view. A field name must always end in a colon, and it can be no more than 15 characters long, including spaces. A label or any other type of descriptive text you want to include in a database form must *not* end with a colon, but it can be up to 256 characters long. You enter labels and text into a form exactly as you enter field names. For example,

☐ Return to form view, and click at the top of the screen, about 3 inches along the X axis.

☐ Type *Honest Abe's*, and click the Enter button.

Because you didn't type a colon at the end, Works accepted the text as a label rather than as a field. Now type a longer label:

◻ Click to place the insertion point slightly to the right of the first label, and type *We specialize in Lincolns*. Click the Enter button.

When you create labels, Works lets you apply boldfacing and other character styles to them so they will stand out from the remainder of the form. You cannot change the font or font size, however, unless you want to change the font or font size of the entire form. You have two separate labels here, so apply different character styles to each:

◻ Click on *Honest Abe's* to select it, and then use the Toolbar buttons to boldface and underline the text.

◻ Click on the second label, and use the Toolbar buttons to boldface, italicize, and underline *We specialize in Lincolns*.

That's it. Abe's inventory form now bears the dealership's motto:

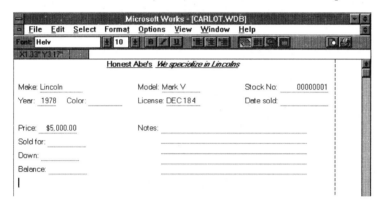

You can use labels for other, more informative text as well. For example, you could add a label to the Notes section of your form reminding the person filling out the form to be sure and include mileage, overall condition, and any repair work done to make the car more salable.

Three commands on the Edit menu help you manage labels:

■ Position Label, which appears instead of Position Field when a label is selected, lets you move the label to a new location.

- Delete Label, which appears instead of Delete Field when a label is selected, deletes a label.

- Duplicate Label, which always appears on the menu, but it is grayed out unless a label is selected, makes a copy of a label and turns the mouse pointer into a hand so that you can move the duplicate anywhere on the form.

Making Calculations

You've seen some ways, such as list view and the Fill commands, in which the database resembles the spreadsheet, at least in operation. These two applications also overlap considerably in their ability to perform calculations. The spreadsheet can take values from various cells, tuck them into a formula, and produce a new value, in a different cell. The database can also use values from one or more fields to calculate the entry that belongs in another field.

You can use formulas to perform any of the following operations:

- "Normal" calculations, such as totals

- Calculations, such as averages, highs, and lows, that are performed by built-in functions

- Proposed responses, such as area codes or city and state names, that you don't want to type for each record.

NOTE: *This chapter doesn't include an example showing a proposed response, but such a formula is simple to create: Highlight the field where the item is to appear and type an equal sign followed by the text you want — for example, =“Chicago (note the double quotation mark for text) in the City field if Chicago appears more often than any other city. Works will fill in the field for you. To enter a different city, highlight the field, and type over the proposed response.*

In your sample form, you created fields for the selling price of a car, the down payment, and the balance owed. The balance requires simple subtraction, but unless you enjoy the practice, there's no need to do it yourself because Works can do it for you:

- ☐ Click on the Balance field.

- ☐ Type an equal sign followed by *Sold for–Down,* and click the Enter button. You should see $0.00 in the Balance field and a formula in the formula bar, as shown in the illustration at the top of the next page.

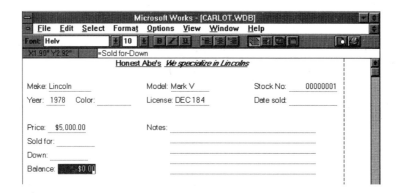

Works inserted a $0.00 in the Balance field because both the Sold for and Down fields in this entry are empty. To verify that your formula works,

☐ Click on the Sold for field, type *4500,* and click the Enter button.

☐ Click on the Down field, type *1200,* and click the Enter button.

Now Works has some figures to work with, so it displays $3,300.00 in the Balance field.

Creating formulas in the database is quite similar to creating them in the spreadsheet. However, you must type database field names to enter them into a formula, whereas you can point to cells to include their references in a spreadsheet formula.

The following example returns to your simple STOCK database form to show some ways to incorporate functions in fields:

☐ Save or close the CARLOT database, and open the STOCK database.

☐ Create the fields shown in the following illustration:

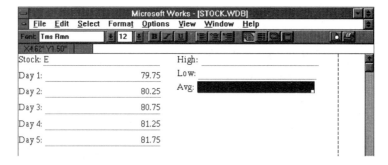

Now you can use three Works functions, MAX, MIN, and AVG, to fill in the new fields. MAX finds and displays the highest value in a set of cells or fields you specify; MIN finds and displays the lowest value; and AVG calculates the average value. For each of these functions, you'll specify the fields Day 1 through Day 5 as the values for Works to examine:

☐ In the High field, type =*max(day 1, day 2, day 3, day 4, day 5)*. Type the field names, including spaces, as they appear in the form. If you don't, Works will display the message *Reference not valid or wrong operand type*. Click the Enter button when you're done typing. Notice that Works displays the highest stock price in this field.

☐ In the Low field, type =*min(day 1, day 2, day 3, day 4, day 5)*, and click the Enter button. Now Works displays the lowest stock price.

☐ In the Avg field, type =*avg(day 1, day 2, day 3, day 4, day 5)*, and click the Enter button. This time Works calculates the average value for the five days and displays the result.

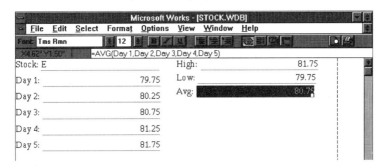

Even though you entered the functions for only one stock, Works applies them to the same fields in all records:

☐ Click the List View button, or scroll through form view to see the other records in the database. Each record now shows the high, low, and average prices for different stocks.

Protecting Your Database

After you've gone to the trouble of building a form and entering data, you'll want to ensure that your information is protected from damage or inadvertent change. Chapter 7 described how to protect data in a spreadsheet: You turn on the Locked attribute with the Style command on the Format menu and then choose the

Protect Data command from the Options menu. Protection in the database works much the same way, except that you can apply protection to forms as well as data by using these procedures:

- To protect a form, switch to form view, and then choose Protect Form from the Options menu.

- To protect an entire database, choose the Style command from the Format menu, verify that Locked is turned on, and then choose Protect Data from the Options menu. You can protect a database from either form view or list view.

- To protect some fields but not others, verify that Protect Data is turned off. Select, in turn, each field you *don't* want to protect and turn locking off with the Style command. After you've unlocked all appropriate fields, protect the rest by choosing Protect Data from the Options menu.

Hiding Information

While you work, you can also hide fields and records, temporarily removing sensitive or unneeded parts of your database from view. You hide fields in list view the same way you hide them in the spreadsheet: by changing the field width to 0. When you want to redisplay the field, use the Go To command, which displays a dialog box listing the names of all the fields in your form. Click on the field you want to move to, and then use the Field Size command to increase the width of the hidden field.

You can hide records in either list view or form view with the Hide Record command on the Select menu. In list view, select the record or group of records you want to hide, and then choose the command. In form view, scroll to each record and hide it. To redisplay hidden records, choose the Show All Records command from the Select menu.

USING A DATABASE

Organizing and constructing a database can require a fair amount of time and planning, especially if you want to design a complex form or enter hundreds or thousands of records. After the form is designed, however, you don't have to bother with sorting or alphabetizing the records you enter, because that's what Works is for. If your database form duplicates a paper form, the only real limitation on you or your data-entry person is likely to be typing speed. After the records are entered, the database is ready for use whenever you need it, and that's what the next sections are about.

Sorting Records

After you create a database, you want to organize it so that it's easy to reference — alphabetically by last name, numerically by serial number, chronologically by date, and so on. With Works, such sorting is a breeze. As you saw in Chapter 7, Works can sort based on up to three columns (fields), so duplicates grouped by one pass through the database can themselves be neatly arranged in the next pass. Sorting on multiple fields this way produces results comparable to the listings in a telephone book: alphabetic by last name, followed by alphabetic by first name, followed by alphabetic by middle name or initial.

Alphabetic and numeric sorting can go either up or down. An upward, or ascending sort, goes from A to Z and from 0 to 9. A downward, or descending sort, moves in the other direction — from Z to A or from 9 to 0.

Sorting on Multiple Fields

You can sort records in either list view or form view. Of the two, list view gives you a better feel for the results because you can see a number of sorted records at one time. If you sort records in form view, Works displays only the first record in the sorted database until you scroll to see the remaining records.

Your CARLOT database is handy for experimentation, so open the file, if necessary. Display the database in list view. Sort the database alphabetically by Make, using Model as a second sort field to alphabetize cars of the same make, and Year as a third field to sort cars of the same make and model chronologically:

□ Choose the Sort Records command from the Select menu. Works displays this dialog box:

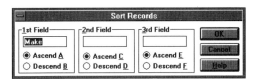

When you perform a sort on multiple fields, you list the most important field first, in this case, the Make field, which Works should propose. If it does not,

□ Type *make* in the 1st Field box. An ascending sort, which Works proposes, is fine, so go on to define the second sort field.

□ Click in the 2nd Field box, and type *model*. Again, an ascending sort is best, so finish up by specifying the third sort field.

□ Click in the 3rd Field box, and type *year*. The ascending sort Works proposes would list the oldest cars first, so refine the sort by clicking the button next to Descend. Now Works will list the cars from newest to oldest.

□ Click OK to carry out the sort. Here's the result:

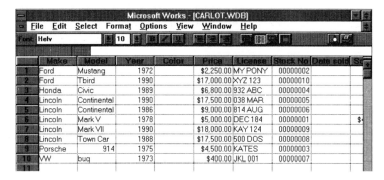

If a field on which you sort contains different types of entries, such as text for some records and numbers for others, Works sorts in the following order:

■ For an ascending sort, the order is text, times (such as 12:00 A.M.), numbers, and then dates (January 1, 1992).

■ For a descending sort, the order is dates, numbers, times, and then text.

When field entries contain mixtures of text and numbers, however, Works places combinations of numbers and text ahead of text and numbers in an ascending sort, and reverses the order in a descending sort. To see this in action, do an ascending sort of the license numbers in the CARLOT example. This produces: 038 MAR, 500 DOS, 814 AUG, 932 ABC, DEC 184, JKL 001, KATES, KAY 124, MY PONY, and XYZ 123.

Refining an Alphabetic Sort

In an alphabetic sort, Works pays no attention to differences in capitalization, so *baby* goes before *Babylon*, but *Mars* precedes *martial*. If you create a database in which capitalization matters — for example, if you want *NEW YEAR* to always precede *New Year* — set up a small field (as small as one character, though two makes it easier to read), and use some type of code, such as 1 for all capitals (NEW YEAR), 2 for initial capitals (New Year), and 3 for lowercase (new year). You can then specify the "capitalization" field as the second sort field to ensure that duplicate entries are arranged in the order you want. The following illustration shows an example of such a database structure:

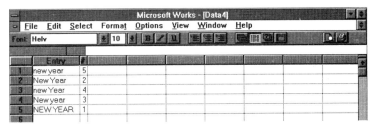

To sort the entries in order, you would specify Entry as the first field (if there were other entries such as Christmas and Easter) and the number sign (#) as the second field:

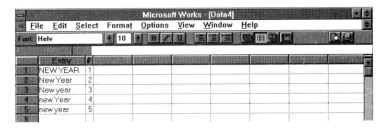

Adding a field such as # won't hurt the appearance of your database because you'll probably use list view to print and display such records. In list view, you can hide fields by dragging their boundaries or setting their widths to 0, the same way you do when you hide columns in a spreadsheet.

SEARCHING FOR INFORMATION

As useful as sorted databases are, you often need more specific information about their contents. You will often find that you need to search a database: to find a particular record or group of records or to find all the records that match one or more criteria.

To find specific records, all you need is some bit of information — some text, a unique value, or a field entry — that Works can use to separate the record or records you seek from those that don't interest you at the moment. To find records that match certain criteria, you switch into query view and provide Works with a "description" of the information you seek.

Finding Related Records

To find one or more records that have some information in common, use the Find command on the Select menu. You can work in either list view or form view. Suppose, for example, you want to find all the records for Lincoln Continentals in the CARLOT database. Starting in list view,

◻ Choose the Find command from the Select menu. Works displays this dialog box:

◻ Type *continental* (uppercase or lowercase).

Notice that the proposed find in the Match box specifies the next record. To see what happens,

◻ Click OK to carry out the command, with the proposed response.

Starting from the current location of the selection, Works scans the database and moves the selection to the next occurrence of the word *continental*. If the current selection is near the end of a database, Works skips to the top and keeps going if it doesn't find a match by the time it reaches the last record.

Notice that when you carry out a Find command and specify only that Works find the next record, the entire database remains available for viewing. Now see what happens with the same command when you specify a different type of match — all records:

◻ Choose the Find command again, but this time click the button next to All records.

◻ Click OK to carry out the command.

This time your screen changes considerably. You told Works to find *continental* in all records, and Works responded by displaying *only* the records in which the text appears. One command, but two entirely different results.

The Find command works the same way in form view, but the result of specifying all records is less noticeable — at first — because you see only a single record at a time in form view:

◻ Click on the Form View button to switch to form view. Works displays the form at the top of the next page.

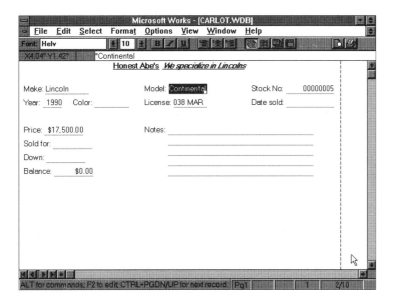

Notice that the status bar indicates that you are looking at record number 1 and that the Find command selected two records from your database of ten records.

☐ Click the forward scroll button in the horizontal scroll bar. Works displays another record for a Lincoln Continental.

☐ Click again, and you see a blank form. Works has reached the end of the Continental records and has no more to display, at least in terms of your last Find command.

☐ To see the entire database once again, choose Show All Records from the Select menu. Scroll through the records in form view, or switch to list view. Both views will display all of the database records.

As you work with a Works database, make a point to remember or jot down what you've been doing with it. This is especially important if you search for specific records, switch to another document, and then return to the database. If you're momentarily disoriented because the database doesn't appear to be complete, check the Status bar. Then try choosing the Find command. Works will continue to redisplay the last text you searched for until you close the file or quit. If that doesn't help, use the Show All Records command in either list view or form view.

Using Wildcards

Chapter 7 introduced the concept of using wildcard characters to find information in one or more spreadsheet cells. You can use the same characters, the asterisk (*) and the question mark (?), in the database to broaden a Find command. The asterisk, you might recall, can stand for any number of other characters, whereas a single question mark can represent any one character. So, for example, specifying *m** in your CARLOT database would cause Works to display all records having a field entry containing an *M* followed by any number of characters. Specifying *198?* in a Find command would cause Works to display all records beginning with 198 and ending in any other character (1988, 1986, 1989).

Wildcard characters can be useful in helping you find "generic" information, but remember that Works does not distinguish between whole words and parts of words. Use wildcard characters in the database in the same way you would use them in the spreadsheet: Be sure to include enough specific text to narrow the selection to what you really want to find. For example, if you were to type *c** to tell Works to find all Continentals in the CARLOT database, you'd be in for a surprise. The specification is broad enough that Works would also include every entry in which the letter *C* is followed by one or more characters: Town Car, the Civic, the Porsche, and even the Lincoln Mark VII.

Queries and Query View

When you want Works to apply some "judgment" to a database search, you turn to *query view*. In appearance, query view is identical to a blank database form. In purpose, however, it is far different. Query view is where you can really give Works and your own database skills a good workout. (Marginal pun intended.) This is where you can define exactly the information you're looking for. In the process, you can incorporate mathematics, logic, relational operators, such as greater than and less than, and even logical operators, such as AND, OR, and NOT.

About Queries in General

The ability to query a database is subject for an entire book in its own right because this is the single area in which you exert the most control over computer software. Computers are information machines, storehouses for knowledge. By extension, database programs are your keys to manipulating information.

More than any of the other Works applications, databases and query view are yours to personalize.

Fashioning a Query

When you use the Find command, you tell Works to search for records that contain certain information. After it finds that information, you have a group of records that are related in some way. When you use query view, you take the search process one step further: Instead of visually scanning the results of a Find command for those records that match certain qualifications, you tell Works to do it all.

You can, for example, use the Find command on a personal database to give you the names of all relatives named Hubbard. With query view, you can tell Works to narrow the field by showing you any and all relatives named Hubbard who had six or more children and are now over the age of 90.

As usual, you can use the CARLOT database to develop a feel for using query view:

□ Click the Query View button to the right of the List View button on the Toolbar. Works displays a familiar sight:

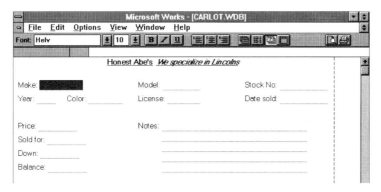

Notice that the right-hand compartment in the status bar shows *QUERY* to indicate that you are in query view. Now instead of using the form you created to enter information, you use the fields to specify records you want to see. For example, suppose you want to see the records for all Lincolns, regardless of model:

□ Verify that the highlight is in the Make field, type *lincoln* (again, uppercase or lowercase doesn't matter), and click the Enter button.

Nothing much happens, so

□ Click the List View button. Works displays the following:

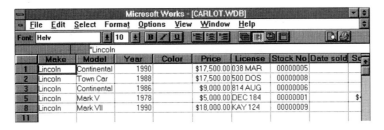

That's easy enough, but it's only the start — even with a database as small as this one. Besides, using query view so far isn't much different from sorting the database on a single field (Make). But this is where the fun starts. Try telling Works you want to see all Lincolns that cost more than $9,000.00:

□ Return to query view, click in the Price field, and then type *>9000*.

□ Click the Enter button in the formula bar, and click the List View button again.

Now all you see are the records for Lincolns that cost more than $9,000.00. Want to see more? How about all cars built from 1975 to the present that cost less than $6,000.00:

□ Return to query view, click in the Make field, and press Del to erase the entry.

□ Click in the Year field and type >=1975. The entire entry won't show, but don't worry about it.

□ Click in the Price field and type *<6000*.

□ Click the Enter button, and then click the List View button again.

Now you have a list you could give to a customer looking for a relatively recent but inexpensive car:

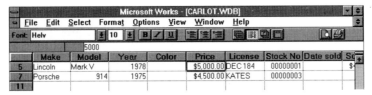

Viewing Other Records

Each time you've queried the database, Works has displayed only the records you wanted to see. Where did the others go, and what if you want to see them?

Whenever you use the Find command or execute a query, Works hides all the records that don't match the text or criteria you specified. To see those records instead of the ones you requested, choose Switch Hidden Records from the Select menu. This command causes Works to swap the two sets of records, hiding the ones you asked to see and displaying the others. You can switch back and forth as many times as you want. Each time, Works will replace the records currently on display with the alternate, hidden set:

- ☐ From list view, choose Switch Hidden Records from the Select menu. Works displays all records other than the post-1975, under $6,000.00 cars you requested in the last example:

	Make	Model	Year	Color	Price	License	Stock No	Date sold	Sc
1	Lincoln	Continental	1990		$17,500.00	038 MAR	00000005		
2	Lincoln	Town Car	1988		$17,500.00	500 DOS	00000008		
3	Lincoln	Continental	1986		$9,000.00	814 AUG	00000006		
4	Honda	Civic	1989		$6,800.00	932 ABC	00000004		
6	VW	bug	1973		$400.00	JKL 001	00000007		
8	Lincoln	Mark VII	1990		$18,000.00	KAY 124	00000009		
9	Ford	Mustang	1972		$2,250.00	MY PONY	00000002		
10	Ford	Tbird	1990		$17,000.00	XYZ 123	00000010		
11									

Microsoft Works - [CARLOT.WDB] — File Edit Select Format Options View Window Help — Font: Helv 10 — 17500

- ☐ Choose Switch Hidden Records again, and the set you requested comes back into view.

- ☐ To see the entire database, choose Show All Records from the Select menu.

When you work with queries, Works doesn't allow you to display both hidden and non-hidden records simultaneously, but if you want to compare two sets of records in a database, there is a way to do so. Apply your query and save the file twice — once under its real name and again under a temporary name, such as TEMP.WDB. Open both files and tile the two document windows. If the records you want to see aren't displayed, switch into query view and reapply the query to each document. Switch into list view, and use the Switch Hidden Records command to display one set of records in one document window, the other set in the second window. To discard the duplicate when you no longer need it, close the extra copy of the database without saving. When you return to Windows or the DOS prompt, delete the duplicate file to keep your hard disk uncluttered.

Applying Judgment to Queries

The queries you've used so far are the type you'll most likely need on a day-to-day basis for selecting records, but that's not the only way to run this dog and pony show. When you fill in more than one field in query view, you're entering an implied AND as part of your query, as in "Show the records for all cars built after 1975 *and* priced under $6,000.00."

Works understands more than AND, however. As described in Chapter 7, Works also responds to OR, as well as NOT, and even NOT EQUAL. To symbolize these words in a query, you use the following operators:

- The ampersand (&) for AND, as in "Find the records that match both A *and* B."

- The pipe (¦) for OR, as in "Find the records that match A *or* B."

- The tilde (~) for NOT, as in "Find the records that do *not* match A."

- The less than and greater than signs (< >) for NOT EQUAL, as in "Find the records that are *not equal* to A."

With these operators, you can go even further in your quest for truth by including more than a single criterion in a query field. For example, suppose you want to see all Lincolns that were built before 1985 or cost less than $10,000.00. You can construct the query in either of two ways.

The first method is easy to use because it helps you construct a "plain English" query that matches your form and, probably, the way you perceive your data:

- ☐ Switch to query view, and type *lincoln* in the Make field.

- ☐ Click on the Year field, and type *<1985¦ price <1000.*

- ☐ Click on the Price field, press Del, and click the Enter button to erase the old query.

- ☐ Click the List View button, and you see two entries that match your criteria: a 1986 Continental priced at $9,000.00 and a 1978 Mark V.

- ☐ Choose Switch Hidden Records from the Select menu, and you'll see that the Lincolns not chosen are all too new and too expensive to match the criteria.

In this example, you told Works first to find all the Lincolns, and second, to display the ones that were either built before 1985 or cost less than $10,000.00.

The result would have been the same if you had typed the second condition in the Price field instead, as *<10000 | year <1985*. The real point, however, is that you broke your query into parts that parallel the way you think.

The second approach to constructing the same query might be less intuitive at first, but it can provide you with a foundation for understanding what Works is doing. In this approach, you essentially formulate the query in Works language rather than your own. To try it,

☐ Click Show All Records and switch to query view.

☐ Click on the Year field, press Del, and click the Enter button to clear the field.

☐ Click in the Make field, and type

```
=make ="lincoln"&(year<1985|price<10000)
```

☐ Check your typing and verify that you've enclosed *lincoln* in double quotation marks. (Works insists on this.) Click the Enter button.

☐ Switch to list view, and you'll see the same results you did before.

In this example, you "wrote" your query in such a way that Works could "read" it. Notice that you started the query with an equal sign to indicate you were entering characters you wanted Works to evaluate. Your first instruction was *make ="lincoln"*. In constructing a query in this form, you must specify the fields you want to search and enclose any text in double quotation marks.

You also used parentheses. They function much as they do in the spreadsheet, by grouping conditions (year *or* price in this example) to guarantee that Works will treat the conditions as a unit. If you hadn't used parentheses, Works would interpret the query as "Search for records in which either the make is Lincoln, *and* the year is before 1985, *or* the price is less than $10,000.00." The resulting display would include not only the 1986 Continental and the 1978 Mark V, but the Honda, VW, Porsche, and Mustang, all of which are under $10,000.00.

Different Types of Queries

Databases are as varied as the people who use them. Scientists, teachers, accountants, consultants, engineers, students, businesspeople, charity workers, and clerics all use databases in one form or another, on paper or on computer. Because databases and the types of information they hold can be so varied, the hands-on examples showing how to query them stop here. To help you get started on your own queries, the following paragraphs describe the various ways you can tell Works to search a database.

Greater than (>) and less than (<). Use these operators to find records in which a certain value is greater or less than a value you specify. Although previous examples showed how to use these operators with numeric values, you can also use them with text, as long as you remember to enclose the text in double quotation marks. In a listing of dogs, for example,

- Specify *>24* to find all breeds taller than 24 inches.

- Specify *>"samoyed"* to list all breeds that come after samoyed in the alphabet.

Combined > and < . Use these operators in combination to find records within a specified range. Again, you can use them with either numbers or text, enclosing the text in double quotation marks. Because you are specifying more than one criterion, you must include the AND operator (&) to show you want items that are greater than X and also less than Y. For example,

- Specify *>10 & <100* to find all records containing a value from 11 through 99.

- With text, specify *>"cocker" & <"doberman"* to find all breeds alphabetically between cockers and dobermans, excluding the two you use as criteria.

Logical operators. Use the AND operator (&) to find records that satisfy more than one condition. Use OR (¦) to find records that match at least one condition you specify. Use NOT (~) and NOT EQUAL (<>) to find records that do not match the conditions you specify. You can enclose conditions within parentheses, in the same way as you group math operations, to control the way Works evaluates them. The following examples assume you are entering a query in a field named Grade. The form includes fields for the grades, grade average, days absent, and midterm grade.

- Specify *avg >95 & absence <4* to find all students who qualify for an A.

- Specify *midterm>=70&((avg>50&avg<80)&absence<8)* to find all students who qualify for a C on the basis of a 70 on the midterm and an average grade between 50 and 80, plus less than eight absences.

Math operators. Use any of the following math operators, all of which should be familiar from the spreadsheet: + (addition), – (subtraction), * (multiplication), / (division), or ^ (exponentiation). As in combined queries, use parentheses to group calculations you want to be treated as a unit.

- Specify *(Price–Sold for)>1000* in the CARLOT database to find all records in which the selling price was more than $1,000.00 below the original price.

- In a parts inventory, specify *(on hand*unit price)* to find the total value of the parts you currently have in stock.

Works functions. Use built-in functions, such as AVG, MIN, and MAX to search for records meeting criteria you have to calculate. Works includes many functions. For reference, the built-in functions are described in Appendix C.

PAGE SETUP AND PRINTING

Page setup and printing in the database is familiar from the other Works applications. As in the word processor and the spreadsheet, you can set page margins, include headers and footers, and specify page size and numbering. The following sections deal with database-specific printing options.

Page Setup in List View

Because the database operates in different views you have a number of different choices when it comes to page setup. In list view, you set up pages much as you do in the spreadsheet, so most of the Page Setup & Margins dialog is familiar right from the start:

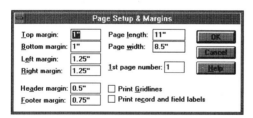

As in the spreadsheet, you can choose to print or omit gridlines. The only real difference in this dialog box is the Print record and field labels option. If you turn this option on, Works will include field names across the top of the page and row numbers (a complete pageful) down the left side. If a database is too wide to print on one page, Works repeats the row numbers but prints the appropriate labels above the field names on the next page. If you choose to print field names, use Print Preview to verify that all fields are wide enough to print the entire field name. You could be quite frustrated after printing a long database, if you find that some field names are truncated on paper.

Page Setup in Form View

In form view, the Page Setup & Margins command produces a considerably different and more elaborate set of options than you've encountered. None are difficult to use, however. When you choose the Page Setup & Margins command, Works displays this dialog box:

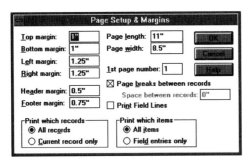

Following are the options specific to form view and their meanings:

- The Print which records box lets you choose whether to print all records in the database, or only the one currently displayed. (Remember, you view one record at a time in form view.) By default, Works assumes you want to print all records.

- The Print which items box lets you choose to print the entire form — field names, labels, descriptive text, and so on — or data entries only. The default is All items, rather than Field entries only.

- Page breaks between records, which is turned on by default, assumes that you want to print one record per page. Turn it off to print multiple records on each page.

- Space between records, which is turned off when Page breaks between records is turned on, lets you specify the amount of blank space between records when you print more than one on a page. The default is 0 inches. Though you might expect this to produce a cramped printout, it doesn't. If you use the default, check the layout in Print Preview. Unless you want a lot of extra room, 0 inches between records is sufficient for most of your printing needs.

■ Print Field Lines, which is turned off by default, omits the dotted entry lines in printouts, even when All items is selected in the Print which items box. If you want to print the lines, turn this option on.

As always, use Print Preview to see what Works will print with the settings you've specified. Wasting time and paper on incorrect printouts is never fun.

REFERENCE TO DATABASE COMMANDS

The following table lists and briefly describes the database commands, noting differences where they occur between and among the form, list, and query views described in this chapter. The table does not include commands specific to report view. If you need that information, refer to the end of Chapter 10. For more details, or for tutorial help with any command, don't forget about the online help and tutorial program.

The File Menu — for manipulating entire files

Create New File	Opens a new database; starts you in form view.
Open Existing File	Opens a previously saved file; starts you in the view you were last using when you saved the file.
Close	Closes an open file; prompts for instructions if you have any unsaved changes.
Save	Saves a file under the current name.
Save As	Saves a file under a new name or on a different disk.
Save Workspace	Saves the status of your Works "desktop" so you can return to the same documents in your next session.
Print Preview	Shows what your work will look like when printed; accessible from both form view and list view. Unavailable in query view.
Print	Prints a database from list view or form view. Unavailable in query view.
Page Setup & Margins	Sets margins, page number, page size, and print options in list view and form view. Unavailable in query view.
Printer Setup	Defines or modifies your printer and its settings. Unavailable in query view.
Exit Works	Quits Works; prompts for instructions if you have open files containing unsaved changes.

(continued)

continued

The Edit Menu — *for managing database entries*

Cut Record (form view)/Cut (list view and query view)	Deletes the selected record or field, temporarily saving the information on the Clipboard.
Copy Record (form view)/ Copy (list view and query view)	Copies the selected record or field to the Clipboard.
Paste Record (form view)/ Paste (list view and query view)	Pastes a record or field from the Clipboard into the database at the current location.
Clear Field Entry	Deletes information from the selected field.
Position Field (form view only)	Lets you move fields around to position them on a form.
Delete Field (form view only)	Deletes the selected field.
Duplicate Label (form view only)	Makes a copy of a selected label (descriptive text).
Delete Record (form view)/ Delete Record/ Field (list view)	Deletes the currently selected record, making the information irretrievable. In list view, can delete either a record or a field. Unavailable in query view.
Insert Record (form view)/ Insert Record/ Field (list view)	Inserts a blank form for a new record. In list view, can insert either a record or a blank field. Unavailable in query view.
Fill Right (list view only)	Copies selected information into adjoining cells in a row.
Fill Down (list view only)	Copies selected information into adjoining cells down a column.
Fill Series (list view only)	Fills a set of selected cells with numbers.
Delete Page Break	Removes an inserted page break. Unavailable in query view.
Insert Page Break	Inserts a page break; useful in determining which portions of a large database or form are printed on each page. Unavailable in query view.

(continued)

continued

Field Name (list view only)	Names a new or inserted field.
Headers & Footers	Opens a dialog box for entering and editing headers and footers. Unavailable in query view.
Delete Query (query view only)	Deletes a query from a field; equivalent to pressing the Del key.

The Select Menu — *for navigating in and viewing a database (not available in query view)*

Entries (list view only)	Selects a range of cells using arrow keys.
Record (list view only)	Selects an entire record.
Field (list view only)	Selects an entire field (column).
All (list view only)	Selects an entire file, including blank cells.
Go To	Moves the highlight to a specified field.
Find	Searches a database for specified characters.
Apply Query	Repeats the last query.
Hide Record	Hides the selected record from view.
Show All Records	Displays all database records after some have been hidden via commands or because of a query.
Switch Hidden Records	Displays the set of records temporarily hidden by a query.
Sort Records	Sorts a database alphabetically or numerically on up to three fields.

The Format Menu — *for controlling the appearance of a database or a form (not available in query view)*

General, Fixed, Currency, and so on	Formats a selected field or cell for the specified format.
Font	Applies a different font to a database or form.
Style	Applies a character style, such as italic, to a database, form, or form label.
Field Size	Sets the field width.
Show Field Names (form view only)	Turns the display of field names on and off.

(continued)

continued

The Options Menu — *for controlling Works and protecting data*

Works Settings	Sets up Works to operate according to your preferences.
Dial This Number	Calls a highlighted number for voice, not computer, communication.
Show Toolbar	Turns the Toolbar on and off.
Show Field Lines (form view)/ Show Gridlines (list view)	Turns field lines or gridlines on and off. Unavailable in query view.
Protect Data	Protects data from deletion or change, if locking is already turned on. Unavailable in query view.
Protect Form (form view only)	Protects a form from change.
Snap To Grid (form view only)	Causes fields to snap to an invisible grid; useful for aligning fields horizontally and vertically.

The View Menu — *for choosing a view and creating a report*

Form	Switches to form view.
List	Switches to list view.
Query	Switches to query view.
Create New Report	Creates a report from a database; for more details, refer to Chapter 10.

The Window Menu — *for controlling onscreen windows*

Cascade	Overlaps open document windows.
Tile	Resizes open windows, fitting them side by side on the screen.
Arrange Icons	Arranges minimized documents at the bottom of the screen.
Split (list view only)	Splits a window.

The Help Menu — *for when you're stuck*

Various commands, including Index, Basic Skills, and Tutorial, provide onscreen help in using Works. Commands named Form view (in form view), List view (in list view), and Query view (in query view) call up an overview of the Works database.

10
Creating Reports

Databases are wonderful things, but large ones can be a nuisance to align and print, especially if you want to show only selected fields or summarize subgroups of printed records. With Works it's easy. In the same way the word processor gives you graphics and the spreadsheet gives you charts, the database gives you reports.

After you've created a database, you can generate up to eight different reports for it, including in each one whatever fields and records you want. You can name a report, duplicate it, and delete it with ease when you no longer need it. You can also include titles, notes, labels, and calculations in your report, as well as the usual headers, footers, and page numbers.

Although you can preview the reports you create, the Works report generator is not really meant for saving selected parts of a database for later viewing. It is, instead, an easy-to-use means of formatting and printing the results of your queries.

Use the CARLOT database you created in Chapter 9 to experiment with reports. Start Works, if necessary, and open the CARLOT file. Maximize the application and document windows, and choose Show All Records to ensure that Works displays the complete database.

A STANDARD REPORT

Works comes with a built-in design for a standard database report. You can customize the report before printing, but in many instances you'll find that the standard report is all you need. You can create a standard report from form view, list view, or query view:

□ Click the Report button on the Toolbar, or if you prefer, choose the Create New Report command from the View menu. Works displays the large dialog box shown at the top of the next page.

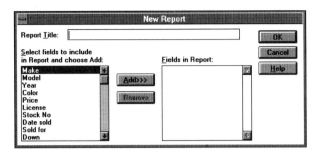

At the top of the dialog box is the Report Title box where you type a title for your report. If you leave the space blank, Works will omit a title. The two large boxes dominating the lower part of the dialog box are where you define the report.

The box to the left contains all of the field names in the database from which you're creating the report. The field names are listed in the same order they appear, from left to right, in list view.

The box to the right, headed Fields in Report, is blank to begin with.

The Add and Remove buttons let you choose the fields to include in your report. Highlight a field in the left-hand box, click Add, and Works immediately duplicates the field name in the right-hand box, for inclusion in the report-to-be. If you make a mistake, highlight the field name in the right-hand box, and click Remove. Out it goes.

Defining Report Fields

When you're creating a report, you can choose as many fields as you want, in any order you want. If you're not sure whether to include a particular field, choose it anyway. You can remove it later, and deleting an unwanted field is faster than adding one later.

The order in which you choose field names determines the order in which Works will display and print them in your report, so you can arrange database fields any way you want in a report. You can, for example, list price before make and model in a CARLOT report. Think a bit, however, before you go romping through the list of field names, clicking here and there. Works adds field names to the end of the list in the Fields in Report box. If you enter fields willy-nilly, the only way to rearrange them in this dialog box is to remove and re-enter them.

To create a report with your CARLOT database,

☐ Type *Honest Abe's: All cars* in the Report Title box.

Now include the Make, Model, Year, and Price fields in the report:

☐ The highlight is already on Make, so simply click the Add button.

288

□ Works moves the highlight to the next field in the list. You want Model, so click Add again. Do the same for Year.

□ You want to skip Color, so click on Price to highlight it, and then click Add again.

□ To see how easy it is to remove a field if you change your mind, click Add to include License in your growing list of report fields.

□ To omit the License field, click on its name in the right-hand box. Notice that Works now dims the Add button and makes the Remove button active. Click the Remove button.

□ You don't want to include any other fields in the report, so click OK.

Adding Statistics

No report yet. Works displays another dialog box. The Report Statistics dialog box shows some of the sophistication of the report generator. Ease of use in a program usually, if not always, implies a lot of forethought, hard work, and behind-the-scenes programming activity. In this instance, the Works developers assumed that you would find certain statistics to be valuable in many database reports. Instead of leaving the definition and creation of those statistics up to you, they designed the capability into the report generator, setting up this dialog box:

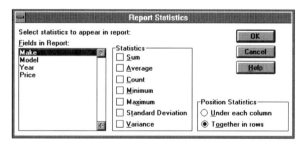

Works displays the fields you chose to include in the report in the Fields in Report box. The Statistics box lists a set of standard calculations you can choose from, such as Sum, Average, and Count (number of items). The Position Statistics box lets you decide whether to print the relevant statistics under each column or group them together in rows.

You can mix and match field names and statistics. For Honest Abe's report, include a count of the cars, as well as the minimum and maximum prices in the list:

◻ The highlight should be on Make in the Fields in Report box, so click the box next to Count to tell Works to list the number of cars. (Note that this is not the number of models. You'll see how to do that later.)

◻ Click on the Price field name, and click on the boxes for both Minimum and Maximum in the Statistics box.

◻ To group the statistics in rows, verify that Together in rows is selected in the Position Statistics box. Click OK to finish up.

You've finished defining your report, so Works displays a message:

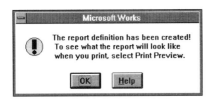

If you look at the screen behind this message, you see that the "report" you've created doesn't look like the report you probably expected. This is because you are looking at the *report definition,* not the actual formatted report. The message tells you that the report-generation process is complete and error-free and that you can see the report itself by clicking the Print Preview button. Click OK to eliminate the message. This is the report definition you should see:

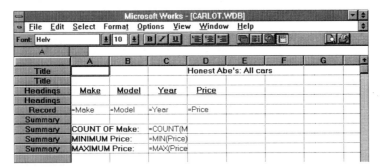

Before you go any further, satisfy your curiosity by clicking the Print Preview button on the Toolbar and zooming in twice to see what a standard report looks like. You should see something like this:

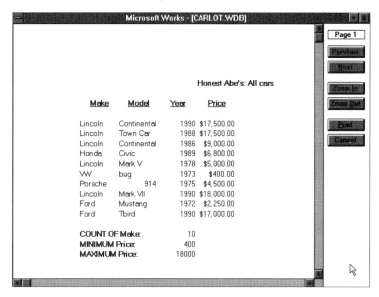

NOTE: *The order of your records might differ if you've saved and closed the file or sorted it in some way.*

Works uses the field widths you set up in list view as the column widths when it creates a report. If your data prints completely in list view, it will also print without problem in a report. Be sure, however, to use Print Preview freely when creating a report, especially if you use one font or font size in list view and a different one for your report. If any of the columns are too narrow to hold complete entries, Works will truncate text at the right edge, and it will display and print the number signs (########) in place of numbers. You can see any such problems in Print Preview, so catch them before printing to save yourself some frustration later on. To widen columns, either drag the column boundary, as you do in the spreadsheet and the database list view, or use the Column Width command on the Format menu.

If you notice any problems with column width, fix them now. When you're finished, click the Cancel button to leave Print Preview.

The Report Definition

The report definition now on your screen is an outline of the report you just generated. Use the report definition to tailor reports to your own specifications. You can, for example, add subtitles or formulas of your own. Because Works displays the report definition, rather than the report itself, you can modify a standard report without having to view or manipulate the actual records in it.

The parts of your report are laid out in a grid comparable to the display you see in list view. In the report definition, however, the columns are identified by letter, and the row labels tell you which elements are included in the report. Above the report definition, Works displays a formula bar that you can use for entering information and for displaying the complete contents of any cell (for example, the formula *=COUNT(Make)* in column C of the first Summary row). The box at the left edge of the formula bar displays the letter of the column, but not the row name, where the highlight is currently located.

Works uses these standard names for row labels when you generate a report:

- *Title* — the title of your report, or any other identifying text you care to include. By default, Works boldfaces the title you type when you create a report, and centers the title above the fields you include in the report. (This is not necessarily the same as centering them on the page, especially because a report containing many fields can require more than one page to print them all.) Titles appear only on the first page of a printed report.

- *Headings* — field names or other identifiers you want to use as headings for the columns in your report. Unless you change the headings, Works uses the field names you chose, displaying and printing them in bold, underlined characters centered above each column.

- *Record* — the names of the fields to be included in the report, each in a separate column. Each field name is preceded by an equal sign, making it a formula of sorts. When generating the report, Works uses this row to find the required data for each record you choose to include.

- *Summary* — the statistics you chose to include in the report. Each summary row identifies and gives the formula for one statistic. By default, Works identifies the statistic by name and prints the text in bold characters and the actual statistic in normal type.

Although you don't see them on your report definition yet, Works also recognizes two additional row types: *Intr fieldname* and *Summ fieldname*. You use these rows after you've sorted a database into groups (for example, by model of car in the sample database):

- *Intr,* presumably short for *internal, intra, inter,* or some other word meaning *within,* inserts rows between groups in a sorted report (Lincoln, Ford, and so on). You can use this row type to add blank space between groups or to place headings or other information at the top of each group.

- *Summ,* short for *summary,* inserts a summary row between groups, giving you a quick means of including subtotals and other statistics for each group. Summ rows calculate intermediate statistics, such as the number of Lincolns on hand. Summary rows, on the other hand, provide statistics on the report as a whole, for example, the total number of cars in Abe's car lot.

BASIC FORMATTING

If you zoom in on your report in Print Preview, you'll notice that the column headings are poorly aligned above the entries. This happens because the headings are centered, whereas the text entries are left-aligned and the numeric entries (including the 914 model number for the Porsche) are right-aligned.

To align the column headings, you must change the formatting of either the headings or the column entries. Here's one solution:

- In the Headings row, select Make and Model by extending the highlight. Click the Left button on the Toolbar to make them left-aligned. Leave the Year and Price headings centered.

- In the Record row, select =Model and left-align it so that all entries in this column will have the same alignment. Now the 914 will fall neatly into place beneath the other model names.

- Again in the Record row, select =Year, and click the Center button on the Toolbar. This both aligns the column under the heading and increases the space between the Year and Price fields, which were squeezed together because the entries in both columns, being numeric, were right-aligned.

Preview the report again. It should look like this:

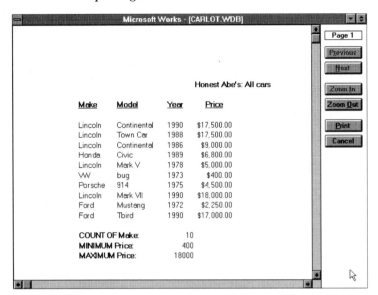

ROWS AND COLUMNS

You can add and delete rows and columns whenever you want to modify a report. You can add new field names and entries, insert extra blank lines or columns, and make room for additional titles, text, or statistics.

Adding and deleting columns in a report is similar to doing the same in the other Works modules. Select the column to the right of the position where you want to add a new column, and choose Insert Row/Column from the Edit menu. To delete, select the actual column you want to delete, and choose Delete Row/Column from the Edit menu.

Adding a New Row

Adding a row to a report differs slightly from adding rows in the other modules. You use the Insert Row/Column command, as usual, but when working with a report definition, you always refer to rows by type. Notice that some rows in your form have titles but no column entries. Works included these rows to add blank space to the printout. Even though the rows aren't functional in the sense that they contain information, they still belong to one row type or another. Their names indicate where blank rows will appear: one beneath the title, another beneath the column headings, and a third between the printed records and the summary statistics.

Suppose you want to add a subtitle to the report:

☐ Click on the blank Title row to select the entire row. As in list view, when you select an entire row (or column), Works bypasses the dialog box that asks whether you want to insert a row or a column.

☐ Choose Insert Row/Column from the Edit menu. Works displays a new type of dialog box:

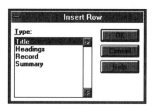

This dialog box shows the types of rows already in your report definition. The type of row Works highlights corresponds to the type of row you select before choosing the command. Here, for example, you selected a Title row, so Works proposes adding another of the same type:

☐ Click OK to add the row.

The new row appears above the one you selected. If you had chosen to add a different row type, such as Summary, Works would have inserted the row in the appropriate section of the report definition, even though you had selected a Title row before choosing the command. If you add a row in the wrong place, delete it with the Delete Row/Column command from the Edit menu.

Modifying a Column

Now that you've added another Title row, enter some text in it:

☐ Highlight the cell in column A, and type *March 1992.*

Here's a snag. Unlike text, which Works will display across several empty columns, dates and other numeric information are confined to the width of the column in which you type them. If you're still using the default column width of 10 characters, the column is too narrow to display the entire entry, so Works fills the cell with number signs (#). Go to Print Preview, and notice how Works displays the new entry — number signs there, too.

The obvious solution in this case is to widen the column:

☐ Drag the column boundary slightly to the right, increasing the width by two characters. If you want to check the width, choose the Column Width command from the Format menu.

☐ For appearance, click the Bold button to darken the text.

Inserting an extra Title line might have piqued your curiosity about aligning titles on several different lines. The title you originally added is centered on the page. Centering the subtitle, however, would have centered it *within* column A, not *between* the page margins. You could insert the subtitle under the main title, but doing this would not center the subtitle under the title, like this:

Honest Abe's: All cars

March 1992

And if you widened the column a little, as you did earlier, you would see something like this:

Honest Abe's: All cars

March 1992

Because you are working with cells in a report definition, your formatting options are not as unlimited as they are in a truly text-based application such as the word processor. As a result, you'll sometimes find yourself tinkering and fine-tuning to get the results you want. Here, for example, if a centered title wasn't that important, you could cut the main title (Honest Abe's: All cars) to the Clipboard, reinsert it in column A, and then use the Left button to align both titles evenly with the left margin, like this:

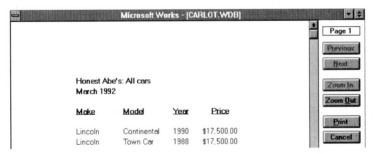

If you really wanted both titles centered, you could resort to a little trickery. When creating the report, you could type the subtitle in the Title portion of the

New Report dialog box. After the report was created, you could then type a centered header by using the &C header code in the Headers & Footers dialog box, like this:

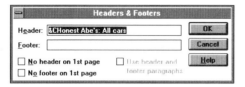

In this case, you would have to do some tinkering with the formatting and, possibly, move the subtitle to the left to center it properly. You could not boldface the header, and it would appear on all pages of the report, but you would have two centered titles:

SELECTING RECORDS

After you've created a report definition, you can choose to include in it any set of records in the database by jumping out to query view and specifying the records you want to see and print. For example, suppose you want to see a list of Lincolns only:

□ Click the Query View button to move to query view.

□ Specify the records you want by typing *lincoln* in the Make field.

□ Switch back to report view, and click the Print Preview button. (You can't go directly from query view to Print Preview.)

Instead of a list of all the cars in the database, you now see only the Lincolns. Works has also recalculated the statistics so that they are accurate for the cars you included in the report.

If you return to query view and specify another set of records, Works will adjust the report again to include the set you specified. Note that even though Works includes commands for naming, duplicating, and deleting reports on the View menu, a specific query does not "stick" to a particular report. When you change the query, all of the reports change to reflect the new specifications.

If you sort a database, and you want to keep the sorted report for future reference, save the database under a different name. Works will save the query and the report so you can view and print the selected records simply by opening the database under its new name and switching to report view.

GROUPING RECORDS

Displaying and printing selected records is one way to use database reporting. Another is to group records in the order that you want. In a product database, for example, you might want to print all or most of the records, but group them by category, price, stock number, and so on.

You've seen how sorting works in the database. You can sort records on up to three fields, specifying an ascending sort or a descending sort. In report view, you can refine the output by telling Works to break up the groups, instead of listing them one after the other, and you can specify whether you want the entries grouped alphabetically, according to the first letter in the field. In the CARLOT database, for example, you might want to see the cars grouped by make:

◻ First, switch to list view, and choose Show All Records so you can view the entire database.

◻ Switch back to report view.

◻ Now choose Sort Records from the Select menu. Works displays this dialog box:

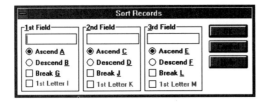

Unlike the Sort Records dialog box you see in list view, this dialog box includes a Break option and a 1st Letter option (currently dimmed) for each sort field. The Break option tells Works to group similar entries, such as all Lincolns. The 1st Letter option, which is available only when you've checked Break, lets you group the entries alphabetically. If you don't choose 1st Letter, Works breaks the groups whenever any portion of the sort field changes (for example, Johnson and Johnston would form two groups).

To see how grouping works,

◻ Type *make* in the 1st Field box.

□ Click in the Break checkbox to turn it on. You can leave the 1st Letter option unchecked. It doesn't make any difference here because the car makes will naturally fall out alphabetically. If, however, you specified a second sort field, such as Model, you could turn on the 1st Letter option for that field to group models alphabetically within makes. Under Lincoln, for example, Continentals would be in one group, the Mark V and VII in another.

□ Click OK to carry out the command.

Summ Rows

When your report definition reappears, notice that Works has inserted a new row, Summ Make. Works creates a Summ row whenever you group records. The Summ Make row tells you that Works will insert statistics for each group within the report. By default, Works uses a COUNT function for any fields containing text entries (Make and Model, in this example), and it uses a SUM function to total each field containing numeric values (Year and Price). In creating these statistics, Works uses field names, for example, the COUNT of (Make), the SUM of (Price), and so on. Handy, and easy to decipher.

You've no doubt noticed that Works made a mistake by totaling the years in each group. If you don't want to include a statistic Works sets up, or if you want to delete one that's wrong, all you have to do is edit the Summ row:

□ Switch back to the report definition, if necessary.

□ Click in the cell containing =SUM(Year). Choose the Clear command from the Edit menu, or press Del and click the Enter button in the formula bar.

□ Switch to Print Preview, and you can see that the offending statistic is gone.

Inserting Your Own Rows and Formulas

If you prefer, you can replace the Summ rows that Works inserts with those of your own creation. You can include text and formulas, if you want:

□ Extend the highlight to cover columns A through D in the Summ Make row. Clear them by choosing the Clear command from the Edit menu.

□ Click in the cell under =Year in the Record row.

□ Type *Subtotal:* and click the Enter button.

□ Click in the cell under =Price.

- ☐ Type the formula =*SUM(Price)*, and click the Enter button again.

- ☐ Check Print Preview. This time you'll see the Works summary replaced by subtotals of your own.

You can insert other row types and calculations, too. For example, now that you've created subtotals, you ought to have a total at the bottom of the report:

- ☐ Click the cell in column C of the blank row below the last summary row.

- ☐ Type *Total:* and click the Enter button. Notice that simply entering information caused Works to add a new Summary row. Type a SUM function, =*SUM(Price)*, into the cell in column D.

- ☐ Check Print Preview. You'll now see a total below the other summary statistics.

- ☐ For practice, return to the report definition, and format the words *Subtotal:* and *Total:* for bold. Format the SUM cells for currency. Select your new Summary row, and insert an extra row above it to separate the row visually from the rest of the report.

FIELDS AND FIELD ENTRIES

The final way to modify a basic report definition is by adding field names, field entries, and field summaries (statistics). This is where you sometimes need the Intr *fieldname* row type, described in the section "The Report Definition." Works uses the following definitions:

- ■ Field name — the name of a database field. When you insert a field name, Works places the name in whatever cell you selected, in any row type. When you preview or print the report, the field name appears as ordinary text.

- ■ Field entry — the name that refers to the entries in a field, for example, =Model in the preceding examples. When you insert a field entry, you tell Works to replace that name with actual entries from the database records in the field you specify. For example, if you inserted =License as a field entry in your report, Works would replace it with the actual license numbers of the cars listed in the report.

- Field summary — a statistic (Sum, Avg, Count, Min, Max, and so on) that you insert in a report in relation to a particular field. A field summary belongs in a Summ *fieldname* row. It is an easier way of inserting the type of formula you created earlier as =SUM(Price) in the Summ Make row.

You can choose to insert field names for either of two reasons: to add a field you didn't include in the original report definition, or to save typing time while constructing a formula or mathematical calculation or, if you want, while inserting text. Field entries, of course, enter the picture only if you want to include additional data from the database. You need both field names and field entries to add extra fields to a report.

Inserting Field Names and Field Entries

You can add fields and field entries to a report whenever you want, and you can do so in any way you want. To save a little typing, however, you can use the Insert Field Name and Insert Field Entry commands on the Edit menu. Suppose, for example, you decide you want to include the License number for each of the cars in your report:

◻ To avoid cluttering the report you've created, click in the cell in column F of the Headings row. Choose Insert Field Name from the Edit menu. Works displays this dialog box:

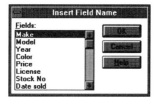

◻ Click on License to select it, and then click OK.

As easily as that, you can add a field name to any part of your report. When Works inserts the name, it doesn't add any special formatting, so you must take care of the formatting on your own:

◻ Click the Bold and Underlined buttons on the Toolbar to make the new heading match the others.

Adding a field entry will be a snap now, because the action is practically a duplicate of what you just did:

☐ Click in the cell in column F of the Record row.

☐ Choose Insert Field Entry from the Edit menu, and then choose License from the box. Click OK to insert the entry.

☐ Click Print Preview. You'll now see all the license numbers on the report.

Inserting Intr *fieldname* Rows

The Intr *fieldname* row type is useful in situations such as creating extra spacing or internal headings between groups in a sorted database. You can also use it for inserting text at the head of each group in the database.

In this example, suppose you decide you want to repeat the headings at the top of each group in the report:

☐ Click on any row title to select the entire row.

☐ Choose the Insert Row/Column command from the Edit menu.

☐ Because you've grouped the database records, Works now presents you with an Intr row type, based on the first field you sorted, Make. Choose Intr Make, and click OK to insert the new row:

Regardless of the row you selected, Works inserts the Intr Make row above the Record row. Now to see what you can do with this,

☐ Click in column A of the Intr Make row, and type *Make.*

☐ Press Tab and in each column repeat the heading that appears in the Headings row. When you've finished, duplicate the formatting of the original headings in the headings you just typed.

☐ Now switch to Print Preview:

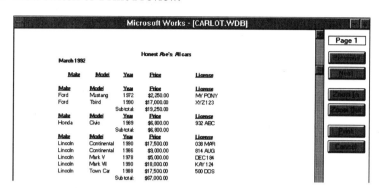

Each group of cars is now neatly laid out under its own headings. Notice, however, that Works displays two sets of headings at the top: one from the original Headings row, and the second from the *internal* headings row you just inserted. To take care of that,

☐ Select the Headings row, and delete it.

To make your report look better,

☐ Select the entire Intr Make row, and insert another of its kind above it.

Inserting Field Summaries

You created a field summary of your own when you entered the SUM formula in the Summ Make row. Inserting summaries with the Insert Field Summary command on the Edit menu is simpler and much like choosing from the Statistics dialog box Works presents when you create a report for the first time. Field summaries, as mentioned in "The Report Definition," earlier in this chapter, belong in Summ *fieldname* rows. To see how simple it is to add a summary,

☐ Click in the cell in column A of the Summ Make row.

☐ Choose Insert Field Summary from the Edit menu.

Add a count of the number of cars in each make. (True, Works did this for you, when you added the Summ Make row.)

☐ The field name Make is already highlighted, so all you need do is choose the type of statistic you want. Click the button next to COUNT, and click OK to complete the command.

☐ Check Print Preview. The new statistic now appears below each group.

Saving a Report

When you create a report and want to save it for future reference, you can give it a name of up to 15 characters as follows:

□ Choose the Name Report command from the View menu. Works displays this dialog box:

In the Reports section of the box, Works lists the reports (up to eight) that you've created for this database. In this dialog box, you have one report with the default name Report1. To change its name,

□ Click in the Name box, and type *oldcars*.

□ Click the Rename button to change the name from Report1 to Oldcars.

□ Click OK to complete the command.

□ Open the View menu. You now see *oldcars* listed at the bottom, where Works displays the names of the reports associated with the current database.

The related Delete Report and Duplicate Report commands on the View menu work much like the Name Report command. Delete Report, as you would expect, eliminates a report you no longer want or need. This command is useful when you want to throw away a mistake or eliminate one or more reports when you bump up against the eight-report limit in the report generator. To delete a report, choose the Delete Report command, select the report, click the Delete button, and then click OK. To duplicate a report, use the same procedure but choose the Duplicate Report command. When you duplicate a report, Works gives it a default name, such as Report1. Use the Name Report command to change the name of the duplicate.

REPORT FORMATTING AND PRINTING

You've done a fair amount of formatting in this chapter, and you've seen the default settings Works uses for headings, titles, and summaries. Most of the formatting you do when creating reports is the same as the formatting you do in any other application. As in the spreadsheet and the main database module, remember that a change in font or font size applies to your entire report; you cannot use one font for titles, another for headings, and a third for data.

Your most important ally in preparing a report for printing is the Print Preview button. Aside from being interesting to use, Print Preview is an invaluable means of seeing what you'll get before you get it — WYSIWYG in full-page displays.

Page Breaks

Like the other Works applications, the report generator lets you insert and delete manual page breaks to arrange your printed output. You can insert page breaks either between rows or between columns.

Inserting a page break between rows is useful when you want to print groups on separate pages. For example, if you insert a page break above the Headings or an Intr *fieldname* row in the report definition, each group will start on a new page. If you use this approach, however, bear in mind that your titles will also print on a page by themselves, so format or lay them out accordingly. A better solution would be to create a blank Summ *fieldname* row just before the summary rows and then insert a page break before the blank row.

Inserting a page break between columns is your obvious choice when printing a report that is too large to fit on a single sheet of paper. By inserting a vertical page break of this type, you can determine where Works will break pages between printed fields.

Page Setup & Margins

The Page Setup & Margins command in the report generator is simpler than it is in the database or the spreadsheet. Aside from the usual margin settings and page-size specifications, you have only one additional option, Print all but record rows:

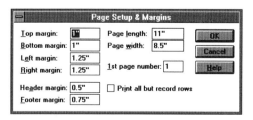

Click in this checkbox if you want to print your report *form,* including headings and summaries, but not the data entries themselves.

REFERENCE TO REPORTING COMMANDS

The following table briefly describes the various menus and commands available in the report generator. Use these descriptions as reminders or for reference. Tutorial help is available through the Help menu.

The File Menu — for manipulating entire files

Create New File	Opens a Works application with a new blank document.
Open Existing File	Opens a previously saved file; starts the application used to create the document if the application is not already running.
Close	Closes an open file; prompts for instructions if the file contains unsaved changes.
Save	Saves a previously saved file under the same name.
Save As	Saves a file under a new name, on a different disk, or in a different directory.
Save Workspace	Saves the current Works desktop environment so it can be duplicated in the next session.
Print Preview	Switches to preview mode, which displays a document as it will be printed. In the report generator, this is the only way to see what a finished report will look like.
Print	Prints a document; lets you specify the entire document or a range of pages, as well as draft (fast) printing mode.
Page Setup & Margins	Sets the margins, page size, and beginning page number of the document; in the report generator, also lets you choose whether to print records or the report "form" and summaries only.
Printer Setup	Defines or redefines a printer to work with Works. Use this command to change from portrait to landscape printing if your printer has the capability.
Exit Works	Quits Works; prompts if any open files contain unsaved changes.

The Edit Menu — for modifying a report

Cut	Removes selected information and places it on the Clipboard.
Copy	Copies selected information to the Clipboard.
Paste	Inserts the contents of the Clipboard into a document at the current location of the highlight.

(continued)

continued

Clear	Clears the contents of the selected cell, row, or column. Cleared contents cannot be retrieved.
Delete Row/Column	Deletes a row or column from a report definition.
Insert Row/Column	Inserts a row or column into a report definition; inserted rows must be selected from a list of available row types presented in the command's dialog box.
Insert Field Name	Inserts a field name into a report definition; often inserted in Intr *fieldname* rows.
Insert Field Entry	Inserts a field entry into a report definition so that data represented in that field can be included in a report; inserted in Record rows.
Insert Field Summary	Inserts one of the report generator's basic statistics for a selected field; inserted in Summ *fieldname* rows.
Insert (Delete) Page Break	Insert and delete horizontal or vertical page breaks.
Headers & Footers	Inserts and formats running heads and running feet.

The Select Menu — *for selecting cells and sorting records*

Cells	Extends the selection to multiple cells.
Row	Selects an entire row in a report definition.
Column	Selects an entire column in a report definition.
All	Selects the entire report definition grid, including blank rows and columns.
Sort Records	Sorts records on up to three fields in ascending or descending order; also inserts breaks between sorted groups and can break groups alphabetically.

The Format Menu — *for controlling the appearance of a report*

General, Fixed, Currency, and others	Applies the specified format to numeric values.
Font	Changes the font for a report.
Style	Applies character styles (italics, bold, underline) and alignment (general, left, right, center) to selected characters.
Column Width	Changes the width of a column; default in the report generator corresponds to the column width used for the same field in list view.

(continued)

continued

The Options Menu — *for controlling Works*

Works Settings	Tailors Works for specific preferences.
Dial This Number	Dials a highlighted number for voice, not computer, communication.
Show Toolbar	Turns the Toolbar on and off.

The View Menu — *for creating and managing reports*

Form, List, Query	Switches to the specified view.
Create New Report	Creates a new report definition for the current database.
Name Report	Assigns a name of up to 15 characters to an existing report.
Delete Report	Deletes specified reports.
Duplicate Reports	Makes a copy of a specified report, assigning a generic name, such as Report1, to the copy.

The Window Menu — *for controlling the window*

Cascade	Overlaps open windows.
Tile	Displays open windows side by side.
Arrange Icons	Arranges icons for minimized documents along the bottom of the screen.

The Help Menu — *for getting out of a jam*

Report View	Provides specific help with reporting. Additional commands are standard throughout Works Help.

Part III

Information at
Your Fingertips

Information at Your Fingertips defines Microsoft's vision for personal computing. Part III shows how Works blends this vision with reality. The final three chapters introduce you to information sharing of two types: computer-to-computer communications and information exchange among the three Works applications. Both types of sharing, as you'll see, open the door to a more flexible electronic workplace where information of any type can truly be as close as your keyboard.

11

Online with Windows Terminal

In earlier chapters you encountered references to the Dial This Number command on the Options menu. If your computer is equipped with a modem for communications, this command dials the phone number of someone you want to talk to. You can call anyone — business contacts, coworkers, customers, your dentist, or the person who clips your dog — simply by displaying and highlighting the person's phone number and choosing one command.

Dialing a phone number is one way Works and your computer can help you communicate with other people. Another way is through *telecommunication,* a process that lets you become part of the large and still growing group of people who rely on computer-to-computer hookups to gather information, transfer files, bat ideas back and forth, and keep in touch with one another.

Before you can use your computer for any type of data transfer, you must set it up so it can use your phone line to "hook up" with another computer. Earlier, non-Windows versions of Works included a special communications module for doing this. Your version of Works doesn't need such a module because, as a Windows-based program, it can use Windows Terminal, the communications program that is part of the Accessories program group.

Computer communications depends on having someone to call, so this chapter won't give you any hands-on examples to try. It will, however, explain some of the terminology and help you develop an understanding of how Terminal can help when you go on line with the world. All you need are your computer, a phone line, a modem, and Windows Terminal.

THE PROCESS OF COMMUNICATION

After you've installed a modem, computer communications boils down to several operations that you perform in sequence. Briefly, you

1. Set up your computer and modem to communicate.

2. Dial the phone number to which the other computer (called the *remote* computer) is connected.

3. Log in. You do this on a bulletin board or on a commercial service, which is open to many people. Logging in is the way you identify yourself as a legitimate user.

When you finish communicating, reverse the steps:

1. Log out to tell the remote computer you've finished.

2. Disconnect (hang up) so neither you nor the other computer leaves the phone line open.

3. Save your communications settings if you want to reuse them at another time.

MODEMS AND WHAT THEY DO

A modem is a piece of hardware that handles the "three C's" of remote computing: calling, connecting, and communicating. Although your computer can "think" for itself perfectly, without a modem it cannot pass information to other computers except by using files stored on disk.

The word *modem* is short for *modulate/demodulate,* which describes exactly what a modem does. To send information, a modem *modulates* the electrical signal output by a computer, in a sense embedding the data in a sound wave that can travel over a telephone line much as radio stations "embed" music in their AM and FM signals. When receiving information, the modem *demodulates* the incoming carrier wave, retrieving the bits of data and reconstructing them in a form the computer can use.

The Language of Communications

When you connect your computer to another computer via modem, however, you must ensure that the two computers "speak" the same language, transmit at the same speed, and follow the same rules of etiquette. If you don't, one computer might transmit in a "dialect" the other computer can't interpret, or it might transmit far too fast for the other to follow. Rules of etiquette are needed for the same reasons they are needed in everyday life: to avoid conflicts. These rules of etiquette will prevent situations such as both computers trying to transmit at the same time, essentially trying to shout each other down. Windows Terminal and comparable programs are your means of ensuring that communications sessions proceed smoothly. Terminal takes care of all aspects of a communications session.

The remaining sections of this chapter cover the Terminal features needed for basic communications. Your Windows documentation and Terminal's Help feature are excellent resources for more extensive information on communication.

Although you won't actually connect to another computer, you can start Terminal to see the menus and commands described in this chapter. Terminal, remember, is in the Windows Accessories group. To start it, return to Windows (if necessary), open the Accessories window or choose it from the Windows menu, and double-click on Terminal. Don't worry about looking around in Terminal, even if you have a modem installed and ready to go. Terminal won't try to call out unless you tell it to.

When you start Terminal, you see a typical Windows screen:

NOTE: *If Terminal displays a message asking for your Default Serial Port, click the option (such as COM1:) your modem is connected to. If you don't know, click OK, but do find out the name of your port before you ask Terminal for communications.*

SETTING UP

Setting up for communications means telling Terminal about your modem, specifying the phone number of the computer you want to call, and ensuring that both computers will use the same communications settings while sending and receiving data. Most, if not all, of the information you need for setup should be listed in the documentation for your modem and for the remote computer. If you're connecting two independent personal computers — yours and someone else's, for example — be careful to use the same settings on both.

To set up for communications, you use Terminal's aptly named Settings menu:

If you've never tried communications, some of the terms you see here and in command dialog boxes will look distinctly unfriendly, but don't let them bother you. Communications — and popular services such as CompuServe — wouldn't exist if you needed a degree in science or engineering to get started. From the beginning, then . . . .

Your Modem

Modems vary, not only by make, model, and speed, but in the types of commands they use to start and end phone connections. To tell Terminal which type of modem you have, you use Modem Commands on the Settings menu. Choosing Modem Commands presents you with this dialog box:

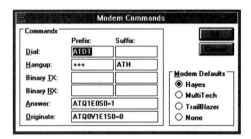

The options in this dialog box let you choose from several standard modem types. When you start out, Terminal displays the commands used by Hayes and Hayes-compatible modems, a particularly widespread group. If you use a different modem, click in the button next to its name in the Modem Defaults box, and Terminal will display the commands appropriate for your choice. Click next to None if your modem doesn't match any of the choices shown. In this case, look in your modem documentation to find what to type in the Commands part of the dialog box.

314

NOTE: *The dial prefix ATDT in the Commands box refers to tone dialing. If you need pulse dialing (as on a rotary phone), change this command to ATDP.*

Phone Numbers

Once you've identified your modem to Terminal, you can tell it who (or what) to call by choosing the Phone Number command from the Settings menu:

When you type a phone number, type it all, including such digits as 9, if you need an outside line, and 1, if you're calling out of your local dialing area. You can use parentheses or hyphens to separate the parts of a phone number, but they're not necessary. (Spaces work too.) An important character to remember, however, is the comma. Use a comma to tell Terminal to pause for two seconds before dialing the next digit. For example, if you dial 9 for an outside line, you can type the number as *9,1-800-555-1000* to have Terminal pause after the 9. If you use call waiting, help your communications session go smoothly by disabling the feature temporarily. Your phone book will give you the details.

In the remainder of the dialog box you can

- Specify the number of seconds (Terminal proposes 30) that you want to wait for a connection. If the receiving computer does not open the line within that time, Terminal will stop trying to connect (assume a *timeout*).

- Check Redial After Timing Out if you want Terminal to try again until it makes a connection.

- Check Signal When Connected if you want your computer to beep when it connects successfully.

Terminal Emulation

Terminal emulation refers to the way your computer behaves while connected to another computer. Back in the early days of communications, large computers dealt with specific types of *terminals,* which were smaller units with far less "brainpower" than the mainframes that accepted their output and fed them their input.

When you're using a personal computer to communicate, you often have to tell it to emulate a particular type of terminal by sending and receiving codes for formatting and display characters as the terminal would do. Again, your documentation should tell you which type of terminal to emulate. The most common terminals are the DEC (Digital Equipment Corporation) VT-100 and VT-52. Of these two, the VT-100, which Terminal proposes as the default, is the one most often used by remote services and mainframe computers.

The TTY terminal type represents a literal "dumb" terminal — one that can send and receive only a few basic codes, such as carriage return and tab. Because TTY is a generic choice, it's a good one to try when you don't know what else to use.

Terminal Preferences

Although it seems odd to tell your computer to emulate a terminal in one command and then tell it how to behave in another, you can do it. The Terminal Preferences command from the Settings menu lets you control several aspects of your computer's communications behavior. Choosing the Terminal Preferences command produces this dialog box:

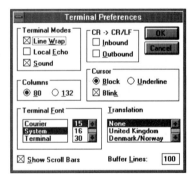

Some of these options are personal preferences. For example, you can choose a cursor shape (block or underline, blinking or nonblinking) you like and an onscreen font and size that seems especially readable to you. The Show Scroll Bars option at the bottom left of the dialog box turns on the scroll bars so you can read text that has already scrolled off the screen.

The Buffer Lines option lets you specify the size of the buffer, in lines of text, that Terminal sets aside for holding incoming information. You can specify from 25 to 400 lines. If you want Terminal to create the largest buffer it can, specify a high number. Terminal will adjust the buffer size to fit the amount of memory it finds available.

The following options might be necessary to display or transmit information correctly. In the Terminal Modes box,

- Line Wrap causes Terminal to wrap lines so that they don't run off the right edge, where they are lost. Choose this option if your screen can display only 80 characters, but you are communicating with a computer that transmits 132 characters per line.

- Local Echo displays the characters you type. Communications is unlike the Works applications in that you don't always see what you type. If the remote computer uses a feature called *remote echo,* it returns (echoes) the characters you type so that you see them onscreen. Turn on Local Echo if your typing doesn't appear on the screen.

- Sound causes your computer to beep whenever it receives a "bell" character, called Ctrl-G, from the remote computer. Ctrl-G is used to get your attention, so leaving Sound turned on is normally a good idea.

In the odd-looking CR -> CR/LF box,

- Check Inbound or Outbound if incoming or outgoing lines of text overrun one another because the cursor does not move down at the end of each line. The symbol CR stands for *carriage return,* the computer character that causes the cursor to return to the left edge of the screen. The CR/LF stands for *carriage return/linefeed,* a combination character that causes the cursor to return and causes it to drop down to a new line. Checking Inbound or (if you're told to do so) Outbound will turn carriage returns into carriage returns plus linefeeds when you're communicating with a computer that deals with carriage returns only.

In the Columns box,

- Specify 80 or 132 characters per line, depending on what your display can handle and how you want it to behave. Most computer screens display 80 characters per line. Choose 132 if your display can manage it (not all can) or if you're communicating with a computer that uses a wide line width. If your display cannot hold 132 characters per line, remember to choose the Line Wrap option in the Terminal Modes box to ensure that no text is lost.

In the Translation box,

■ Specify a different country if you are going to send and receive information in a different language. The country you choose determines the characters Terminal uses. Your choice must be one that the remote computer can recognize.

Communications Parameters

Now you come to an important group of settings — the communications parameters, without which you cannot transfer information between your computer and another. The communications parameters settings determine how fast your modem sends and receives data, as well as the type of error checking it uses, and the number of bits (binary 1's and 0's) it uses to represent each character. Most important in getting your modem to work at all, use this command to specify what *connector* or *port* your modem uses for sending and receiving information.

The Communications dialog box looks like this:

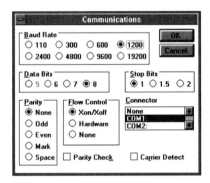

Terminal proposes standard settings for communications parameters, so you might not have to tinker with these at all. If you do, however, you should be able to find the appropriate settings for a particular computer in the documentation that tells you how to connect with the machine. For your own reference, this is what all these settings mean:

■ Baud Rate determines the speed of transmission. Your modem is rated for a certain speed, such as 1200, 2400, 9600, or both 1200 and 2400. This parameter is sometimes called *bps,* which is short for *bits per second,* as in "a 1200-bps modem." Technically, bps describes transmission speed more accurately than does the older term *baud rate.*

■ Data Bits refers to the number of binary digits used to represent each character. During transmission, each data bit is sent as a high or low "blip" in a data stream. Most transmissions use either 7 or 8 data bits.

■ Stop Bits tells the receiving computer where each character ends. As you can see from the choices — 1, 1.5, or 2 — stop bits aren't actual bits. (You can't have half a bit.) Stop bits are actually timing intervals between characters.

■ Parity indicates a form of error checking that uses the setting of an eighth (parity) bit to determine whether a character has been transmitted correctly. Parity checking is used when systems transmit with 7 data bits.

■ Flow Control keeps the buffer from overflowing, with consequent loss of data while you're transferring a file. Xon/Xoff, a standard method, causes Terminal to send a signal to the remote computer that pauses transmission when the buffer is full. This process is called *handshaking*. You might have to choose either Hardware or None if the remote computer uses a different type of handshaking, or none at all.

■ Connector identifies the serial port your modem is connected to. COM1 is the first serial port (or the only one if you have a single serial port), COM2 is the second serial port, and so on up to COM4, the last possible serial port you can have.

■ Parity Check displays the byte (character) where an error was detected if you specified any form of parity other than None. If you don't turn Parity Check on, Terminal displays a question mark where each error occurred (if any).

■ Carrier Detect uses a signal from the modem to tell Terminal whether a connection has been established. Turn this option off if you have trouble connecting even after double-checking all other communications parameters.

SAVING YOUR SETTINGS

The preceding sections describe how to enter a phone number you want to call and how to decipher and select the communications settings you need to connect successfully with a remote computer. After you've finished, you can save the settings in a file by choosing the Save As command from the File menu.

When you choose this command, Terminal displays a familiar-looking File Save As dialog box asking you to type a name for the settings file and, if you want, to specify a disk or directory. Although the file you save isn't one that you can display and work with as you can a letter or other document, Terminal will save it on disk with the extension TRM.

The next time you want to connect with the same computer, simply choose the Open command from the File menu, specify the filename, and Terminal will read all your settings — including the remote computer's phone number — into memory.

CALLING AND LOGGING IN

After your computer and modem are set up and ready to communicate, you can go on line by simply choosing Dial on the Phone menu. After you choose Dial, Terminal displays a small dialog box showing the number it is calling. The dialog box also shows the time remaining until Terminal stops trying to connect if the remote computer doesn't answer.

After you've established a connection, the remote computer might ask you to log in. Logging in gives the remote computer a way to identify you as a legitimate caller. Login procedures generally involve typing your name and a secret password. The service you use provides this information. If you want, you can assign login sequences and other commands to the function keys on your keyboard. Then, you can replay a command by pressing the function key with which it is associated. Terminal's Help facility and your Windows documentation both describe how to do this.

SENDING AND RECEIVING FILES

Communications provides you with a ready means of transferring your Works files from place to place simply by establishing a phone connection between your computer and the remote computer.

Computer files can travel in either of two forms: as *text files* or as *binary files*. Text files are also known as ASCII files. ASCII, short for American Standard Code for Information Interchange, is a set of codes used to translate letters, numbers, and punctuation marks into a form that all computers can work with. ASCII files can contain tabs, carriage returns, and other simple formatting, but they cannot include any unusual or program-specific formatting, such as superscripts or italics.

Binary files, on the contrary, can contain all manner of codes and unusual characters, and so cannot be translated into plain ASCII text. Program files, such as Works itself, are always binary files. Document files you create with Works are also binary files, although you can save them without formatting by choosing the Works Save As command and specifying a format such as *Text* or *Text (DOS)* in the Save File as Type portion of the dialog box.

Sending Files

Although you can send and receive both text and binary files with Terminal, the commands and methods differ. The following sections describe both types of file transfer.

Binary Files

Transferring binary files is easier and potentially more accurate than transferring text files. After you've connected with the remote computer, you simply tell Terminal the type of *protocol* you want to use, name the file to transmit, and choose the Send Binary File command on the Transfers menu.

When you transmit binary files, the sending and receiving computers follow some extremely formal rules, or protocols. These protocols are analogous to those used in diplomatic relations. Luckily, the only people who really need to understand communications protocols are programmers and system designers. Mere mortals can simply choose the protocol to use and be done with it. Terminal supports two common protocols for binary file transfers: XModem/CRC and Kermit.

To send a binary file, do the following:

- ☐ Connect the sending and receiving computers.

- ☐ Specify the protocol for your computer with the Binary Transfers command from the Settings menu.

- ☐ If you are working on the receiving computer, specify a name and directory for the incoming file with the Receive Binary File command on the Transfers menu.

- ☐ If you are working on the sending computer, choose the file to send with the Send Binary File command on the Transfers menu.

That's it. During the transfer, Terminal displays messages at the bottom of the window that tell you the name of the file being transferred, how far the transfer has progressed, and the number of times (if any) that errors caused the program to back up and retry the transmission.

If you're using the XModem/CRC protocol, Terminal can retry up to 20 times; if you're using Kermit, Terminal can retry up to 5 times. In either situation, if Terminal reaches the maximum number of retries, it cancels transmission. Both the sending and receiving computers also have a Stop button displayed in the status report. Click Stop if you have to terminate the transfer.

Text Files

When you send a text file, you can't rely on a file-transfer protocol, so you must give Terminal a little more information than you do when you send a binary file. To begin, you choose Text Transfers from the Settings menu. The command produces this dialog box:

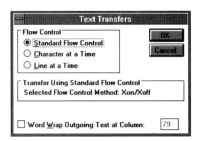

The Flow Control portion of the dialog box lets you tell Terminal to transmit the file either by using the flow control method you set with the Communications command or by sending the file either one character at a time or one line at a time. Both Character at a Time and Line at a Time are much slower than Standard Flow Control, which in the case of Xon/Xoff can use the buffer as a reservoir to keep data moving. Exactly how slow depends on the choices you make in a "subdialog box" that appears when you select Character at a Time or Line at a Time. For example, if you select Character at a Time, you see this dialog box:

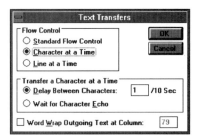

In this dialog box, you can select the length of time Terminal waits before sending the next character. You can also tell Terminal not to send another character until the last character is transmitted back (echoed) as verification that no error occurred. The choices for Line at a Time are comparable.

The Word Wrap Outgoing Text at Column option lets you determine the length of each line. You can specify up to 132 characters. To choose the maximum line length, type 131, not 132, to leave room for Terminal to add a special end-of-line character (^M).

When you're ready to transfer a text file,

- Connect the sending and receiving computers.

- If you are working on the sending computer, specify the name of the file with the Send Text File command on the Transfers menu. Check Append LF if you want Terminal to add a linefeed character to each line; use the default Strip LF if you're certain that the receiving computer will be able to interpret carriage returns as both "return to left margin" and "start a new line."

- If you are working on the receiving computer, specify a name and directory for the incoming file with the Receive Text File command on the Transfers menu. Check Append File if you want to "tack" the arriving file onto the end of an existing file. Check Save Controls if you want to keep any internal formatting that might remain in a file that was originally created with formatting (as with Works) but specially saved as an ASCII file for transmission. Check Table Format if you're receiving data in column format and you want Terminal to insert a tab wherever it encounters two or more blank spaces in the arriving document.

During the actual file transfer, Terminal displays the file onscreen as it transmits the data. At the bottom of the window, you see a status report telling you the name of the file and the amount sent (or received). Stop and Pause buttons in the status report let you terminate or temporarily stop transmission from either the sending or the receiving computer.

If you want to see a file either before or after transmission, use the View Text File command on the Transfers menu.

LOGGING OUT AND HANGING UP

You must take care of two simple but important tasks when you want to end a communications session: logging out and then hanging up.

If you're communicating with a remote computer that requires you to log in, remember to end your session by logging out. Logging out is never difficult and can be as simple as typing *bye*. Regardless of how it's done, logging out tells the remote computer that you're officially checking out. Be sure to log out if you're connected to a computer on which you pay for connect time. If you hang up without logging out, you could end up paying for time you didn't use.

Your final step in ending a communications session is to choose the Hangup command from the Phone menu. Hanging up disconnects you from the remote computer, the same way you end a phone call by hanging up the phone.

12

Moving Data from Place to Place

The chapters in Parts I and II showed you the basics of using the Works modules to create documents, spreadsheets, and databases. Along the way, you saw how to use Microsoft Draw to enliven a word-processed document with drawings and clip art, and you used the spreadsheet's charting feature to give graphic impact to your data.

Real-life work often requires such blending of different types of information. Aside from drawings and charts, you might sometimes want to include rows and columns of spreadsheet values in a financial statement created with the word processor, or you might need to move inventory balances from a database file into the spreadsheet where you track your needs for new materials. This chapter describes how Works can help you merge data from different documents by allowing you to easily move data from one Works application to another.

Through much of this chapter, you'll experiment with small or incomplete documents in the three Works applications. This will let you concentrate on what you're doing rather than on creating the examples themselves. After you've gone through the basics, however, you'll find a summary example at the end of the chapter. To begin,

- □ Start Works, if necessary.

- □ Create a new word processor document, and turn on Show All Characters on the Options menu if it's not already checked.

- □ Maximize the application window, but *not* the document window. Leaving the document window at its default size will often enable you to use the title bars to switch quickly from one document window to another.

- Create two additional new documents, one in the spreadsheet and one in the database. Again, do not maximize the document windows.

Now enter some data in each window:

- In the Word1 window, type *This is word processing.*

- In the Sheet1 window, type the following values in columns A and B:

	A	B
Row 1	100	200
Row 2	300	400
Row 3	500	600

- In the Data1 window, create three fields named *Last:, First:,* and *Middle:,* and type the following data to create three sample records:

Last	First	Middle
Agassiz	Louis	
Audubon	John	James
Darwin	Charles	Robert

WHAT YOU CAN MOVE, AND WHERE

You can select and move (or copy) information from any Works application to any other Works application:

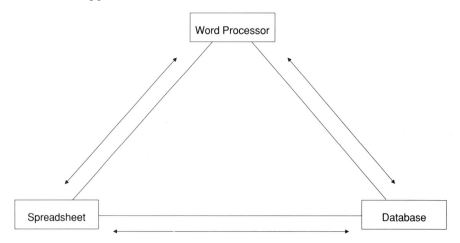

Although the Works spreadsheet and database are valuable applications, the word processor is more flexible in terms of accepting data from other applications, including programs other than Works that run under Windows 3.0.

Within any of the three Works applications, you can cut and paste or copy and paste freely to move information around. Between the word processor and the spreadsheet (not the database), you can also use a more sophisticated *Paste Special* procedure that lets you create a link between the copied information and the original data in the spreadsheet. After you create such a link, Works can update the copy in the word processor whenever you change the same or related information in the contributing spreadsheet.

Knowing roughly what Works is doing when you use data-transfer commands will make you feel more confident as you move data from place to place. All you need is a basic understanding of the three data-transfer mechanisms Works supports: cut and paste (or copy and paste), linking, and embedding. Each is described separately in the following sections.

CUT AND PASTE

Both cut and paste and copy and paste use the Clipboard as a temporary storage place for information you want to duplicate or move. The two procedures differ in only one way: Cut and paste moves the information from one location to another, whereas copy and paste duplicates it. Other than this, cut and paste and copy and paste work as described in earlier chapters:

1. Select the information you want to place in a different document.

2. Cut or copy the information to the Clipboard.

3. Select the location in the receiving document where you want to paste the information.

4. Paste the contents of the Clipboard into the receiving document.

Because Works is both integrated software and a Windows program, you can use the Clipboard as a way station whether you're moving information within a document, between documents in the same application (such as the word processor), or between documents in different applications.

Cut and paste and copy and paste are simple ways to move data from one application to another. Because the applications differ in the way they treat data, however, you will see some differences in the way Works handles the information. These differences are all logical, and one in particular — the effect of moving a table from the word processor to a database — can impress a confirmed technophobe. The following rules will help you know what to expect when you transfer information:

- Spreadsheet to word processor: If you paste the contents of multiple cells into a word-processed document, Works arranges the incoming data in rows and columns separated by tabs 1 inch apart.

- Database to word processor: If you paste one or more records into a word-processed document, Works, again, arranges the data in rows and columns separated by tabs.

- Word-processed tables to spreadsheet: If you paste a table separated by tabs into a spreadsheet, Works places each table entry in a separate cell.

- Word-processed tables to database: If you paste a word-processed table separated by tabs into the database, Works "reads" across the table and turns each row of entries into a separate database record. If you're working in list view, Works places each entry in a separate cell. If necessary, Works also creates fields with default names (Field 1, Field 2, Field 3, and so on) for the entries. If you're working in form view, you can paste the table into a blank form with the Paste Record command, and Works will create default field names and fill in as many blank forms as you have rows in the table.

- Word-processed text to spreadsheet or database: If you paste a string of text — words, a sentence, or a paragraph — into either the spreadsheet or the database, Works inserts the entire block into the cell or field containing the highlight.

- Database to spreadsheet: If you paste database records into the spreadsheet, Works inserts field entries in columns and records in rows.

The following examples show you some of the different ways you can copy and paste between applications.

Pasting from the Spreadsheet

To try copying and pasting between Works applications, start by moving information from the spreadsheet to the word processor:

□ Select cells A1 through B3 in the spreadsheet, and copy their contents to the Clipboard.

□ Place the insertion point in a blank new paragraph below the sample text in your word-processed document.

□ Choose Paste from the word processor's Edit menu.

Your word-processed document will look like this:

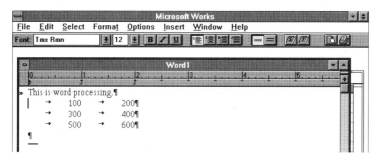

Works pastes in the values you copied to the Clipboard, adding tabs to align the cell contents in your word-processed document. By default, Works sets the tabs 1 inch apart. You can alter these settings by dragging the tab markers to the left or right on the ruler. If necessary, you can also use the Replace command to replace the tabs with blank spaces, commas, or any other character you like. For example, to replace the tabs with three blank spaces, you would choose the Replace command, type ^t in the Find What box, and press the Spacebar three times in the Replace With box.

Pasting from the Database

Pasting from the database to the word processor is similar to pasting from the spreadsheet:

□ Switch to the database document, and click the List View button to see your records in list view.

□ Select all three records, and copy them to the Clipboard.

□ Return to the word-processed document and paste the records into a new paragraph.

Your word-processed document will look like this:

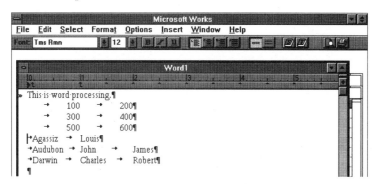

When you paste from the database, Works again separates fields with tabs. Unlike the material from the spreadsheet, however, the first field from the database is only slightly indented by the first tab. The other tabs are 1 inch apart. The word processor adjusts the tabs to simulate left or right alignment and accommodate the source data. Once again, you can replace the tabs with blank spaces or other characters if you want.

Formatting Pasted Data

After you've pasted spreadsheet data or database records into a word-processed document, you can select the information and format it in any way you like. For example, you might want to format the current word-processed document as follows:

□ Select the copied spreadsheet values.

□ Use the Toolbar to format them in a font and size you like, such as Helv 10.

□ Click the Center button on the Toolbar to center the data.

□ Select the three database records.

☐ Use the Border command on the Format menu to draw an outline border around them.

☐ Narrow the border by dragging the right indent marker on the ruler to the left.

Your screen should now look something like this:

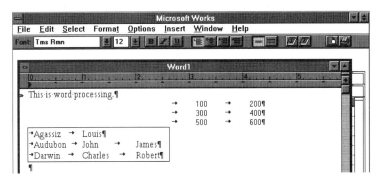

 When you select several paragraphs and create a border around them as you did here, you cannot remove the border by reselecting the same paragraphs. Works defines a border for *each* paragraph, so to remove a border, you must select the paragraphs one by one and turn off the border for each with the Border command.

Pasting from the Word Processor

Although you're more likely to paste from the spreadsheet or the database to the word processor rather than the other way around, you can move text from a word-processed document into either a spreadsheet or a database. To see how this works,

☐ Select the original text, *This is word processing*, in the word-processed document, and copy it to the Clipboard.

☐ Switch to the database. If you're in list view, select the cell in row 4 of the field headed First, and choose Paste. If you're in form view, move to a new record, highlight the dotted line for First:, and choose Paste Record.

When you paste a block of word-processed text (not a table separated by tabs) in list view, Works inserts the text in the field you selected. If you are in list view and select a cell that does not have a field name, Works pastes the text into the selected cell and gives the column a default name, such as Field 5, like this:

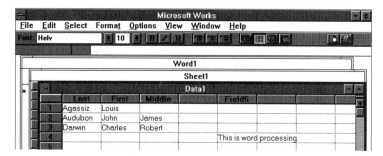

In contrast, when you paste word-processed text in form view, notice that Works pastes the text into the first field, regardless of the field you selected. If you select a blank part of the form, Works still pastes into the first field.

To see what happens when you paste from the word processor into the spreadsheet,

□ Switch to the spreadsheet, and click on cell A4 to select it.

□ Choose Paste from the Edit menu. (You don't have to copy from the word processor because the text you copied earlier is still on the Clipboard.)

As in the database list view, Works pastes the incoming text into the cell you selected.

Pasting Tables to the Spreadsheet

Now see what happens when you move a table from the word processor to the spreadsheet and the database. Your last experiments created ready-made tables in the word processor, but you should start from scratch with a new table so you can easily distinguish old data from new:

□ Switch to the word processor, and place the insertion point at the beginning of a new paragraph.

□ Click on the ruler to set left-aligned tabs at 1 inch and 2 inches.

☐ Type the following, pressing the Tab key between entries:

Quarter	Two bits	$0.25
Dollar	Buck	$1.00
Ten dollars	Sawbuck	$10.00
Thousand	Grand	$1000.00

☐ Select the entire table, and copy it to the Clipboard.

To move the table into your spreadsheet,

☐ Switch to Sheet1, click on cell D1 to select it, and choose Paste.

Your screen should look like this:

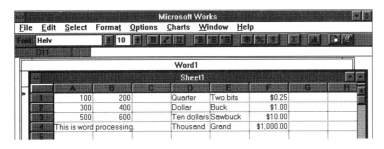

Each table entry becomes a cell entry in the spreadsheet.

Pasting Tables to the Database

Your database document already contains a form and a few records, so to see how Works moves the table into a database, start with a blank new document:

☐ Choose Create New File from the File menu, and click Database to open a new document.

You can paste a table into a blank form like the one on your screen or into a form with field names you've assigned. To try the latter,

☐ Create the three fields Name, Slang, and Amount.

☐ To paste in the table, choose Paste Record from the Edit menu.

Works produces this:

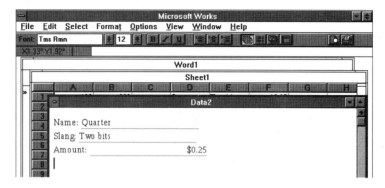

Now here's the interesting part. You now see only the entries in the first row of your word-processed table:

☐ Click the next button (the one with the right-pointing arrow-head) in the horizontal scroll bar.

Works displays a form containing a record for the second row of your table. Scroll through form view some more, or switch to list view, and you'll see that Works pasted the entire table into the database as field entries for four separate records.

If you had pasted the table into a blank form, you would see pretty much the same results, except Works would assign default names to the three fields corresponding to the columns in your table. You could change these default names by selecting each and typing in the name you wanted.

WINDOWS BUZZWORDS: LINKING AND EMBEDDING

You can ignore the twin *concepts* of linking and embedding until the sun turns blue without affecting your ability to use Works in any way. By now, however, you've probably developed a feel for the underlying sophistication that helps make Works intuitive and easy to learn, so you might enjoy some additional insight into this automated data manager.

Linking and embedding are two ways that Works and other Windows programs can help you update information quickly and with ease. Linking establishes a connection between a Works spreadsheet and a word-processed Works document you copy spreadsheet information into. When you create such a link, changes you make in the original document are automatically reflected in the word-processed copy. Basically, linking is like giving a one-way radio to the original. When you update the original, it sends a message to the copy: "Hey, change this and this."

Embedding, which you used when you inserted a drawing in a word-processed document, lets you create a document or drawing in one program and insert your work in a document controlled by another program. In effect, embedding is like giving a transmitter to the embedded data (called an *object*). When you double-click on the embedded object, it sends a message to the originating program: "Come get me, I'm going to be changed."

Both linking and embedding are based on the idea that you should be able to access any type of information without having to start a separate application or close one document and open another. In essence, linking and embedding take the concept of the Clipboard one giant step further toward truly usable software. Instead of using part of your computer's memory as a temporary stopping place for information traveling from one document to another, you can form direct connections between the information you move around and the documents or programs that you take the information from.

The ability to update data in more than one place is the most important difference between linking or embedding and copy and paste. Linking and embedding can always take you back to work on your original data; copy and paste immediately "forgets" where the copy came from and, thus, cannot help you transfer changes from the original to a duplicate version.

The advantage of both linking and embedding over cut and paste or copy and paste is that both forms of data transport leave the work of managing applications and data files to Works, rather than to you. When you're busy or in a hurry, that's a significant advantage. If you're overworked or tend to be forgetful, linking and embedding can help ensure fewer loose ends and help you keep your documents accurate and up to date.

Linking

Linking within the Works applications operates in one direction: from the spreadsheet to the word processor. With linking, you can create an invisible connection between a chart and a word-processed document or between a spreadsheet and a word-processed document. Like an internal note from Works to itself, a link remains "attached" to copied information even after you've closed the document or quit Works. Because the link is permanent, it ensures that any changes you make to the chart or to the data in the spreadsheet are automatically reflected in the word-processed document.

Linking a Chart

Linking a chart to a word-processed document is so simple it's fun — at least after you've gone through the work of producing the chart to begin with. The Works terminology is a bit confusing, however, because you link a chart to a word-processed document with the Chart command on the *Insert* menu. You'll insert a chart into a sample document in the following examples.

Linking with the Spreadsheet

Linking spreadsheet data is based on a variation of copy and paste in which you select and copy data to the Clipboard as usual, but then paste it into a word-processed document with the Paste Special command (rather than Paste). The Paste Special command — in the word processor only — lets Works establish a link between the original document (and application) and the pasted copy. Because this link exists, the copied information has a direct line to the source document, and Works can update the copy whenever you change the original.

The only Works application that can accept linked data is the word processor, and the only Works application that can provide linked data is the spreadsheet. You can also create links between certain Windows applications, such as Microsoft Excel, and the Works word processor. The remainder of this discussion, however, assumes that the linking you'll do will be within Works.

To try out linking, close your sample files and create new ones in the word processor and the spreadsheet:

☐ Select each open document in turn, and choose Close from the File menu. When Works asks if you want to save the changes, click No.

☐ When your screen is clear, create the new documents as usual, with the Create New File command.

☐ Now enter the following nonsense data into the spreadsheet:

	Column A	Column B
Row 1	20	60
Row 2	30	70
Row 3	40	80
Row 4	50	90

Inserting a Chart

Because charts are so easy to insert and so useful in all kinds of printed materials, start by charting the data in your sample spreadsheet and then inserting the chart into the word-processed document:

◻ Select cells A1 through B4.

◻ Click the Chart button to create a bar chart.

◻ So you can see what's happening, tile the three document windows.

◻ Click in the word processor window to make it active.

◻ Choose the Chart command from the Insert menu.

Works displays this dialog box:

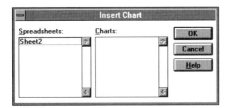

You use this dialog box to choose the spreadsheet and chart you want to insert. Now do the following:

◻ Click on the spreadsheet name (Sheet2) to select it.

◻ When Works displays Chart1 in the Charts box, click on it, and then click OK to complete the command.

The chart you selected quickly appears in the word processor window. To see it better,

◻ Maximize the word processor window.

The chart is rather large, so scale it to a more manageable size:

◻ Click on the chart to select it.

◻ Choose the Picture command from the Format menu. (You used the Picture command in Chapter 5 to scale the drawing you inserted in a sample document.)

□ To keep the inserted chart from intruding on your other examples, yet keep it large enough to view, scale it to 50 percent of its original height and 75 percent of its original width.

The chart should look like this:

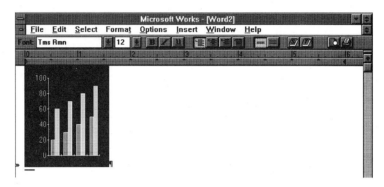

□ To work with the other documents, tile the windows once more.

Linking Spreadsheet Data

When you want to link spreadsheet information to a word-processed document, form the habit of saving the spreadsheet as a first step. Works will not create a link unless the originating document has been saved, so begin by doing the following:

□ Save the spreadsheet in your WKSBOOK directory, naming it SSLINK.

□ Copy cells A1 through B4 to the Clipboard.

□ Switch to the word processor and make room for the copied data by creating a new paragraph.

□ Now choose Paste Special from the Edit menu.

Works displays this dialog box:

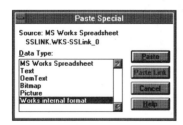

At the top of this dialog box, Works identifies the source of the data you've copied to the Clipboard, in this case, the Works spreadsheet. When you're pasting from within Works, the dialog box also shows the name of the source document. The text reading *SSLink_0* tells you that Works will consider the data you copied to the Clipboard as the basis for link number 0.

For the spreadsheet, if you replace the Clipboard contents and choose the Paste Special command, Works sets up a new link number for the contents of the Clipboard. For example, if you were to select the same cells and copy them to the Clipboard a second time, the new set would replace the old. If you then chose the Paste Special command, Works would propose *SSLink_1* for the data, even though the values were identical to those you copied earlier.

Below the identifying text, in the Data Type box, Works displays several options that are essentially formats you can choose from for the data you plan to paste. Once again, these items vary according to the type of information on the Clipboard and the application (such as Windows Paintbrush or Windows Notepad) you used to create the Clipboard contents.

When you're working with spreadsheet data, the highlighted option (in this case, Works internal format) pastes the data in as columns separated by tabs. The same happens if you choose Text or Oem Text. (OEM stands for Original Equipment Manufacturer; Oem Text enables Works to paste the full range of characters, including lines, accented letters, and special graphic symbols, that are supported by your computer.) If you select Bitmap or Picture, Works pastes in the cell contents as a dot-by-dot or a drawn image, duplicating the cells as they appear in the spreadsheet, including the gridlines.

None of these options, however, allows you to link the source document with the copy. If you click on any of them, you'll notice that the button labeled Paste Link remains grayed out and unusable. To forge a link with the spreadsheet,

□ Click on MS Works Spreadsheet.

□ The Paste Link button becomes active; click on it.

A short while later, your word-processed document holds a copy of the cells in the spreadsheet.

Updating a Link

Updating a link when your documents are open is very simple:

□ Click on cell A1 in the spreadsheet.

□ Type *200*, and press Enter to change the cell contents.

As soon as you press Enter, Works updates not only the spreadsheet, but the copy in the word processor. Try it again:

▢ Change 30, 40, and 50 to 300, 400, and 500 in the spreadsheet.

Each change you make is immediately reflected in the word-processed document (and, of course, in the chart created from the spreadsheet values).

You've probably noticed that Works did not update the chart you inserted in the word-processed document, even though you linked the chart to the word processor with the Chart command on the Insert menu. The reason for the non-update is simple, though potentially frustrating: You changed the name of the spreadsheet when you saved it (from the default SheetX to SSLINK in the WKSBOOK directory).

Works associated the new filename with the linked *data* in your word-processed document, but it has not yet associated the new filename with the chart you inserted. You'll change that shortly, but for now (and in the future) remember that links are sometimes tenuous things, and a small detail can leave you scratching your head for awhile.

Opening a Linked Document

Meanwhile, what happens if you update the spreadsheet when the word-processed document is closed? To see,

▢ Save the word-processed document, again in your WKSBOOK directory, under a name such as WPLINK, and close the file.

▢ Change the values in column B of the spreadsheet to 600, 700, 800, and 900.

▢ Save the spreadsheet. (This isn't a necessary step for the example, but it's useful to form the habit of saving files after making substantial changes.)

▢ To reopen your word-processed document, choose its name from the list at the end of the File menu.

Before opening the document, Works displays the following dialog box:

□ Click Yes, and a few moments later your word-processed document appears onscreen, complete with updates to the linked
data. Notice that Works *still* has not updated your chart.

Closing a Linked Document

When Works saves a linked spreadsheet, it also saves the link information that
defines the spreadsheet's connection(s) to word-processed documents. If you
try to close a linked spreadsheet without saving, Works displays a dialog box
like this:

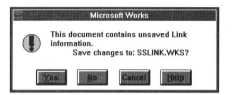

Remember that link information refers to the connections between the
spreadsheet and copies you've made elsewhere. If it's important to update those
copies automatically, click Yes to save all relevant information.

Editing a Linked Object

You edited linked cells when you closed the word-processed document and
changed values in the spreadsheet. At other times, you might be working on the
word-processed document and decide to modify information in the source. This
is where you can see how fast, easy, and intuitive linking can make your work:

□ Close the spreadsheet. Click Yes if Works displays its "unsaved
link information" message.

□ Click on the linked data in the word-processed document to
select it. (Notice that you select it all, much as you select an entire
drawing you insert in a document.)

□ Open the Edit menu, and you'll see a new item, Edit MS Works
Spreadsheet Object. Don't choose it, however.

Whenever you highlight linked or embedded information in a word-
processed document, Works adds an Edit Object command to the Edit menu.
The full name of the command changes to reflect the type of object — drawing,
spreadsheet cells, whatever — that you've highlighted. To edit the object, choose

the command, and Works will start the source application (the spreadsheet here) and display the source document. There's a faster method, though:

□ Close the Edit menu, and instead double-click on the linked data in your word-processed document.

Almost instantly, Works displays the source spreadsheet. As you can see at the top of the application window, it has also started the spreadsheet application for you. All with two clicks of the mouse.

Editing a Link

Now it's time to update that chart. In addition to editing linked data, you'll sometimes have to edit (modify or cancel) the link itself. For example, you might redefine a spreadsheet after you saved it under a new name or in a different directory. You do this type of editing with the Links command on the Edit menu. The Links command offers several ways to affect a link. To see them,

□ Close the spreadsheet document.

□ If necessary, highlight the linked data in the word-processed document. Choose the Links command from the Edit menu.

Works displays a large dialog box:

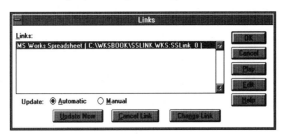

In the box labeled Links, Works identifies the link for the data you've selected. The remaining options are as follows:

■ Update — Automatic, which is the default, updates linked information whenever you change the original; Manual lets you choose when to update.

■ Update Now — Updates linked data.

■ Cancel Link — Breaks the link, essentially turning the copied data into ordinary, non-updatable information.

■ Change Link — Lets you change the identification of the source document. For example, you can change the drive letter or directory if you move the file. You will use this button to update the chart in your document.

- Play — Starts the source application.

- Edit — Also starts the source application and displays the source document for editing. Use either Play or Edit if the source program is the Works spreadsheet.

You've selected the linked data in your word-processed document, so try out the Edit button:

□ Click Edit.

Works starts the spreadsheet and displays the document from which you linked data.

For something a little more useful, update the chart at long last:

□ Tile the windows so you can see both documents.

□ Click on the chart to select it.

□ Choose the Links command again.

This time, Works displays its "understanding" of the chart's identification: *Chart (SheetX:ChartY)*. To update the link and, therefore, the chart in your document,

□ Click the Change Link button.

Works displays a dialog box that is almost identical to the dialog box displayed by the Open Existing File command. Here, however, you want to redefine the name of the link, so

□ If necessary, use the File Name and Directories boxes to find the spreadsheet.

□ Click on the filename to select it, and then click OK.

The dialog box disappears, and when your word-processed document returns to the screen, the chart is updated to reflect the latest information in your spreadsheet.

When you're working with your own documents, remember the "problem" you encountered here with your linked chart. Although you'll probably be working with named files most (if not all) of the time and will seldom encounter this situation, the real point of the example is this: Clever as it is, Works cannot anticipate everything you might choose to do.

Computers and their software are so reliable and so fast that people often forget they are machines and sets of instructions. Imagination and leaps of intuition are still in the province of humans, so when a small but irritating problem arises, keep your sense of humor and think small — small in the sense of assuming you might have overlooked some detail that seemed insignificant to you but is significant to Works.

Embedding

Embedding, which you saw in Chapter 5 when you used the Draw module from the word processor, forms a direct connection between an object you insert in a document and the program you use to create the object. When using Draw, for example, you temporarily leave the word processor to create a drawing, and you embed the drawing in your word-processed document by exiting Draw. To edit the drawing later on, you open the word-processed document and double-click on the drawing to call Draw once again.

Using Note-It

In addition to drawings, Works also lets you embed the electronic equivalent of stick-on tags in word-processed documents. Your tool for this is a program called Microsoft Note-It, which appears as Note-It on the word processor's Insert menu.

Note-It is useful for drawing a reader's attention to comments, notes, questions, and even editorial judgments. The program is also fun to use:

☐ Create a new word processor document, and type the following, so you'll be able to compare your note with some text: *This is a sample paragraph to show the default size of a note in relation to some document text.*

☐ Press Enter to start a new paragraph.

☐ Choose Note-It from the Insert menu.

Works displays a large, graphical dialog box:

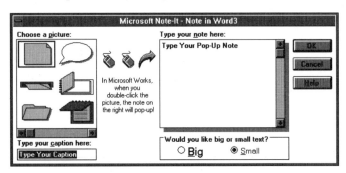

The title bar in the dialog box identifies both the Note-It program and the file into which Works will insert your note. The boxes labeled Choose a picture, Type your caption here, and Type your note here are the parts of the dialog box where you create the note. The picture you choose appears in your word-processed document to show that a note exists. The caption is text that appears with the picture to identify the note. The note itself is text that remains hidden until the reader chooses to view it by double-clicking the Note-It picture.

To create a sample note, first choose a picture. Note-It includes many interesting and (if you have a color monitor) colorful pictures, so

- Scroll through the graphics in the Choose a picture box. When you reach the ladybug, click on it to select it.

- To caption the note, move to the caption box by pressing Alt-C, instead of clicking with the mouse.

Alt-C both moves to the edit box and selects the words *Type Your Caption*, so as soon as you begin to type a caption, the existing text will disappear. If you used the mouse to place the insertion point in the caption box, you would have to drag over the text to select it. Using the keyboard instead is a small matter, but more efficient in this case.

- Type the caption *Note to Editor*.

- Press Alt-N to move the highlight to the box where you type the body of your note.

Once again, using the keyboard instead of the mouse both moves the highlight and selects the text, so all you have to do is type. Note-It wraps lines for you, so you don't even have to worry about pressing Enter at the ends of lines. To create the text,

- Type the following: *The highfalutin' language in this section really BUGS me. Please replace the five-dollar words and fancy jargon with good, plain, explanatory prose.*

That's your note. The last part of the dialog box gives you a choice of making your text big or small. Unless you want to make your note really stand out, small is fine.

- To leave the Note-It dialog box and insert the note, click OK.

After a short while, the picture and caption for the note appear at the location of the insertion point. To see what the page looks like,

- Click the Preview button.

□ If the entire caption doesn't appear, zoom in on the preview page.

□ Click Cancel to leave Print Preview.

Reading and Editing Notes

After you've inserted a note, you or anyone else can read the text associated with the note in either of two ways. The easiest method is to double-click on the picture.

Works displays this:

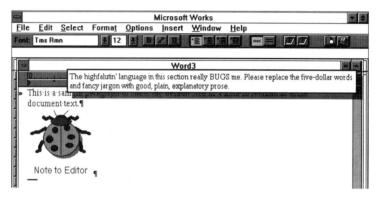

To clear away the text,

□ Click anywhere within the application or document windows.

Whenever you select a linked or embedded object in a document, recall that Works adds an Edit Object command to the Edit menu. When you insert a note in a document, this command gives you a means of both displaying and editing the note:

□ If necessary, select the picture by clicking on it.

□ Open the Edit menu, and choose MS Note-It Object.

Works displays this dialog box:

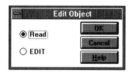

□ To view the note, select Read and click OK. To start Note-It so you can edit the note, select EDIT and click OK.

The body of a note can contain about 25 lines of 40 characters each, so your instructions, questions, complaints, or observations can be fairly detailed. While constructing or editing a note, you can use the following keys and key combinations:

- Ctrl-X to cut selected text.

- Ctrl-C to copy selected text.

- Ctrl-V to paste cut or copied text.

- Backspace or Del to delete characters.

- Up arrow and Down arrow to move up and down a line at a time.

- Ctrl-Left arrow and Ctrl-Right arrow to move left or right a word at a time.

Note-It has a clear, well-organized on-line Help file, if you need to know more about this feature. After you've embedded a note in a document, you can do the following:

- Size the picture and caption with the Picture command on the Format menu. If your caption is relatively long, be aware that making the picture too small can truncate some of the letters or words in the caption. If you want to embed a picture and scale it down, keep your caption short.

- Delete a note by selecting it, and then use either the Cut or Delete command on the Edit menu, or press the Del key.

- Move a note by selecting it, cutting it, and pasting it into the new location. You can use the regular Paste command to do this.

- Copy a note by selecting it, copying it, and pasting it back into the document. Again, you can use the Paste command. Double-clicking on the copy displays the same note text as the original, so copying is a useful way to embed a number of identical notes — for example, a red warning flag and the text *Check this* — in many places in a document.

- Print a note picture (not the text) when you print the document. To avoid printing notes, select and delete them before printing.

AN EXTENDED EXAMPLE

Now that you're familiar with the methods you can use to move information from place to place, you can use the following examples to practice. The three documents you create in this section are typical Works documents. By combining these three documents you can create a letter that contains text, spreadsheet data, database records, and graphics. The finished letter won't be long, but creating it will show you how to comfortably jump from one document to another.

The foundation of this example will be a letter:

☐ Begin by closing your open files — don't bother to save them.

☐ Next, create a new word processor document.

☐ Maximize the document window, and type the text shown in the following illustration. Format all paragraphs for single spacing.

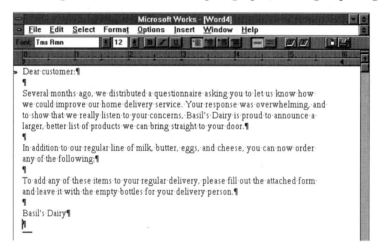

Now create a spreadsheet:

☐ Widen columns A and C to fit the text; format cells B3 through B8 and I3 through I8 for currency with two decimals.

☐ Format columns D through H for 5 characters.

Your spreadsheet will look like this:

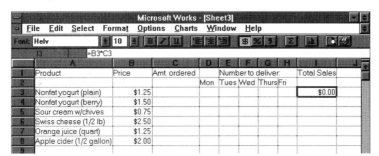

Assume that Basil will be using this spreadsheet to track new orders, determine how many must be delivered each day, and total the sales. The example doesn't make use of any formulas, but you can see the formula for calculating sales by product in the formula bar in the illustration.

Now use the database to create an order form:

☐ Copy cells A3 through C8 to the Clipboard.

☐ Create a new database document and create the four fields Product, Price, Amount ordered, and Total.

☐ Choose Paste Record to fill in the Product and Price fields.

☐ Switch to list view, format the prices for currency, and adjust the column widths so all entries and field names are displayed.

Your database should now look like this:

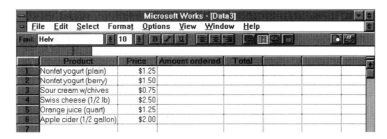

☐ Switch to report view. Skipping the Report Title box, add the four fields to a new report.

- ☐ Click on OK for each dialog box until the report appears.

- ☐ Type *Basil's Order Form:* in the Title row, formatting the text for boldfacing and underlining. Left-align the Product heading, and right-align the Price and Total headings.

- ☐ Select the Headings row, and use the Insert Row/Column command to add a second Title row for more space at the top of the form.

- ☐ Click in column A, and type *Name:* two lines below the Summary row. Type *Address:* and *Phone:* in the following two rows, using the Down arrow key to move from row to row. On the next row, type *Please circle your delivery day: M T W Th F,* spacing the letters out evenly.

Your finished report should look like this:

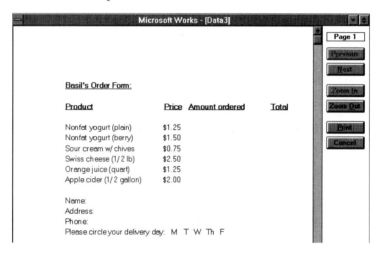

Those are your sample documents. Save them before you continue.

Combining Your Data

To see how truly integrated Works is, add a logo to Basil's rather plain letter:

- ☐ Place the insertion point at the beginning of the letter, in front of the word *Dear.*

- ☐ Press Enter to create a blank paragraph. Place the insertion point in the blank paragraph.

□ Choose Drawing from the Insert menu. Expand the Draw window a bit if necessary, so you can see all the tools down the left edge.

Instead of designing a logo with a dairy theme, make use of the clip art library that comes with Works:

□ Choose Import Picture from Draw's File menu.

□ In the dialog box that appears, change to the CLIPART directory under MSWORKS, and double-click on *2doorvan.wmf* to insert it in the drawing area.

□ Using the square, dark resize handles surrounding the van, reduce the size of the picture to 1.5 inches high by 3 inches wide.

The van is nice, but not very distinctive, so make use of Draw's ability to overlay objects:

□ Click on the A to choose the Text tool.

□ Click in a blank part of the screen and type *Basil's*.

□ Format the text for a font size that will fit the side panel of the van — 10 points or so — and make the text both bold and italic.

□ Select the formatted text, and move it onto the upper side panel of the van.

Your graphic should now look like this:

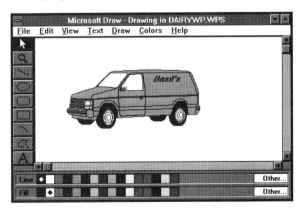

□ Using the same procedure, type and format the word *Dairy*, and move it into position below *Basil's* on the van.

Now embed the van in your word-processed letter:

☐ Choose Exit and Return from the File menu, and click Yes when Draw asks if you want to update the letter.

☐ Center the van and preview the results. If you want more space between the logo and the first line of text, format the *Dear customer* line for two or more lines of space before the paragraph with the Indents & Spacing command.

There's your graphic. Now it's time to add the list of new products Basil wants to introduce:

☐ Move the insertion point to the blank paragraph above the paragraph that begins *To add any of these.*

☐ Switch to the spreadsheet document and select cells A1 through B8. Copy them to the Clipboard.

☐ Return to the word processor, and insert the Clipboard contents. Insert the copied cells and link the copy to the original document by choosing the Paste Special command, selecting MS Works Spreadsheet as the data type, and clicking the Paste Link button.

Now if Basil decides to change prices or add new items before the letter goes out, the word-processed copy will reflect the latest version of the product list in the spreadsheet. When the linked cells appear in the letter,

☐ Fine-tune the appearance and layout of the cells by centering the paragraph, and adding a line of space above and below.

Finally, turn your attention to the order form that will accompany each letter. The form, remember, is a database report. You might expect to simply print as many copies as you need and have someone attach a printed form to each letter by hand. With Works, this is not necessary:

☐ Select, or create and select, a blank paragraph at the end of the letter, after *Basil's Dairy.*

☐ Switch to report view in the database, and open the Edit menu.

Works displays a command called Copy Report Output, which copies the *report,* not the *report view form,* to the Clipboard. That's what you want, so

☐ Choose Copy Report Output, and then switch back to the word processor.

☐ You can't link database information to a word-processed docu- ment, so choose the Paste command.

Immediately, Works adds the order form to the end of the letter. Pretty good! All you have to do now is

☐ Choose Page Break from the Insert menu to ensure that the order form appears on a separate page.

You're done. Save your files because the next chapter uses this letter to show how Works can help you create personalized form letters.

13
Form Letters and Sample Files

This, the last chapter in the book, covers two different but useful topics: How to create form letters and labels for mass mailings, and how to use the sample files that come with Works as the basis for organizing and giving structure to your own business or personal data. Beyond this, a little experience at using Works in real-life situations is all you need to see where and how this program can make your work easier, faster, and more organized.

CREATING A FORM LETTER

To produce a form letter, you need two pre-existing Works documents: a basic letter (or other word-processed document) and a database of names and other information that you'll call on to personalize the letter. After you've created these two documents, you can put the form letter together on your own or with the help of a WorksWizard. The WorksWizard ensures that the form letter is constructed correctly, but as you'll see, doing it on your own is hardly fraught with pitfalls. After you're familiar with both methods, you might find yourself switching from one to the other, using whichever approach best suits your immediate needs.

To try out the following examples,

□ Start Works, if necessary, and open the letter you created in Chapter 12. Click Yes when Works asks if you want to update the links in the document.

□ Maximize both the application and document windows.

☐ Open a new database document, and create the form shown in the following illustration:

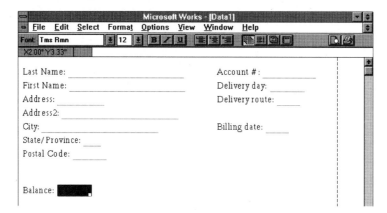

If you want to match the field sizes exactly, set the fields as follows:

Set	To	Set	To
Address	8	Delivery day	6
State	3	Delivery route	4
Postal Code	6	Billing date	4
Account #	9	Balance	6

Format the Balance field for currency.

☐ Save the file in your WKSBOOK directory under the name MAILING.

☐ Now switch to list view, and adjust column widths and create a set of records in the database, as shown in the following two illustrations:

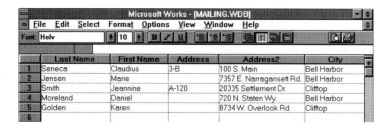

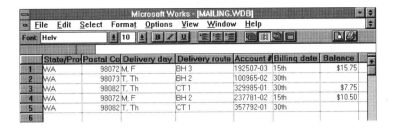

With these preliminaries out of the way, you can create your form letters.

The Word-Processed Document

A form letter can be so simple that it includes little more than the recipient's name and address:

Dear (NAME):

You may already have won $1,000,000 in our fabulous, all-cash sweepstakes! All winning entries have already been picked, and (NAME) living at (AD-DRESS) in (CITY, STATE) could be the lucky winner!

Or, depending on how many fields your database includes and how many you want to incorporate, a form letter can be much more personal:

Dear (NAME):

Long time, no see! How are (SPOUSE) and (CHILDREN)? Bet you had a great birthday party on (BIRTHDAY) . . . and so on.

A form letter doesn't have to be a letter at all. It can be a brochure, a catalog, a memo, a pamphlet, or any other type of document. The difference between a regular letter and a so-called form letter is that you include database fields wherever you want Works to insert personalized data in the letter. That data is often a person's name and address, but as you'll see later, it can also extend to the person's account number, billing date, or outstanding balance. If you're creating a catalog or putting together a price quote, the letter can incorporate part numbers, prices, available colors and sizes, or any other database information.

To create a form letter, start with the word-processed document containing the text you want for the body of the letter. To turn the document into a form letter, you then insert *placeholders* that show Works where you want the personalized information to appear. Each placeholder is the name of an existing field, such as First Name, in a database you've already created. On screen, a placeholder is distinguished from surrounding text by chevrons that, as you'll see shortly, look like small double arrowheads.

Using the WorksWizard

You can use the Form Letters WorksWizard to create a simple letter with the recipient's name, address, and if you choose, a salutation. Before you use this WorksWizard, you should know something about how it works, so you can avoid missteps and extra effort.

The Form Letters WorksWizard is designed to work hand-in-glove with the Address Books WorksWizard, and that means it is designed to recognize the field names used by the Address Books WorksWizard — First Name, Last Name, Postal Code, and so on. If you created the database on your own, the Form Letters WorksWizard can use your database only if you use field names spelled *exactly* as they appear in a database created with the Address Books WorksWizard. You won't break the Form Letters WorksWizard if your own field names differ, but to use the WorksWizard, you'll have to modify your database before you can continue.

Your sample database includes the correct field names, so you won't have any problems. If you create your own mailing lists without the Address Books WorksWizard, however, you can verify your field names by checking a file named FIELDS.WPS in the MSWORKS directory. To see what this file looks like,

- □ Choose Open Existing File from the File menu.

- □ Change to the MSWORKS directory, and double-click on the file named FIELDS.WPS.

The file gives all the details you need to create appropriate field names for the Form Letters WorksWizard. Now look at what the WorksWizard can do:

- □ Close FIELDS.WPS.

- □ Choose Create New File from the File menu, and click on WorksWizards in the Create New File dialog box.

- □ When the WorksWizards dialog box appears, double-click on Form Letters.

- □ Take a few moments to read the opening screen. When you finish, click the Next button at the bottom of the instruction box.

The next screen asks whether you created your database with the Address Books WorksWizard. In this instance, you didn't, so

- □ Click item 2, I created my address book with Works.

- □ Click the Next button.

The next screen bears out the need for the Form Letters WorksWizard to find exact field names. Notice that the screen refers you to FIELDS.WPS if you need help. Your database has the correct fields, so

- ☐ Click the Next button.

- ☐ Click Yes when the WorksWizard asks if the database is open.

- ☐ Click the Next button, and press the *number* of MAILING.WDB when the Window menu opens at the top of the screen. Use the numbers in the top row of the keyboard; the WorksWizard doesn't respond to your numeric keypad.

- ☐ Click Next again, and click Yes when the WorksWizard displays the correct database. Click Next.

Now the WorksWizard swings into a flurry of activity, checking your database for the fields it needs and following up by checking the other fields in your database. If you had made a mistake, the WorksWizard would tell you so with a message like this:

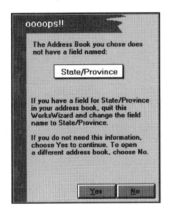

To fix the error, you would click No (you do not want to continue), and then click Exit when the next screen appeared.

When the WorksWizard finds that all is well, it moves on to the next phase by asking about your word-processed document. You have a letter you want to change, so

- ☐ Click 1, Change a letter into a form letter, and then click the Next button.

- ☐ Click Yes when the WorksWizard asks if the document is open and click Next again.

☐ When the Window menu opens at the top of the screen, press the number of your word-processed document. Click Next.

☐ Click Yes when the WorksWizard displays your document. Click Next.

Now the WorksWizard asks whether you want to include an address, a salutation, or both:

☐ Click 1, Include Address only. Click Next.

The next set of screens asks for information that tells the WorksWizard how to format the address in your document. Your sample mailing will go to residents of Washington state, so

☐ Click 1, North or South America. Click Next.

☐ Click 1, United States. Click Next.

The next screen (you're getting close to the end now) displays the field names the WorksWizard can insert. Those that appear in your database are displayed in dark characters. Choose the fields you want:

☐ Click next to all of the items, from First Name through Postal Code. Click Next.

In the next screen, the WorksWizard gives you a chance to go back and change any choices you made. If your choices are all right,

☐ Click Next.

Now the WorksWizard pulls a rather clever rabbit out of its electronic hat. It asks you where to insert the address:

☐ Place the insertion point in front of the *D* in *Dear* and click. Click Next.

☐ Click Insert Fields when the WorksWizard tells you it will insert the address fields into your letter.

As you watch, the fields appear in your letter in the designated location. The spacing has a definite "airiness" about it because each new paragraph is taking on the formatting of the *Dear Customer* paragraph. Don't worry, you'll fix the spacing in a moment. When the WorksWizard is finished, it asks what you want to do next. The formatting isn't quite right, so you don't want to save the letter yet. Instead,

☐ Choose 4, Exit the WorksWizard to print the letters. (You won't be printing yet, but the WorksWizard doesn't have to know.) Click Next.

You have a little more work to do, so

☐ Exit the WorksWizard by clicking 2, No, don't save the changes.

☐ Click Next, and the checkered flag appears.

☐ Click Exit.

You've gone through a pretty extensive procedure, but if you've ever tried to create a form letter with a nonintegrated program, you'll appreciate the ease with which you made it all happen. Notice, for example, that the WorksWizard has included a blank space between First Name and Last Name, and another between State/Province and Postal Code. It has even included a comma and a space after City. Except for cleaning up the paragraph spacing, your job is done.

To finish up,

☐ If an extra space appears in front of *Dear,* delete the space.

☐ Select the paragraph containing the First Name and Last Name fields, and format it for 1 blank line above with the Indents & Spacing command.

☐ Select the remaining address fields, and format them for 0 space above with the same command.

Previewing and Printing

When you create a form letter, it's a good idea to preview some of the finished letters to verify that the printed output will be exactly as you expect. If you click the Preview button on the Toolbar, Works displays the form letter with the database fields, not the names and addresses that will replace them. To preview form letters as they will be printed,

☐ Choose the Print Form Letters command from the File menu.

Works displays this dialog box:

The Preview button is what interests you now:

☐ Click Preview.

Works displays your first personalized letter:

Notice that this address is four lines long because it includes both an apartment number (3-B) and a street number (100 S. Main). Not all of your recipients live in apartments, however. To see what happens with their addresses,

☐ Click the Next button twice to move to the first page of the letter to Marie Jensen.

Exactly as you want it. Works is smart enough to omit the first address field if it's blank.

There's no need to print these sample letters, but if you want to do so,

☐ Verify that your printer is turned on.

☐ Choose the Print Form Letters command again, and click the Print button.

☐ Choose the number of copies (of each letter) you want when the Print dialog box appears.

That's it. Notice that you must print form letters with a special command. If you were to choose Print instead of Print Form Letters, Works would print the version with the database fields, not the personalized letters. As always, you can use the Page Setup & Margins and the Printer Setup commands before printing to change the page layout or any printer settings, such as paper size.

You don't need this document for any more examples, so save it only if you want to use it for later experiments, and then close the file.

Creating Form Letters on Your Own

Using the Form Letters WorksWizard is easy as long as your database fields match the fields used by the Address Books WorksWizard, and as long as you don't want to include more than the address and, possibly, a salutation. If you want to use different field names in your database, or you want to insert personalized information in the body of your letter, you use the Database Field command on the Insert menu. This command lets you select existing fields in a database and insert placeholders wherever you want in a document.

To create a form letter and insert placeholders, follow these steps:

□ Create or open a document in the word processor.

□ Open the database containing the fields you want. You cannot insert placeholders unless the database is already open.

□ Working from the word processor, choose the Database Field command from the Insert menu.

□ Select the field name you want to insert, and click OK to complete the command.

You use the Database Field command for each field name you want to insert. The process can be repetitive if you're inserting many field names, but it's no more difficult than using the Form Letters WorksWizard. After you're experienced with the procedure, you might find this do-it-yourself approach faster, especially if you don't need the help of the WorksWizard in formatting addresses for different countries.

To try creating a form letter from scratch, put together a reminder to customers who are tardy paying their bills:

□ Be sure that your MAILING database is still open. Remember, Works cannot insert fields unless the database is open.

□ Create a new document in the word processor.

▢ Center the first paragraph and type the following, pressing Enter where you see [Enter] below:

```
Basil's Dairy[Enter]

P.O. Box 23[Enter]

Route 17[Enter]

Cowvalley, WA 98072[Enter]
```

▢ Format the blank paragraph for left alignment and two blank lines above.

▢ Choose Special Character from the Insert menu. When the dialog box appears, choose Print long date to have Works insert the correct date in the finished letter.

▢ Press Enter, and then format the resulting paragraph for zero lines above.

So far, your document should look like this:

Now you're ready to insert the recipient's name and address, all from database fields:

▢ Choose Database Field from the Insert menu.

Works displays this dialog box:

In the Databases box, Works lists the names of all open databases, in this case, the one you created earlier and named MAILING. In the Fields box, Works displays the names of all fields in the highlighted database. The Field name box at the bottom displays the name of the field currently selected in the Fields box (none as yet). To insert the recipient's name and address,

☐ Click on First Name in the Fields box, and click OK.

A placeholder for the field appears in your document:

When you used the WorksWizard, it took care of blank spaces for you. Here, you do it for yourself:

☐ Press the Spacebar once to leave a blank after First Name.

☐ Insert the Last Name field by choosing it from the Database Field dialog box.

☐ Press Enter to move to a new paragraph, and then insert the Address field.

☐ Press Enter again, and insert the Address2 field.

☐ Press Enter, and insert the City field.

☐ Type a comma and press the Spacebar to punctuate your paragraph-to-be, and then insert the State/Province field.

☐ Press the Spacebar again, and insert the Postal Code field.

For the salutation,

☐ Press Enter, and then format the new paragraph for one blank line above.

☐ Type *Dear Customer:* and press Enter.

Now it's time for the body of your letter, complete with additional database fields. The new paragraph will have the same formatting as the preceding one, so get straight to business. Type the following letter, inserting the appropriate database field wherever you see a field name in parentheses and all in capitals. Press Enter where you see [Enter], and insert *date* with the Special Character command.

```
We regret to inform you that your account, number (ACCOUNT #) is overdue. Your
normal billing is sent out to you on the (BILLING DATE) of every month. As of
*date*, we have not received payment on your outstanding balance of
(BALANCE).[Enter]

Please remit (BALANCE) as soon as possible. If you have already sent payment,
please disregard this notice.[Enter]
```

For the closing,

☐ Format the new paragraph for two lines of space above.

☐ Type *Sincerely,* and press Enter.

☐ Format this paragraph for zero lines above, and type *Basil's Dairy*.

That's all there is to creating a form letter on your own. Save it in the WKSBOOK directory as BILLSDUE.WPS.

This is what it looks like:

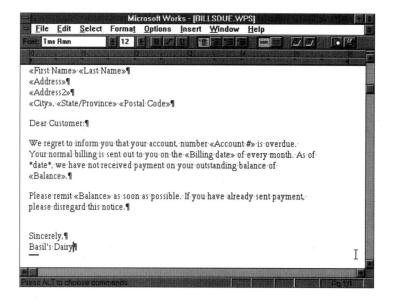

Selecting Records to Print

If you were to print your form letter now, Works would print a letter to everyone in your database, whether or not the person's payment is late. To see this,

▫ Choose Print Form Letters.

▫ Click the Preview button, and zoom in on your document.

▫ Use the Next button to scroll from one letter to the next.

Notice that Works displays letters for Marie Jensen and Karen Golden, even though their records don't show an outstanding balance. Before you print, you'll want to be more selective about the recipients of the letter.

Because one Works application can communicate with another, selecting records to include in a form letter requires only one extra step, a visit to query view in the database. Use query view to choose the records you want, and let Works do the rest:

▫ Click the Cancel button to leave Print Preview.

▫ Switch to the database, choose list view, and scroll to the right.

Three of the five records show an unpaid balance. To select only those records for use in the form letter,

▫ Click the Query View button.

▫ Click in the Balance field, and type >0.

▫ Switch back to list view, and this time you see only the records with a value greater than 0 in the Balance field.

▫ Switch to the word processor, and choose Print Form Letters.

▫ Click the Preview button, and scroll through the letters again.

This time, Works displays letters only for the people who owe money to the dairy. Because one Works application is so thoroughly compatible with the others, sending letters to selected people in a database is as simple as that. And, of course, you're not limited to one set of records after you sort a database. By simply changing the query, you can sort the same database again and again, to send different letters to different groups of people. For example, you could type *15th* in the Billing date field to find customers who need to receive notices that their billing date will change from the 15th to the 20th of each month.

MAILING LABELS AND ENVELOPES

Printing mailing labels and envelopes is comparable to printing form letters: Once again you make use of both the word processor and a database of names and addresses. You use the word processor to create a document containing the database fields you want to print, and you use the database, as usual, to supply the information you need. You can choose to print only selected records, rather than the entire database. The main difference between printing addresses and printing letters is in the layout, margins, and page sizes you specify for the labels or envelopes.

Mailing Labels

To print mailing labels, you can use either the third of the three WorksWizards, or you can use the Print Labels command on the File menu in the word processor. Like the Form Letters WorksWizard, the Mailing Labels WorksWizard requires the same field names, with the same capitalization and punctuation, that the Address Books WorksWizard uses; if you use a database of your own creation, be sure that the fields exactly match the ones listed in the file FIELDS.WPS.

You're experienced enough with the WorksWizards to be comfortable using the Mailing Labels WorksWizard on your own, so this section will describe how to set up a label document and print addresses with the Print Labels command. Most of this explanation is actually a step-by-step description of the work the WorksWizard does for you.

Although a mailing-label document doesn't look much like a document in the traditional sense, it's your starting point for printing labels. The document itself is simply a set of paragraphs containing the database fields you want to use to print the labels. Using the sample database, you can easily construct such a document:

- ☐ Create a new document in the word processor.

Normally, you would use the Database Field command to insert the required fields in your new document. Right now, however, you have an easier way:

- ☐ Switch to your BILLSDUE form letter.
- ☐ Select the address fields you inserted at the beginning of the letter, and copy them to the Clipboard.
- ☐ Switch to the new document in the word processor, and paste the copied fields in.

□ Delete the extra paragraph mark at the end of the document to be sure you don't throw off the spacing when you print the labels. (Delete the paragraph mark by placing the insertion point in front of it and pressing the Backspace key.)

That's your document. Because mailing labels are sometimes on the small side, format these lines for smaller type if you can:

□ Select all of the lines, and format them for a font and size such as Helv 10.

You're halfway done. Next, tell Works how to print the labels. Mailing labels are arranged on sheets in various ways. Some sheets have two labels across, others have three. The size of the labels varies too, as can the spacing between them. Because the size and layout of the labels vary, you must tell Works how many labels to print across each sheet and how far apart the labels are spaced, both vertically and horizontally. That's why you have the Print Labels command:

□ Choose Print Labels from the File menu.

Works displays this dialog box:

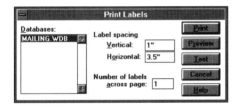

When printing labels, measure the distance from the top of one label to the top of the next, and type that measurement in the Vertical box under Label spacing. Measure the distance from the right edge of one label to the right edge of the next, and type that measurement in the Horizontal box under Label spacing. Type the number of labels per row in the box titled Number of labels across page. To avoid wasting time and labels, click the Test button to test print two experimental rows of labels.

NOTE: *Small errors in measurements can add up quickly as Works prints down or across a page of labels. An error of 1/16th of an inch, for example, throws off printing by half an inch by the time Works reaches the eighth row of labels on a page. When measuring the distance between the labels, be as exact as possible. The WorksWizard recommends you try for measurements to the hundredth of an inch or centimeter. Many label manufacturers provide these measurements either on the back of the package or on a sheet inside the box. Check for this information — you might save yourself some time.*

You'll use the default label spacing for this example, but to see how labels print,

☐ Type *2* in the box titled Number of labels across page.

☐ Click the Preview button to see how your labels will look.

Even though your document contains only one set of database fields, Works repeats this set as many times as needed to print a separate label for each record. To actually print the labels, you would click the Print button in the dialog box for the Print Labels command. Before actually printing, Works displays the Page Setup & Margins dialog box so you can set the correct margins, page length, and width for your sheets of labels. Be sure not to overlook the margin settings. In addition, if you change the page length or width, remember to set the same page size with the Printer Setup command. Page measurements in both commands must match, so if you forget, Works will prompt you to make the adjustment before it will print your labels.

Refining Your Labels

Notice that mailing labels, unlike form letters, don't automatically close up the lines of an address if one of the fields (Address) is blank. If you don't want those blank lines to print, there's an easy solution:

☐ Click Cancel to return to your document.

☐ Select all lines of the document, and copy them to the Clipboard.

☐ Open a new document in the word processor, and paste in the copied lines.

☐ Select the paragraph (including the paragraph mark) containing the Address field and delete it.

Now you have two different label documents, one for four-line addresses and one for three-line addresses. To select records for each type of label,

☐ Switch to the database document, and choose Show All Records and then Sort Records from the Select menu.

☐ Type *address* as one of the sort fields, and click OK.

The Sort Records command sorts the database so that records with entries in the Address field are separate from records without entries in the same field. To select the records to print,

☐ Select the two records with entries in the Address field.

☐ Choose Hide Record from the Select menu.

☐ Switch to the label document with three-line addresses (the one you want for the remaining records).

☐ Choose Print Labels and click Preview.

Now you see "labels" laid out with no intervening blank lines because your commands to sort and hide selected records left only those that fit the three-line label document. To print the records with four-line addresses, you would follow the same procedure, hiding the records with no entries in the Address field, and then printing from the alternate label document. To save the two documents for future use, you could give them related names, such as LABELS4 and LABELS3, that are easily recognizable.

Envelopes

To print envelopes, you follow the same overall procedure as for mailing labels, but the way you format and print them differs. If your printer is capable of printing single envelopes, set up an envelope document in the word processor and then use the Print Form Letters command to print the envelopes. If your printer uses form-feed envelopes that are attached to continuous sheets, use the Print Labels command.

Setting Up the Envelope Document

The following example shows how to print both a return address and the address of the recipient:

☐ Open a new document in the word processor.

☐ Type the return address, as shown in the following illustration:

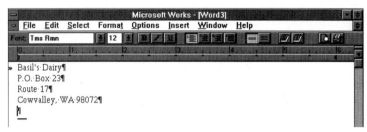

If you didn't have all your sample documents, you would insert the recipient's name and address with the Database Field command. You've already created this part, however, so

☐ Switch to your four-line mailing-label document.

☐ Select the name and address fields, and copy them to the Clipboard.

☐ Switch to the new document, and paste the copied fields into a new paragraph.

☐ Format the return address for the same font and font size as the copied fields.

That completes the *content* part of your envelope document. The formatting you choose now depends on whether you'll be printing single envelopes or those attached to form-feed sheets.

Printing Single Envelopes

Before you try printing single envelopes, you might want to check your printer manual for instructions specific to your make and model of printer. The following basic procedures apply to printing envelopes in general. Specific settings, however, are for Hewlett-Packard LaserJet printers.

To print on single envelopes, you set up the "page" to match the layout you need and the size of the envelopes on which you'll print. First, take care of the page size and margins:

☐ Choose the Page Setup & Margins command.

The important settings here are the top and left margins, to position the addresses at appropriate distances from the top and left edges of the envelope. You might need to experiment to find your own preferences, but for this example

☐ Set the top margin to 2.25 inches, and then set the left margin to 1.75 inches.

Next set the page length and width. For a LaserJet printer, these should be the same as standard paper in landscape orientation, so the following settings will work:

☐ Type *8.5* in the Page length box and *11* in the Page width box.

☐ Click OK to complete the command.

If you change the page size in the Page Setup & Margins command, but not in the Printer Setup command, Works will display a message telling you about the discrepancy when you try to preview or print the envelopes. To change the page size,

☐ Choose the Printer Setup command, and change the orientation to landscape. While you're at it, change the paper source — to manual feed or to an envelope bin — if necessary. Click OK.

If you don't see an appropriate page size, leave the defaults. Even though Works warns of the difference in page sizes, you can override the warning, as you'll see later.

To position the recipient's name and address on the envelope (again, these settings are for a LaserJet printer),

☐ Place the insertion point in front of the First Name field.

☐ Choose the Indents & Spacing command.

☐ Set the left indent to 3.5 inches, and set Space before paragraph to 7 lines. (Again, you'll probably choose settings you prefer for your own envelopes.) Click OK.

☐ Select the remaining paragraphs in the recipient's address, and set the left indent to 3.5 inches for all.

To print the envelopes, you would use the Print Form Letters command. Here, preview the results:

☐ Choose the Print Form Letters command, and click the Preview button.

If the page size you set does not match the page size defined in the Printer Setup command, Works will display this warning:

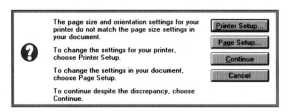

You can click the Printer Setup button if you forgot to change the page size. If you could not match the envelope size, however,

☐ Click the Continue button.

Works moves on to show you how your addresses will print. Because you're using the Print Form Letters command here, you don't have to worry about blank lines appearing in recipients' addresses. Works will close up the lines for you.

NOTE: *If part of the address in Print Preview slips to the left margin, try saving the file. The next time you preview, the problem should disappear.*

Printing Form-Feed Envelopes

To print form-feed envelopes, you start with the same basic document in the word processor but use different page and indent settings, and you use the Print Labels rather than the Print Form Letters command. The following lists describe the commands you use but do not present hands-on examples to try.

To set the page size and width:

☐ Choose the Page Setup & Margins command.

☐ Set all margins, including header margins, to 0 inches.

☐ Type appropriate values for the page length and page width, as exactly as possible. Note that these measurements are much more significant with form-feed envelopes than they are with single envelopes. Standard measurements are 11 inches for the page length and 10 inches for page width.

☐ Use the Printer Setup command to set the same page size, if possible. If not, remember that you can click the Continue button when Works displays a message about the discrepancy between the page sizes in the Printer Setup and the Page Setup & Margins commands.

To align the addresses on the page, format the first line of the return address, the rest of the return address, the recipient's name, and the recipient's address separately:

☐ Select the first line of the return address. Your page margins are 0, so use the left indent to specify how far from the left edge this line will print. For example, type *.25* to start printing a quarter of an inch from the edge.

☐ Also for the first line of the return address, specify the size of the envelope flap, plus the amount of room you want to leave above the line. For example, if the flap is 1 inch and you want to start printing a quarter of an inch from the top of the envelope, set the space before to 1.25 inches by typing *1.25in*. You can type a measurement in inches here, even though you usually specify the space before in number of lines. Works will convert the inches to lines for you. Click OK when you're finished.

☐ Select the remainder of the return address, and set the left indent to the same value you used for the first line.

☐ Place the insertion point at the beginning of the recipient's name, and set the left indent to an appropriate value, such as 3.5 inches. Position the line several lines below the return address by pressing Enter as many times as needed.

☐ Position the recipient's address by selecting all of it and setting the left indent to the same value you used for the name.

To print the envelopes:

☐ Choose the Print Labels command.

☐ Measure the distance from the top of one envelope to the top of the next, including the flaps, and type the value in the Vertical box under Label spacing. For standard envelopes, 5.5 inches is accurate. In the Horizontal box, type the width of the envelope page, for example, 10 inches.

☐ Set the number of labels across page to 1.

From here, you can either preview the envelopes, test print some, or print them all. If Works tells you the page sizes don't match in the Printer Setup and the Page Setup & Margins commands, click Continue to override the objection.

SAMPLE WORKS DOCUMENTS

You've covered most of Works now. This section points you to some sample files that come with Works, and that you can use as models for setting up and organizing your own information. Deciding how you want to design a letter, spreadsheet, or database is not always easy, so one good approach is to look at comparable examples created by experts. In these sample files, you have the advantage of seeing how the Works designers decided to set up particular types of documents. These documents are formatted for you, and they also contain sample entries, formulas, and, where needed, instructions on their use. Because these samples are interconnected to some degree, you will have the opportunity to practice moving data between documents.

The sample documents are all stored in the MSWORKS directory. To see their names,

□ Choose the Open Existing File command from the File menu. When the Open dialog box appears, double-click on msworks in the Directories portion dialog box.

You should see a list like this:

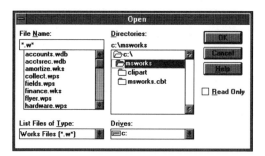

Because these samples are actual Works documents, they have the typical Works extensions: WPS for the word processor, WKS for the spreadsheet, and WDB for the database. You can use these samples as is, or you can use what you learned in Part II to modify them to suit your own needs and preferences.

Copying the Sample Documents

Until you're satisfied with your own versions of these documents, you might want to keep the originals unchanged. The files don't require a lot of disk space, so one easy way to have your cake and eat it too is to copy the samples into a working directory, leaving the originals where Works put them. To do this, leave Works temporarily:

- ☐ Click the Minimize button in the application window's title bar (labeled *Microsoft Works*).

- ☐ Choose Main from the Window menu in the Windows Program Manager.

- ☐ To see a list of the sample files, double-click the File Manager icon in the Main window. This starts a secondary "shell" program that lets you work with directories and files from within Windows.

When the File Manager starts, it takes a short while to read disk information into your computer's memory. When it's ready to go to work, you see a window like this:

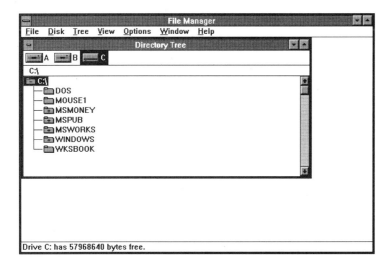

□ If you do not see a directory named MSWORKS, the File Manager is showing you information about a different drive. Click on the letter of the drive on which you installed Works (probably drive C).

□ Double-click on MSWORKS, and you see a list like this:

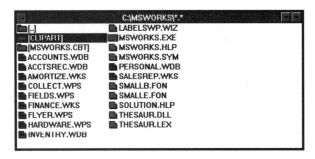

This directory contains some critical program files — including the Works program itself, MSWORKS.EXE — in addition to the sample documents. You *do not* want to take chances with these files, so sort the listing to group the WPS, WKS, and WDB files together:

□ Choose By Type (which means "by extension") on the File Manager's View menu. Now the sample documents should be grouped at the end of the list, beginning with ACCOUNTS.WDB and ending with HARDWARE.WPS. (If you tried the Address Books WorksWizard in Chapter 3, you should also see your personal address book listed here.)

You're almost done. All you have to do is create a directory for the files and tell the File Manager to copy the samples into the new directory:

□ Choose Create Directory from the File menu.

When the File Manager displays a dialog box asking for the name of the new directory, type a name. To avoid cluttering the MSWORKS directory, begin the name with a backslash (\) to put it in the main (root) directory of your hard disk. For example, if you want to name the directory SAMPLES, fill in the dialog box like this:

☐ Click OK after you've typed in the new directory name.

To copy the files as a group,

☐ Click on ACCOUNTS.WDB to select it. Extend the selection by holding down the Shift key and clicking on the last sample filename, HARDWARE.WPS.

☐ Choose the Copy command from the File menu.

☐ Type the name of your new directory in the To portion of the dialog box that appears, like this:

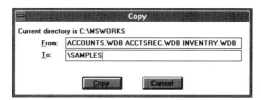

☐ Click the Copy button.

When your computer finishes copying, double-click on your new directory and you'll see all the files listed there. Now you can experiment with the sample documents as much as you want, knowing that the originals are untouched in the MSWORKS directory:

☐ Quit the File Manager by double-clicking the Control menu icon.

☐ Click OK when it asks for confirmation.

If you ever need a new copy of one of the originals, start the File Manager, select the filename in the MSWORKS directory, and use the Copy command to copy the file to your sample directory again. If the File Manager asks you to confirm that you are replacing the version in your sample directory, click Yes to overwrite the unwanted document.

OTHER SOLUTION SERIES PROGRAMS

You might find that Works is all the program you ever need to get things done. You might use it a little, or you might become dependent on it for many different types of tasks. Along the way, you might find yourself wondering about the other programs in the Solution Series.

The choice of adding to your software collection is a highly personal one that depends on what you want to do. If you're curious about the other two programs in the Solution Series, the following brief descriptions will tell you — very roughly — what they do. Because both programs are part of the Solution Series, they have the same easy-to-use design you've seen in Works.

When you start Windows and open the Solution Series program group, you see a question mark icon labeled Series Info.

Double-clicking on the icon produces a Help window that describes the three programs in the Solution Series. Scrolling through the window gives you an idea of Microsoft's goals for the series.

Microsoft Money

Microsoft Money is a financial management program that works basically like an onscreen checkbook and check register for as many accounts, either business or personal, as you need to track. You can use Microsoft Money to perform such tasks as entering transactions, reconciling accounts, and listing transactions by payee and other categories. You can keep track of income and expenses, print checks, do your budgeting, and create different types of reports and summaries. Microsoft Money can also help you at tax time and help you keep track of your net worth. The illustration below shows you what a basic screen looks like in this program:

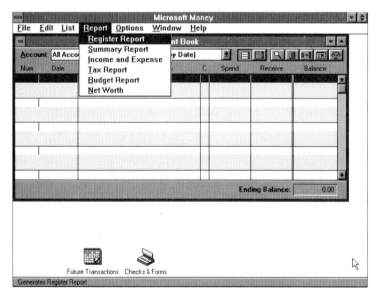

Microsoft Publisher

Microsoft Publisher is perhaps the most fun of the three members of the Solution Series. An entry-level desktop publishing program with a remarkable range of sophisticated capabilities, Microsoft Publisher can help you produce newsletters, brochures, invitations, catalogs, and even paper airplanes. The airplanes, by the way, are created by one of Publisher's PageWizards (relatives of the Works-Wizards). And, like all good teaching tools, they entertain while showing you a great deal about graphics, text, and other features common to desktop publishing. Publisher also offers a PageWizard that helps you create seven frequently used business forms, including a customer refund, expense report, purchase order, invoice, and quote. The following illustration shows you what Publisher looks like. As you can see, its onscreen appearance is already familiar thanks to Works and Windows.

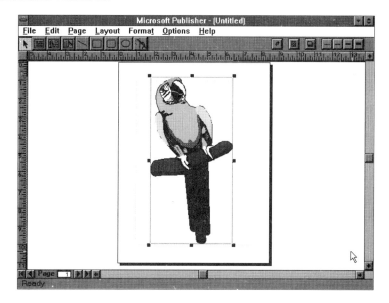

Part IV

Appendixes

The three appendixes in Part IV provide additional information you might find useful. Appendix A tells you how to install Works and Windows if they are not yet on your computer. Appendix B is a table of special characters you can type into your documents. Appendix C is a list of the built-in functions you can use with the Works database and spreadsheet.

A

Installing Windows and Works

Both Windows and Works are extremely easy to install, even if you've never installed software on your computer. These programs are simple to install because each comes with its own "smart" Setup program that does most of the work for you.

INSTALLING WINDOWS

How do you know if you need to install Windows? Start your computer and wait for the DOS prompt to appear. On a computer with a single hard disk, the prompt usually looks like this:

```
C:\>
```

When you see the prompt, type *win* and press Enter, like this:

```
C:\>win
```

If Windows is installed, this command will start it. If Windows is not installed, you'll see the message *Bad command or file name,* meaning that DOS, your computer's bandleader, could not find and start Windows.

If you have to install Windows, you'll find the procedure straightforward. It's helpful, however, to know certain information ahead of time that the Windows Setup program will ask you for. Most of this information — which language you want, whether you have a mouse, and so on — you probably know. You should also know what type of printer you will be using (serial or parallel) and which port, or plug, it's attached to. Serial printers connect to ports named COM, so your choices boil down to COM1, COM2, COM3, or COM4. Parallel printers connect to ports named LPT, so your choices are LPT1, LPT2, or LPT3. If you use a printer with different font cartridges, check the names of the cartridges ahead of time.

To install Windows, follow this procedure:

□ Start your computer, if necessary.

□ Gather your Windows disks together, find the disk labeled Disk 1, and place it in your floppy disk drive. You can use either drive A or drive B if you have two; most people use drive A.

□ Type the letter of the drive containing the Windows disk, followed by a colon. For example, type *a:* if the disk is in drive A. Press Enter.

□ Type *setup* and press Enter again.

At this point, the Windows Setup program takes over. It will check your computer and its attached devices and prompt you for information or for different Windows disks as required. If you're in doubt about any step or you would like more information, press the F1 key, and the Setup program will display Help that tells you more about what is happening.

After Setup announces that it's ready to go, all you need do from here on is follow the instructions that appear on your screen. Take your time; Windows doesn't mind waiting. And remember, press F1 if you have any questions.

INSTALLING WORKS

If you have Works, you presumably have a computer on which it will run. For reference, however, the following list tells you the basic hardware and software requirements for running Works:

■ A computer with an 80286, 80386, or 80486 microprocessor.

■ At least 1 megabyte (fairly standard on new computers) or more of memory.

■ At least one 1.2-MB or 720-KB (or better) floppy disk drive.

■ A hard disk.

■ An EGA, VGA, 8514/A, or compatible video graphics adapter supported by Windows 3; color is both recommended and enjoyable.

■ MS-DOS version 3.1 or later.

■ Microsoft Windows version 3.0 or later.

■ A mouse (not required but recommended).

Before you can install Works, you must have installed Windows, so follow the instructions in the preceding section, "Installing Windows," if Windows does not start on your computer. After you've installed Windows, installing Works is a breeze:

☐ Start your computer and Windows, if necessary. If an onscreen window titled Program Manager or File Manager does not open, press the Ctrl and Esc keys at the same time. When a small window titled Task List appears, point to either the item Program Manager or File Manager with your mouse pointer and double-click (click twice in succession). If you don't have a mouse, use the arrow keys to move the dark highlight to either Program Manager or File Manager, press Tab so that a dotted box moves to the button labeled Switch To, and then press Enter.

☐ Gather your Works disks together, find the one that has the word *Setup* on it, and place the disk in one of your floppy disk drives. (Either will do, though most people use drive A.)

☐ If you have a mouse, point to the File menu name at the top of the Program Manager or File Manager window and click once. (If you don't have a mouse, hold down Alt and press the F key.)

☐ With the mouse, point to the item Run on the menu, and click once. (With the keyboard, press the R key.)

☐ When a box labeled Run appears on the screen, type the letter of the drive containing your Setup disk, a colon, and the word *setup*. If your disk is in drive A, the command looks like this:

```
a:setup
```

If the disk is in drive B, the command is

```
b:setup
```

☐ Click OK or press the Tab key, and then press Enter to carry out the command.

In a few moments, the screen fills with Setup's opening screen. You'll know you're on your way when a notice appears in the upper left corner reminding you to fill out and send your Works registration card to Microsoft.

From this point on, follow the instructions Setup displays. It begins by asking you to type your name and, optionally, your company. After that, aside from asking whether you want a complete or a custom (partial) installation (accept complete), Setup charges ahead on its own, stopping periodically only to ask you to insert a different disk.

When the installation is over, Setup will display a screen giving you the choice of returning to Windows or starting Works. Choose either one. Works is now on your hard disk and ready to go to work.

B
Special Characters

The Works word processor lets you insert special characters, such as different types of hyphens and end-of-line marks. There's another, completely different set of special characters you can use, too. These other characters are generally referred to as *extended* characters and comprise up to an extra 128 characters, in addition to the normal character set, which includes the alphabet and other standard characters.

Like regular characters, the extended characters are identified by code numbers that computers and their programs use to determine which character to display or print. The extended characters include accented letters, currency symbols, and other characters you don't find on the regular part of your keyboard. To insert these characters in a Works document, you type the code numbers as follows:

☐ Press and hold the Alt key.

☐ Type the number of the character you want. Use the *numeric keypad,* and precede the number with a zero (0) — for example, type *0214.*

The table on the next page lists the extended characters that Works recognizes. If you want to print these characters, test them before sprinkling them throughout a document. Not all printers can reproduce extended characters.

EXTENDED CHARACTERS

128	Ç	151	ù	180	'	229	å
129	ü	152	ÿ	181	µ	230	æ
130	é	153	Ö	182	¶	231	ç
131	â	154	Ü	183	·	232	è
132	ä	155	¢	184	,	233	é
133	à	156	£	186	º	234	ê
134	å	157	¥	187	»	235	ë
135	ç	160	<space>	188	¼	236	ì
136	ê	161	¡	189	½	237	í
137	ë	162	¢	191	¿	238	î
138	è	163	£	196	Ä	239	ï
139	ï	165	¥	197	Å	241	ñ
140	î	166	¦	198	Æ	242	ò
141	ì	167	§	199	Ç	243	ó
142	Ä	170	ª	201	É	244	ô
143	Å	171	«	209	Ñ	246	ö
144	É	172	¬	214	Ö	249	ù
145	æ	173	-	220	Ü	250	ú
146	Æ	174	‖	223	ß	251	û
147	ô	175	‗	224	à	252	ü
148	ö	176	°	225	á	255	ÿ
149	ò	177	±	226	â		
150	û	178	²	228	ä		

C
Works Functions

Works includes 57 built-in functions you can use instead of defining your own formulas to do the same work. Every function has a name and must be typed in the following format:

=FunctionName(Argument0,Argument1,...ArgumentN)

where *FunctionName* is the name of the function. Function names are shown all in capitals in this appendix.

Argument0,Argument1,...ArgumentN represent arguments — values — to be used in the calculation. Arguments can be numbers, cell references, range references or names, field names, or other functions. Regardless of form, however, all arguments must represent numbers. For example, if cell B3 is included as an argument, B3 must contain a numeric value.

All functions, like all formulas, begin with an equal sign (=) to indicate that they are to be calculated rather than interpreted as text or values. Arguments, if used, are always enclosed in parentheses. If a function takes multiple arguments, they must be separated by commas.

The following descriptions provide a reference to the Works functions.

ABS(*x*)
Gives the absolute value of *x*. An absolute value is a number stripped of its sign. For example, the absolute value of –3 and +3 is 3.

X must be a positive or negative number.

ACOS(*x*)
A trigonometric function that gives the arccosine (inverse cosine) of the angle whose cosine is *x*.

X must be a value between –1 and +1. The function returns a value between 0 and π radians (0 through 180 degrees).

ASIN(x)

A trigonometric function that gives the arcsine (inverse sine) of the angle whose sine is x.

X must be a value between –1 and +1. The function returns a value between $-\pi/2$ through $\pi/2$ (–90 degrees through 90 degrees).

ATAN(x)

A trigonometric function that gives the arctangent (inverse tangent) of the angle whose tangent is x. The function returns a value between $-\pi/2$ through $\pi/2$ (–90 degrees through 90 degrees).

ATAN2(x,y)

Description: A trigonometric function that supplements the ATAN function by giving the arctangent of an angle defined by x and y coordinates.

X is the x coordinate and y is the y coordinate. If both x and y are 0, the function returns ERR (error). Otherwise, the function returns a value between $-\pi/2$ through $\pi/2$ as seen in the following table:

If x is	If y is	Function returns
+	+	0 through $\pi/2$
–	+	$\pi/2$ through π
–	–	$-\pi$ through $-\pi/2$
+	–	$-\pi/2$ through 0

AVG(range0,range1,...rangeN)

A function that gives the average of the values in the ranges listed as arguments.

Range0,range1,...rangeN are sets of values. They can be entered as numbers, cell or range references, or formulas. Text is always treated as 0. Blank cells are also treated as 0 if they occur in cell references; in range references, they are ignored.

CHOOSE(x,option0,option1,...optionN)

A function that uses the value of x to return the value of the option whose position in the list of arguments corresponds to x. For example, in the function

= CHOOSE(2,20,30,40,50)

the function would return 40, because its position corresponds to 2 (20=0, 30=1, 40=2, 50=3). The value of x cannot be less than 0 or greater than the number of items in the list.

COLS(*range*)

A function that returns the number of columns in *range*. For example,

    =COLS(A1:C1)

returns 3 because the range covers three columns, A, B, and C.

COS(*x*)

A trigonometric function that returns the cosine of *x*, an angle expressed in radians.

COUNT(*range0,range1,...rangeN*)

A function that returns the number of cells in the ranges specified.

Range0,range1,...rangeN can be numbers, cell or range references, or formulas. The function counts cells containing not only numbers, but text and the values ERR and N/A, which are returned by other functions. Blank cells are counted only if they occur in cell (not range) references.

CTERM(*interest rate,future value,present value*)

A financial function that calculates the number of compounding periods required for an investment to grow from the specified present value to the specified future value, given a fixed interest rate per compounding period.

> **NOTE:** *The interest rate is for a single compounding period. For annual and other rates representing more than one period, divide the interest rate by the frequency (such as monthly) at which the interest is compounded. Type the rate as a percent (12%) or as a decimal value (.12).*

DATE(*year,month,day*)

A function that converts a date to a constant number between 1 and 65534, representing the days from January 1, 1900, through June 3, 2079. The values for *year, month,* and *day* must be numbers. For example,

    DATE(1992,1,Z,0)

returns 33623 for January 20, 1992. *Year* can also be a number from 0 (for 1900) through 179 (2079); *month* can be 1 through 12; *day* can be 1 through 31. If the *day* or *month* are outside the normal ranges, the function corrects for the error; it does not return ERR.

DAY(*date*)

A function that returns the number of the day of the month for the date specified as *date*. Using the preceding DATE example of 33623 for January 20, 1992,

    =DAY(33623)

would return 20.

Date can be entered either as a number or as a date surrounded by single quotation marks, for example, =DAY('1/20/92').

DDB(*cost,salvage,life,period*)

A function that uses the double-declining balance method of calculating depreciation of an asset.

Cost is the original cost of the asset; *salvage* is the expected value at the end of the asset's life; *life* is the number of years or other time periods the asset is expected to be usable; *period* is the time period for which you want to calculate the depreciation.

The function calculates depreciation for a given period according to the formula

$$\frac{(value * 2)}{life}$$

ERR( )

A function that returns the value ERR. This function is usually used to display ERR in a specified cell under a specified condition. ERR takes no argument. For example,

=IF(A1<0,ERR(),A1)

displays ERR if the value in cell A1 is less than 0; otherwise, the IF function that contains the ERR function displays the value in cell A1.

EXP(*x*)

A mathematical function that returns the value of the constant 2.71828..., the base of the natural logarithm, raised to the power of *x*. EXP is not for use in calculating exponentiation with other bases.

FALSE( )

A logical function that can be used in other formulas to return the value 0, meaning False. This function is the complement of TRUE(). For example,

=IF(A1>0,TRUE(),FALSE())

returns 1 (True) if the value in cell A1 is greater than 0; otherwise, the IF function returns 0 (False).

FV(*payment,rate,term*)

A financial function that calculates the future value of an annuity in which equal *payments* earn a fixed *rate* per term, compounded over the specified number of *terms.* The function assumes the first payment is made at the end of the first period and calculates future value according to the formula

$$\frac{payment * ((1 + rate)^{term} -1)}{rate}$$

HLOOKUP(*search value,range,row*)

A function that uses a search value to retrieve an entry from a predefined table.

Search value is a value in the top row of the table; *range* is the range comprising the table; *row* is the number of rows that the function is to go *below* the search value to retrieve the desired entry. Arrange the search values in the top row in ascending order, as shown in the following example.

If a table in cells A1 through C4 contains the following,

1	2	3
10	20	30
40	50	60
70	80	90

the formula

=HLOOKUP(2,A1:C4,2)

would return 50. The function would first read across the top row of the range defined by A1:C4. When it found a number equal to the search value, it would go down the specified number of rows (2) and retrieve the value in the cell at that location. The function returns 0 if the target cell contains text. HLOOKUP always searches in the same pattern, across and then down. The complementary VLOOKUP function searches down and then across.

HOUR(*time*)

A function that returns the number of the hour of the day (0 through 23) for the time specified as *time.* Specify *time* as a number between 0 and 0.99999, representing the times between 12 A.M. and 11:59:59 P.M. or enclose the time in single quotation marks. For example,

=HOUR(.9876)

or

=HOUR('8:23:36')

IF(*condition,true value,false value*)

A logical function that returns one of two results, depending on the outcome of a specified condition.

Condition is the condition to evaluate and is often an expression that includes an operator such as greater than (>), less than (<), or equal (=); *true value* is the value that is returned if the outcome of the condition is true; *false value* is the value returned if the outcome of the condition is not true. IF functions can be nested, one inside the other, to refine the results of a conditional statement. For examples, see Chapter 7.

INDEX(*range,column,row*)

A function that returns the value of the cell at the intersection of the specified column and row. Column and row numbers begin with 0, so the intersection of column 0 and row 0 is the first value in the specified range.

INT(*x*)

A function that gives the integer part of the value x. The INT function truncates the decimal portion of a number without rounding up or down. For example,

=INT(3.14)

and

=INT(3.99)

produce the same value, 3.

IRR(*guess,range*)

A financial function that gives the internal rate of return (profit) on the series of cash flows represented by *range*.

Guess is an estimate of the yield; *range* is the reference to the cell range containing the values to be calculated. Typically, a value between 0 and 1 is recommended as a starting point for *guess*.

This function is based on a trial-and-error approach called *iteration* in which the successive calculations are used to refine the initial approximation specified by *guess*. If calculations do not produce a meaningful result within 20 iterations, the function displays ERR.

ISERR(*x*)

A logical function that determines whether the argument is the error value ERR. If the argument produces ERR, the function returns 1; otherwise, the function returns 0. The ISERR function can be used to control the propagation of the ERR error message through related formulas in a spreadsheet. For example,

=IF(ISERR(C15),0,C15)

returns 0 if cell C15 contains an error, but otherwise returns the value in cell C15.

ISNA(*x*)

A logical function that determines whether the argument is the value N/A (not available). This function is similar to the ISERR function in helping prevent the propagation of one value (N/A) throughout related formulas in a spreadsheet.

LN(*x*)

A mathematical function that gives the natural logarithm (base *e*, the constant 2.71828) of x. To provide a valid result, x must be a positive number or a reference to a cell containing a positive number.

LOG(*x*)

A mathematical function that gives the base 10 logarithm of *x*. To provide a valid result, *x* must be a positive number.

MAX(*range0,range1,...rangeN*)

A statistical function that returns the largest (maximum) value in the referenced ranges.

Range0,range1,...rangeN can be numbers, cell or range references, or formulas. The function ignores blank cells in range references, but treats them as 0 in cell references.

MIN(*range0,range1,...rangeN*)

A statistical function that returns the smallest (minimum) value in the referenced ranges. This function is the complement of MAX.

MINUTE(*time*)

A function that returns the number of the minute, from 0 through 59, for the time specified as *time*. Specify *time* as a number between 0 and 0.99999, representing the times between 12 A.M. and 11:59:59 P.M., or enclose the time in single quotation marks. See also HOUR.

MOD(*numerator,denominator*)

A mathematical function that gives the remainder (modulus) of *numerator* divided by *denominator*. For example,

=MOD(10,3)

produces 1 because 10 divided by 3 has a remainder of 1.

MONTH(*date*)

A function that returns the number of the month for the date specified as *date*.

Date can be entered either as a number between 1 and 65534 or as a date surrounded by single quotation marks, for example, =MONTH('1/20/92').

NA( )

A function that returns the value N/A (not available). Works treats N/A as a numeric, not text, value. See also ISNA.

NOW( )

A calendar function that returns a serial number representing the current date and time. The number returned consists of an integer plus a decimal fraction. The integer is the serial number representing the date; the fraction is the serial number representing the time. Unlike DAY, MONTH, MINUTE, and related functions which retain the serial number as a constant value, NOW is updated every time the spreadsheet is recalculated. Compare the related time and date functions.

NPV(*rate,range*)

A financial function that returns the net present value of a series of payments at a fixed interest rate per period.

Rate is the interest rate per period; *range* is the range of cells containing the values to calculate. If the interest rate is annual, but the payment periods are more frequent, divide the rate by the number of periods (such as 12). The range can include a number of cells, but must cover no more than one row or column.

Like other financial functions, NPV assumes that payments occur at the end of periods of equal length. The function uses the formula

$$\text{NPV} = \sum_{i=1}^{n} \frac{Payment\,[i]}{(1 + Rate)\,i}$$

PI( )

A mathematical function that returns the value of π rounded to nine decimal places (3.141592654).

PMT(*principal,rate,term*)

A financial function that calculates the payment per period on a loan or investment with a fixed interest rate over the specified term.

Principal is the amount of the loan or investment; *rate* is the interest rate; *term* is the length of the loan or investment. The rate and the term must correspond to the same periods. If the rate is annual, but the payment is monthly, divide the rate by 12. The function assumes that payments are made at the end of each period. Calculation is based on the formula

$$\frac{present\ value * rate}{(1 - (1 + rate)^{-term})}$$

PV(*payment,rate,term*)

A financial function that calculates the present value of a series of equal payments earning a fixed rate of interest over a specified term.

Payment is the amount per period; *rate* is the interest rate; *term* is the number of periods. The function assumes that the first payment is made at the end of the first period. The calculation (for rates not equal to 0) is based on the formula

$$\frac{payment * (1 - (1 + rate)^{-term})}{rate}$$

Compare this function to NPV.

RAND( )

A statistical function that returns a random number. The number is a decimal fraction from 0 up to, but not including, 1.

RATE(*future value,present value,term*)

A financial function that returns the fixed interest rate per period needed for an investment to grow from its present value to an expected future value in the number of terms specified.

Future value is the value expected at the end of the term; *present value* is the current value of the investment; *term* is the number of periods to be considered. The calculation is based on the formula

$$\left(\frac{future\ value}{present\ value}\right)^{\frac{1}{term}} - 1$$

ROUND(*x,places*)

A function that rounds the value *x* to the number of places specified.

X is the value to be rounded; *places* is the number of places to round. If *places* is specified as 0, the function rounds the value to the nearest integer; if *places* is positive, the function rounds to the right of the decimal point; if places is *negative,* the function rounds to the left of the decimal point.

ROWS(*range*)

A function that returns the number of rows in *range.* Compare to the function COLS.

SECOND(*time*)

A function that returns the number of the second, from 0 through 59, for the time specified as *time.* Specify *time* as a number between 0 and 0.99999, representing the times between 12 A.M. and 11:59:59 P.M., or enclose the time in single quotation marks. See also HOUR and MINUTE.

SIN(*x*)

A trigonometric function that returns the sine of *x*, an angle expressed in radians.

SLN(*cost,salvage,life*)

A financial function that calculates the straight-line depreciation for an asset. Straight-line depreciation assumes a linear reduction in value, so the depreciation amount is the same for any period.

Cost is the initial cost of the asset; *salvage* is its estimated salvage value; *life* is the number of periods the asset is expected to remain useful. The calculation is based on the formula

$$\frac{cost - salvage}{life}$$

SQRT(*x*)

A mathematical function that returns the square root of *x*. The value of *x* must be positive; if it is negative, the function returns ERR.

STD(*range0,range1,...rangeN*)

A statistical function that calculates the population standard deviation of the values in the specified ranges.

Range0,range1,...rangeN can be numbers, cell or range references, or formulas. Blank cells are ignored in range references but treated as 0 in cell references. To calculate the standard deviation of a sample, use the formula

$$STD(ranges)*SQRT(COUNT(ranges)/(COUNT(ranges)-1))$$

where *ranges* includes *range0,range1,...rangeN* for the functions involved.

SUM(*range0,range1,...rangeN*)

A mathematical function that totals the values in the specified ranges.

Range0,range1,...rangeN can be numbers, cell references or ranges, or formulas. Blank cells are ignored in range references and treated as 0 in cell references. For examples, refer to Chapter 7.

SYD(*cost,salvage,life,period*)

A financial function that calculates depreciation of an asset according to the sum-of-the-years-digits method, in which the greatest allowances for depreciation are made in the earliest years in the life of the asset.

Cost is the initial cost of the asset; *salvage* is the estimated salvage value of the asset; *life* is the estimated useful life of the asset; *period* is the period for which depreciation is to be calculated. The calculation is based on the formula

$$\frac{(cost - salvage) * (life - period + 1)}{\left(\dfrac{life * (life + 1)}{2}\right)}$$

TAN(*x*)

A trigonometric function that returns the tangent of *x*, an angle expressed in radians.

TERM(*payment,rate,future value*)

A financial function that calculates the number of periods required for an annuity to grow to the specified future value at a fixed interest rate and a fixed payment per period.

Payment is the amount per period; *rate* is the interest rate; *future value* is the desired future value. If the interest rate is annual, divide the rate by 12 for a monthly payment period.

TIME(*hour,minute,second*)

A function that converts a time to a number between 0 and 0.99999, representing the hours, minutes, and seconds between 12:00:00 A.M. and 11:59:59 P.M. For example,

TIME(*hour,minute,second*)

returns 0.538831.

Hour can be 0 through 23; *minute* and second can be 0 through 59. If the minute or second are outside the normal ranges, the function corrects for the error. If the hour is greater than 23, the value returned is greater than 1.

TRUE( )

A logical function that can be used in other formulas to return the value 1, meaning True. See also FALSE.

VAR(*range0,range1,...rangeN*)

A statistical function that calculates variance — the degree to which the values in the specified ranges deviate from the mean for all values.

Range0,range1,...rangeN can be numbers, cell or range references, or formulas. Blank cells are ignored in range references and treated as 0 in cell references.

To calculate sample variance, use the formula

VAR(*ranges*)*(COUNT(*ranges*)/(COUNT(*ranges*)−1))

where *ranges* includes *range0,range1,...rangeN,* as described above.

VLOOKUP(*search value,range,column*)

A function that uses a search value to retrieve an entry from a predefined table.

Search value is a value in the leftmost column of the table; *range* is the range comprising the table; *column* is the number of columns that the function is to go *to the right of* the search value to retrieve the desired entry. Arrange the search values in the leftmost column in ascending order, as shown in the following example.

If a table in cells A1 through C4 contains the following:

1	10	50
2	20	60
3	30	70
4	40	80

the formula

=VLOOKUP(2,A1:C4,2)

would return 60. The function would first read down the leftmost column of the range defined by A1:C4. When it found a number equal to the search value, it would go across the specified number of columns (2) and retrieve the value in the cell at that location. The function returns 0 if the target cell contains text. VLOOKUP always searches in the same pattern, down and then across. The complementary HLOOKUP function searches across and then down.

YEAR(*date*)

A function that returns the number of the year for the date specified as *date.*

Date can be entered either as a number between 1 and 65534 or as a date surrounded by single quotation marks, for example, =YEAR('1/20/92').

Index

Special Characters

\# (number sign) 291
& (ampersand) 123, 125, *165*, 278, 280
* (asterisk) *165*, 274, 280
\+ (plus) *165*, 280
– (minus) *165*, 280
/ (slash) *165*, 280
: (colon) 42
< (less than) *165*, 278, 280
= (equal sign) *165*, 265
> (greater than) 165, 278, 280
? (question mark) 145, 274
\ (backslash) 94
< > (not equal) 165, 278, 280
^ (caret mark) *145*, *165*, 280
¦ (pipe) *165*, 278, 280
~ (tilde) *165*, 278, 280

A

About Program Manager 15
Accessories program group 6
Add Colors from Selection command *117*
addition (+) operator 280
Address Books WorksWizard 48–56
alignment
   Draw text *116*
   headers and footers 123, 124
   report columns 293
   text on page 79–80
All command
   database *285*
   report *307*
   spreadsheet *205*
   word processor *149*
Alt-Backspace key 72
Alt-Esc key 14, 22
Alt-number key for extended characters 389
Alt-number keys 139
Alt-W key 7

American Standard Code for Information Interchange (ASCII) files 320
ampersand (&)
   database query operator 278, 280
   header/footer codes 123, 125
AND operator (&) 278, 280
applications
   comparison of 41
   data transfer between 43–45, 325–53
application window
   finding "buried" windows 14
   Windows 5
   word processor 29–30
   Works 22
Apply Query command 285
Arc tool 98
Arrange Icons command
   database *286*
   report *308*
   spreadsheet *206*
   word processor *151*
Arrow keys
   database use 57
   spreadsheet use *157*, *188*
   word processor use *68*, 69
arrow mouse pointer 30–31
Arrow tool 98, 99, 100
ASCII files 320
asterisk (*) 165, 274, 280
ATDT/P dial prefixes 315
AVG function 267, 281, 392

B

backslash (\) 94
bar charts 211–12
Baud Rate 318
binary files 320–21
Binary Transfers command 321
bit map 114
bits per second (bps) 318
Bold command *116*
boldface type 36, 78–79, 83, *116*

403

Print date character 126
Printer Setup command
  chart *235*
  database *283*
  report *306*
  spreadsheet *204*
  word processor 122, 133, *148*
Print file number character 126
Print Form Letters command 134, *148,*
  361–63
Print Gridlines command 202
printing. *See also* Print command
  charts 235
  drawings 113–14
  form letters 362–63
  reports 305–6
  single page 134
  spreadsheet 201–3
  word processor 82, 133–34
Print Labels command *148*
Print long date character 126
print merge feature 59
Print page number character 126
Print Preview command
  charts 233, *235*
  database *283*
  report 291, *306*
  spreadsheet 198, *204*
  word processor 82, 91, 130–31, *148*
Print row and column headers 202
Print time character 126
program groups 6–8
Program Manager 6–10, 15
proposed responses 265
Protect Data command 194–95, *206, 286*
protocols 321
pulse dialing prefix (ATDP) 315

Q

Query command 286, 308
query view
  applying judgement to queries 278–79
  fashioning a query 275–76
  operators for 278, 280–81
  overview 42, 274
  types of queries 279–81, 367
  viewing other records 277

Query View button 242
Query View command 367
question marks, searching for 145, 274

R

Range Name command *204*
ranges
  charting nonadjacent ranges 232
  charts and 210
  formulas and names 177–79
  naming 174–77
  overview 157–58
Receive Binary File command 321
Receive Text File command 322
Record command *285*
Record row label 292
records
  adding 255–56
  defined 239
  deleting 256–57
  grouping in reports 298–300
  related records search 272–73
  selecting for form letters 367
  selecting for mailing labels 371
  sorting 269–71, 297–98
  status bar information on 243
Rectangle/Square tool 98, 99
remote computer 312
Replace command 143–45, 149
report definition 292–93
reports
  commands *306–8*
  defining fields for 288–89
  definition 290
  fields and field entries in 300–303
  format 293
  grouping records 298–300
  rows and columns in 294–97
  saving 304
  sorting records 297–98
  standard 287–93
  statistics in 289–91
  user-created rows and formulas in
    299–300
Report View button 42, 242
Report View command *308*
resize handles 98, 102, 111

JoAnne Woodcock

JoAnne Woodcock is currently a master writer/editor for Microsoft Press. She is author of *The Concise Guide to MS-DOS 5.0,* coauthor of *Running Unix* and *Microsoft Word Style Sheets,* and contributor to the *Microsoft Press Computer Dictionary,* all published by Microsoft Press.

The manuscript for this book was prepared and submitted to Microsoft Press in electronic form. Text files were processed and formatted using Microsoft Word for Windows.

Principal word processor: Sean Donahue
Principal proofreader: Carla Thompson
Principal typographer: Michelle Neil
Interior text designer: Kim Eggleston
Cover illustrator: Ron Troxell
Cover designer: Rebecca Geisler
Cover color separator: Color Service Inc.

Text composition by Editorial Services of New England, Inc. in New Baskerville with display type in Avant Garde, using Xerox Ventura Publisher and the Compugraphic 9600.

Printed on recycled paper stock.

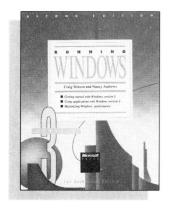
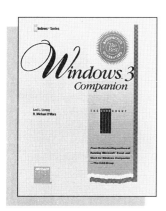

More Titles From Microsoft Press

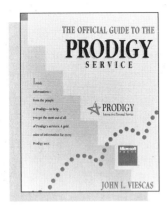

THE OFFICIAL GUIDE TO THE PRODIGY® SERVICE
John L. Viescas

Ready to start telecommunicating? All you need is your computer, a modem, a subscription to the PRODIGY Service, and this book! The PRODIGY Service—one of the country's most popular online services—is so rich in its offerings that many users miss large areas of the service. Or they're uncertain about how to best access information. This guide—the *only* guide authorized by the PRODIGY Service—provides a clear road map to the major PRODIGY services: entertainment, news, shopping, financial data, electronic mail, online encyclopedias, and more. The author has worked extensively with the PRODIGY Services Company to include inside information, solutions to common problems, and tips on accessing the frequently undiscovered gems of the PRODIGY service.

400 pages, softcover $19.95 ($24.95 Canada)   Order Code OFGUPR

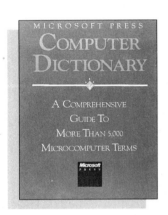

MICROSOFT PRESS® COMPUTER DICTIONARY
Microsoft Press

More than 5000 comprehensive entries make this the standard microcomputer dictionary for classrooms, libraries, and individual computer users (secondary school and beyond). This dictionary especially appeals to users who are involved with personal computers but who are not computer sophisticates. Each entry is written in clear, standard English, and each goes beyond mere definition to provide context. Compiled by a distinguished board of advisers drawn from the computer, business, and academic communities.

400 pages, softcover $19.95 ($24.95 Canada)   Order Code PRCODI

THE PARENT'S GUIDE TO EDUCATIONAL SOFTWARE
Marion Blank, Ph.D. and Laura Berlin, Ph.D.

A gold mine of information for parents and educators! Reviews of more than 200 of today's best educational software programs along with guidelines for selecting and buying the right software. Comprehensive, clearly organized, and packed with information. The core of this guide presents detailed reviews and expert evaluations of software—organized by age group (K-12), subject area, and specific skills taught. The authors, both education professionals, also include advice on selecting software and integrating at-home computer work with in-school curricula. Special information covers software for the learning disabled. A one-of-a-kind resource for parents, educators, librarians, and home-schooling advocates.

400 pages, softcover $14.95 ($17.95 Canada)   Order Code GUPAGU

Microsoft Press books are available wherever quality computer books are sold. Prices subject to change.
Or call **1-800-MSPRESS** for ordering information or placing credit card orders.
Please refer to **BBK** when placing your order.

In Canada, contact Macmillan of Canada, Attn: Microsoft Press Dept., 164 Commander Blvd., Agincourt, Ontario, Canada M1S 3C7. 416-293-8141
In the U.K., contact Microsoft Press, 27 Wrights Lane, London W8 5TZ.